THE VOLUNTARY PRISONERS OF ARCHITECTURAL WORK

Text: Anh-Linh Ngo

The architectural profession is regularly beset by waves of contradictory feelings, oscillating between self-aggrandizement and self-doubt. This inner conflict stems from the schizophrenic experience of architects' daily experience: On the one hand, they witness the profound societal influence architecture can wield as a medium; on the other, they grapple with a sense of powerlessness in the face of market dynamics. The capacity of architecture to materially intervene in the structure of the social fabric and to have a lasting aesthetic-symbolic impact on life contrasts with the sobering realization that, despite this social calling, the architectural profession offers a service primarily to those who can afford it. Architects face an unresolvable predicament: The social aspiration elevates architecture to the level of a societal discipline, while the prevailing political and economic circumstances make living up to that status all but impossible.

Heated debates have once again flared up around the role of architects, some echoing discussions within the editorial team of ARCH+ from the 1970s. At the time, the team was sharply divided into two irreconcilable camps. One group believed that architects, as wage-dependent workers, should join the labor movement. They should, to use the Marxist term, develop a class consciousness and unionize. For this faction, labor unions, as the primary political organizations engaged in class struggle, represented a necessary transition stage toward a socialist society.[1] In contrast, the other group favored a grassroots democratic approach to political struggle, drawing inspiration from social movements that sought alternative forms of collaboration beyond traditional mass organizations, such as cooperative self-help. The second faction aimed to engage with the "immediate *political* dimension, which relates to subjects as subjects and not as wearers of character masks, whether that of the citizen or the seller of labor power as a commodity."[2] Their implied accusation against the orthodox left was that its narrow focus on unions only served to defend economic interests and effectively postponed the "political struggle" until after the "economic struggle."[3]

Nearly fifty years after these intense debates that ultimately led the labor union–oriented faction to resign from the editorial board in 1977,[4] we find ourselves in an era where the subject and its individual economic advancement are at the center of societal discourse. As a result of the increasing individualization and liberalization in the past five decades, the subject has long ceased to define itself as a member of fixed social formations. The concern about being "wearers of character masks" is now obsolete. Today, we all wear the uniform mask of the market. Confronted with the complete commodification of all aspects of life, architects are once again called upon in certain parts of the discourse to develop a class consciousness as workers, to unionize, and to stand in solidarity with other workers. These calls echo familiar themes of the 1970s, now joined by new concerns addressing the construction industry's harmful practices, such as resource consumption, extractive supply chains, and precarious working conditions. This ecological and social awareness marks a discursive progress that extends beyond merely improving the profession's economic standing.

Despite this thematic expansion, the battle is mainly being fought on the economic front now as then: "Because in a society where the relationships between individuals are solely defined through the exchange of commodities—that is, mediated by determinate economic forms—a political movement cannot, in fact, pretend to see past these determinate economic forms."[5] This argument, brought forward by the labor union–oriented faction of ARCH+ editors in the 1970s, simply assumed the commodity nature of society to be a logical necessity. As representatives of the organized left, they added a "class-analytical definition" of social movements, revealing a disregard for the pursuit of alternative economic models: "To recognize them as small producers, trapped in the cycle of simple circulation of commodities, would explain why they are inclined, on the one hand, to understand the products of their labor as the core of their 'political identification,' and, on the other, to fall prey in a special way to the appearance of freedom and equality, where they believe their economic interests are well served."[6]

Putting aside the Marxist jargon of yesteryear, the essence of these and other contemporaneous arguments is making a reappearance in today's debates, albeit often with less theoretical rigor. This phenomenon can be ascribed not only to a lack of theoretical underpinnings in contemporary discourse but also to the affective logic of social media that fuels contentious battles of opinion. Online outrage erupts one day over architects' poor pay, while the next, the spotlight shifts to excessive overtime in design studios, igniting a fresh wave of indignation. Interestingly, the loudest calls for greater shares of the profit and for unionization in architecture come from within the Anglo-Saxon world, i.e., the most thoroughly commercialized societies, particularly as regards academia. In addition, attacks on the bourgeois self-image of the profession, on its "appearance of freedom and equality," are echoed today in similar ways. Especially creativity, ostensibly the core of architectural labor, is now contested, as if it could exist completely detached from social conditions.[7]

Once more, a chasm emerges between theoretical discourse and the incremental yet determined efforts of practicing architects, who strive to organize their work differently, experiment with alternative economic and organizational models, and devise pragmatic strategies to lessen their total dependence on the market while fulfilling their social responsibilities as best as they can. This division within the discipline is documented to some extent within this issue. Perhaps it also reflects a divide between lived experiences: Architects and theorists operating within profit-maximizing, financialized systems—academia included—find themselves opposite a great number of small firms that continue to characterize the profession in Europe. These smaller architecture practices approach client interaction as a societal undertaking. Through their direct confrontation with the design brief, they initiate a form of everyday political activity, characterized by persuasion and the negotiation of priorities, values, and attitudes. Abandoning this fundamental aspect of design work means abandoning architecture.

What is most vexing about the current debate is its utter lack of utopian potential. Hardly any discussion grapples with the societal role of work itself. The situation was quite different in the 1960s and 1970s, when the utopian socialism of thinkers like Charles Fourier was being rediscovered. The generation to come of age during the 1968 protests was fascinated by Fourier's *Theory of the Four Movements and of the General Destinie*s, in which he radically rethought the nature of work at the dawn of the industrial age.[8] Fourier sought to anchor work in the individual's intrinsic drives—its passions, self-love, and communal spirit. People would no longer work out of necessity or financial gain, but in pursuit of self-improvement. This vision was underpinned by an innovative model of collectively managed essential services, a precursor to the present-day concept of a universal basic income. Its architectural manifestation was the phalanstère, a self-sufficient community housed within a single, massive building.

Today's debates are far removed from such radicalism. Instead, capitalism seems to have been internalized as the only viable option. The commodification of human labor—sold to the highest bidder regardless of its intrinsic value—is not fundamentally challenged. Within certain circles, a recurring argument is repeated like a mantra: Architects can only be in solidarity with other workers if they view themselves as architectural workers. It is argued that architectural work must be demystified, treated as no different from any other form of labor. Design, project, imagination, creativity—those are dismissed as vestiges of a bourgeois consciousness,[9] elements of an architectural ideology that distract from the true political struggle. In this way, architectural labor is to be stripped of all conceit; one could also say: of all idealism.

What may initially appear as progressive turns out to be a regression upon closer inspection. There was a time when our analysis of the concept of work was further along. But instead of striving to democratize access to the creative potential of architectural labor—which, despite the profession's problematic aspects, resides in its capacity to envision and shape new worlds—it is now being relegated to the status of ordinary wage labor. This not only negates architecture's productive potential but also disregards the societal role of labor in general. By adopting this perspective, architects make themselves voluntary prisoners of architectural work.[10]

To achieve genuine progress for architectural work, labor itself must first be revolutionized, which means freeing it from its commodity-form. This is not about selling labor power under better terms or decoupling it from "real" life in the sense of a better work–life balance. From an emancipatory standpoint, that would present a rather bleak vision of progress, as the underlying social conditions of labor would essentially stay the same.

Really demystifying labor would require exposing it as a "fictitious commodity," as Karl Polanyi put it in his seminal *The Great Transformation*. This neither entails an emotional detachment from work, nor a negation of its creative potential, nor a clean separation of life from the sphere of work. Instead, it means relocating labor within the broader context of life itself: "Labor is only another name for a human activity that goes with life itself, which in its turn is not produced for sale but for entirely different reasons, nor can that activity be detached from the rest of life, be stored or mobilized."[11] Conversely, this implies that as long as we uphold the fiction of labor as a commodity, we will continue to treat people and their lives as commodities. Polanyi pinpointed this issue as a core problem of contemporary society: "All along the line, human society had become an accessory of the economic system."[12]

This insight suggests that the real revolution consists in re-rooting the economic system within society and thus foregrounding labor's social significance. Only through this paradigm shift can we dismantle the logic of exploiting people and nature. Humanity's ecological survival may well hinge upon the success of this revolution. Thus, when the younger generation, disillusioned with architecture's revolutionary potential, poses the question today, "Why work overtime?," one plausible response emerges: to politicize architecture *within* architectural practice, as the discipline tried to do in the 1970s by aligning itself with social movements. However, such social activism across diverse spheres—committed to social, decolonial, ecological, or other contemporary agendas—will likely never be as well paid as working for capital. This unequal distribution of resources is a direct consequence of the capitalization of our world. As economist Thomas Piketty demonstrates in his study *Capital in the Twenty-First Century*, the return on capital surpasses the potential returns generated by labor.[13] Revolutionizing labor rather than competing with capital may therefore offer the only path forward. This applies to architectural work as well—engaging in non-profit endeavors, noncommercial activities, and even occasional overtime become valuable within this framework. After all, throughout human history, no one has ever been paid a union wage to stage a revolution.

Acknowledgments

This issue was initiated and brought to life by a young generation of current and former ARCH+ contributors led by Jakob Walter, who collaborated on this project with Felix Hofmann, Victor Lortie, and Lukas Meyer—recent graduates and some current students, all exploring their future career paths. I warmly thank them for their critical and thoughtful commitment to having these discussions. Special thanks also go to Olaf Grawert, who, as guest editor, helped shape the focus of this issue based on his practical experience and teaching at ETH Zurich. Sascha Kellermann and Nora Dünser from the ARCH+ team played a major role in the production of the German-language issue, while Nora Dünser and Victor Lortie made this English-language version a reality. I would like to express my gratitude to all of them and everyone who contributed as part of the guest editorial team at station+ at ETH Zurich. The International Architecture Biennale Rotterdam deserves special thanks for co-funding the translation of this publication.

1 Cf. Klaus Brake et al., "Basisdemokratie versus gewerkschaftliche Orientierung," *ARCH+ 28: Glückliche Neue Heimat* (December 1975), 61, trans. the editors.
2 Wolfgang Ehrlinger et al., "Tendenzwende?," *ARCH+ 27* (September 1975), 6, trans. the editors.
3 Ibid.
4 See "Austrittserklärung der Redaktionsmitglieder Klaus Brake, Helga Fassbinder und Renate Petzinger aus der Redaktion ARCH+," (offprint, 1977).
5 Brake et al., "Basisdemokratie," (see note 1), 60.
6 Ibid., 63.
7 See Nick Beech, "Conflagration: The (Self-)Image of the Architect," in this issue, 106–115.
8 Charles Fourier, *The Theory of the Four Movements* (1808), trans. Ian Patterson (Cambridge: Cambridge University Press, 1996).
9 See Beech, "Conflagration" (see note 7).
10 See Rem Koolhaas et al., *Exodus, or the Voluntary Prisoners of Architecture*, 1972.
11 Karl Polanyi, *The Great Transformation* (New York: Farrar & Rinehart, 1944), 72.
12 Ibid., 75.
13 Cf. Thomas Piketty, *Capital in the Twenty-First Century*, trans. Arthur Goldhammer (Cambridge: Belknap Press, 2014).

TO THE PROFESSION

Text: Jakob Walter, Felix Hofmann, Victor Lortie

This issue is dedicated to a profession we—as architects-to-be—have up until now mostly known through internships and short-term employment. After all, we have come to work as editors at ARCH+ slightly bruised by disillusionment: The discrepancy between the holistic approach demanded in our studies and the material contingencies resulting from the reality of being a practicing architect seemed, at least to us, irresolvable.

Working as an architect is akin to an unspoken pact. We stomach the comparably meager material recognition of a university degree because we get the opportunity to work on creative and meaningful tasks—preferably in service to the common good. Yet, among aspiring architects, suspicion is growing about whether that tacit agreement might have fallen apart altogether. On the one hand, a growing number of young professionals, once at ease in a semblance of bohemian frugality, are now increasingly facing real economic precariousness as the cost of living—and most importantly rent—is rising faster than architects' incomes in most places. On the other hand, architects' demands regarding their work have begun to change. Greater awareness of the social, economic, and, most importantly, ecological consequences of the practice, as well as doubts about architecture's ability to solve these problems of its own making, have politicized a new generation of architects. Consequently, many are asking themselves: Why even work overtime anymore?

A little over a year ago, as we were writing the editorial for the German edition of this issue, momentous change still seemed to be in the cards. That feeling was embodied in the heated debates, mostly happening online, about working conditions around the ultimately unsuccessful December 2021 effort by employees of SHoP Architects in New York to unionize. The discourse addressed "architectural workers": Employees in architectural offices were urged to (once again) understand themselves as part of the working class and fight for better working conditions—not as individual economic agents but in solidarity both with one another and with other workers involved in the making of the built environment. These discussions, which we followed with great interest, are symptomatic of a category of solutions principally aiming at improving the working conditions within architectural production. The statistics spread across this issue, first published in early 2023, indeed seem to support this sense of optimism.

In the meantime, however, the bargaining position of architects has rapidly diminished in tandem with the demand for their labor power. Rising material costs, a shortage of skilled construction workers, and inflation have hamstrung the European and North American construction industries, pulling part of the architectural sector down in its fall. Numerous projects have been put on hold or canceled entirely. Offices big and small, until recently desperately looking for staff, have had to furlough or let go of employees to secure their economic survival. And, in times when offices are trying to cut costs, asking for better working conditions is a luxury few can afford. The calls for collective action and unionization have grown perceptibly quieter.

Although the conditions under which, a year ago, we vociferously argued for more self-confidence in the labor force have changed, we would be remiss to resign ourselves to sheltering in place—or elbowing our way through the crisis on our own—while we wait for better times. We explicitly conceived this issue with the conviction that architects can gain agency by shedding the still-prevailing myth of the lone genius and understanding themselves not only as economic subjects but also as political ones by nature of their shared interests. The necessity of this realization becomes all the more urgent in times of crisis. Now is the time to stoke a conscience that can be put to use as soon as the tide turns. After all, a look at the aforementioned pact from both sides reveals that "simply" reducing our impassioned work to labor—and our job performance to the required minimum—is no way forward for a profession whose impact on societies and the planet can be so devastating.

While formulating these pleas and developing this issue, we have repeatedly confronted ourselves with our own biases. ARCH+ is no exception to the rule that architecture and the discourse around it are subjected to the whims of the market and the organizational forms it brings about. The next pages therefore contain many questions we are constantly asking ourselves: What kind of architectural businesses do we want to work in? What are we willing to do under which conditions? The result of that process spawns entirely new parameters for how we conceive our own work: Which factors would define architectural quality if we stopped valuing it for its aesthetics and program and instead began assessing it by means of its organizational form and processes of production? There are many paths to concocting a new pact in which our overtime would not only be worthwhile to us as architects, but to the world we once set out to improve as well.

In the end, this issue is an attempt at reconciling ourselves with the career path we once chose. That, however, doesn't mean that discourse production is an exit strategy to avoid having to engage with the built environment's production. To the contrary: It is a sincere shot at bending the discourse's attention back to the discipline and its agency. Quiet quitting is not the answer; loud dedication is.

FROM THE PROFESSION

THE VALUE QUESTION: "FINANCIAL SELF-PRESERVATION IN AN ERA OF POST-GROWTH"[1]

Text: Olaf Grawert

In 2020, 68 percent of real asset value across the globe was tied to the built environment. Residential real estate (buildings and land combined) made up 46 percent of global net assets, with corporate and government buildings accounting for another 23 percent.[2] This is testament to the considerable influence the built environment exerts both on the values that define our current prosperity and their ability to continue generating income in the future. At the same time, such influence is directly bound up with political and private interests, considering that around 95 percent of global net assets are in private hands, albeit with a highly uneven distribution.[3]

For the same reasons, the majority of European architectural production, at 56 percent, is devoted to private housing.[4] Around 89 percent of European offices work in the private housing sector, making it their most important source of income.[5] It is not exclusively the crises of recent decades that have made (residential) real estate, land included, one of the safest investments available. Every crisis, whether financial in origin or linked to commodities, has resulted in an increase in land and property values.[6] In 2021, the real estate industry accounted for about 20 percent of Germany's gross value added (GVA), nearly four times the value added of the German automotive industry.[7]

Confidence in the safety of the built environment as an investment has ensured the growth of the real estate industry, but it's also reflected in the growing wages of planners. Over the past ten years, the median salary of European architects, adjusted for purchasing power, has risen by 29 percent.[8] From an economic perspective, working in architectural offices is more lucrative than ever, considering that buildings—architects' chief objective and income basis, according to the profession's conventional self-conception—have never been transposed from blueprint to reality to such a great extent. As it happens, this development has followed the rules of the free market, according to which a few offices divide the majority of the market among themselves and conduct architecture as a business, extracting enormous value at a high pace. Such offices lead the annual list of the one hundred biggest offices compiled by the British online magazine *Building Design*, although they barely occupy any space in architectural discourse. The list is topped by the US American firm Gensler with its 2,692 employees. The first European firm is in fifth place: Sweco of Sweden, with 1,264 employees. The first German firm, gmp, has 506 employees and ranks twenty-fifth.[9] Offices of this size are the exception in Europe; the most common type of architectural practice remains the one-person operation, as freelancers and sole practitioners account for 62 percent of registered firms and 30 percent of all architects.[10] However, the market is dominated by the one percent of architecture firms that have over 50 employees, thanks to the high profitability of large-scale, repetitive, and material-heavy projects.[11]

Nevertheless, one-person firms have also profited from the economic boom of recent years, which has made this form of self-employment possible in the first place. Moreover, the shaky situation of the labor market, which faces a dire need for skilled workers, gives applicants a strategic advantage when struggling against problematic working conditions or formulating their own demands. If you're unhappy, you can ask for more money—or found your own firm. Looking squarely to the statistics, we could lean back and think: We have never been better off as (employed) architects, and it has never been easier to establish an economically viable practice. So: *Why are we so unhappy?*

Profit under Protest

As practicing architects, we are confronted these days, both professionally and in university, by a younger generation interpreting the way we build today, as well as contemporary ways of creating value, very differently from previous generations. Where some see economic indicators such as greater investment, rising wages, or increasing construction costs as a chance to profit from broad-spectrum growth, others see symptoms of a polycrisis. As members of a "last generation," they feel directly threatened by the climate crisis, pandemics, wars, and rising inflation. In 2021, 37.9 percent of students in Germany were at risk of poverty.[12] Spread across 500 local chapters, thousands of them staged protests known as Fridays for Future, where they focused on a very different indicator—the fact that the construction industry is responsible for 38 percent of worldwide human CO_2 emissions.[13] This points a finger directly at architects and their supposed *raison d'être*: building.

The younger generation has even gone so far as to challenge values and measurement criteria such as gross domestic product (GDP), arguing it wholly fails to take the unequal distribution of wealth, unpaid labor, or damage to humans, animals, and the environment into account. Natural disasters, accidents, and wars can even have a positive effect on such indicators, as rebuilding efforts are reflected in economic growth, leading to rising GDPs even in the face of humanitarian crises.[14]

As an architect, if you accept this reality, you face the problem of how to establish a professional practice that enables "financial self-preservation in an era of post-growth."[15] What does it mean in practice to pursue objectives other than competition and growth, while taking values like preservation and the common good into account? How can we establish a professional self-conception that reconciles the multiple meanings of the word "value?" So: *What can be done*?

Working in the System Means Working *on* the System

In the short term, we have little choice but to continue practicing in the existing economic system, while continuously politicizing it. In the long term, however, if we hope to remake architecture into a non-destructive practice in service of the common good, the only option is comprehensive economic reform. The transformation of architectural practice must begin in the here and now, from within the current system.

At a professional level, there needs to be a change in the way architects—whether employees, freelancers, or students—show solidarity with each other and unionize. In Germany, architects and engineers are currently represented by the construction trade union IG BAU. In fighting for its members, it advocates for the preservation of jobs—chiming with the real estate industry's unrelenting arguments against changes in construction practices by pointing to the potential loss of jobs. This is where the demands of *Realpolitik* clash with ideological desires: If building less is to be socially responsible and societally accepted, the demands have to consider all stakeholders—especially those who, in the past, have not profited from the boom in construction activity and have only contributed to the prosperity of the upper and middle classes. At the same time, it's critical that all industries involved with land and construction lock arms, because architecture alone has no lobby. Architecture lacks a lever that would make an alternative practice, one led by values, impactful in a systemic manner: the right for associations at the national or state level to bring class action lawsuits against the destruction of the environment by architecture itself, as discussed in this issue with the presidents of the Architects' Council of Europe, the Federal Chamber of German Architects (*Bundesarchitektenkammer*), and the Association of German Architects (*Bund Deutscher Architektinnen und Architekten*).[16]

At an entrepreneurial level, it's necessary to reorientate our approach toward new markets. This would demand new organizational forms in both architecture offices as well as the management of architectural projects. Enormous potential is offered by the renovation of public and private buildings in the vein of the Renovation Wave strategy called for in the European Green Deal. This ambitious goal to decarbonize the existing building stock by 2050, legally binding for EU member states, can be translated into tangible figures: As of now, 25 percent of European buildings have been renovated, which means 75 percent of the work lies ahead of us. At the current 1 percent annual renovation rate, it would take until the end of the century to reach the target.[17] That is three times longer than we have, if we want to reach it by 2050. Our challenge is thus to triple our efforts. This is not only a huge market potential; such a move would also fundamentally shift the construction and architecture sectors away from a material-intensive and toward a labor-intensive economy.

This is because renovation does not merely offer the possibility of reducing emissions; it also creates new jobs in local industries. Well-educated specialists are essential in making our buildings climate-neutral. To update the existing building stock, we need flexible structures that can handle a variety of projects—both large and, most importantly, small. This offers a great opportunity to reform the traditional architectural career path as well. Large offices with conventional hierarchies primarily specialize in new construction, while the emerging renovation market offers opportunities for smaller, more agile organizations, from local craftspeople to small architecture firms maintaining direct relationships with clients and construction workers.

In such a market, values such as preservation and care, which cannot be appraised in today's economy, could attain new value and significance, with the overarching goal of achieving another form of doing business, namely steward-ownership. In this model, the corporation belongs to itself and can never become an object of speculation, as it's not bound to individuals but to a "relation of skills and values." In other words, instead of holding the assets, owners of a company bear responsibility for a company. Control of the company remains with the people who are associated with its aims long-term, demanding an architectural practice based on values instead of profits.[18]

At an individual level, we need to free ourselves from the premises of the industry and redefine the value of planning. In practice, this means decoupling our fees from construction costs and the creation of built objects, in order to resolve the contradiction that architects must build more to be paid better. Standing at the center of our value matrix should be quality of life and the environment, contingency and long-term sustainability. This new definition requires understanding architecture as part of the environment and the market. The forces and ties that affect architects can no longer be understood as constraints, but as tools for rebuilding our profession. In other words: *Let's stop complaining and get to work!*

s+ (station.plus) is a teaching and research platform at ETH Zurich's Institute of Design and Architecture founded in 2017. The + stands for close collaboration between individuals and institutions that understand architecture as a verb. Architecting means imagining, designing, and constructing new sustainable models for living together.

The following members of s+ were involved in the creation of this issue: Professor Arno Brandlhuber, Giacomo Ardesio, Severin Bärenbold, Brigitte Beck, Ludwig Engel, Olaf Grawert, Pan Hu, Alina Kolar, and Meghan Rolvien.

We are grateful for the collaboration of Bing Liu, Sam Ghantous, and Jakob Walter (s+), as well as Franziska Gödicke, Luke Handon, Jonas Janke, Roberta Jurčić, and Jolene Lee (b+).

We are also grateful to our students Paul Barth, Manuel Bokanyi, Leonie Wagner, and Sarah Wirth, who dealt extensively with the statistics for The Business of Architecture, *as well as Ruth Schagemann and the Architects' Council of Europe for providing them.*

1 See Saskia Hebert's talk at the BDA event "Glaube. Liebe. Hoffnung: Wir schaffen das," September 24, 2021, German Pavilion at the Venice Architecture Biennale, *2038: The New Serenity.*
2 Cf. "The Rise and Rise of the Global Balance Sheet: How Productively Are We Using Our Wealth?" *McKinsey Global Institute*, November 15, 2021, accessed June 5, 2024, www.mckinsey.com/~/media/mckinsey/industries/financial%20services/our%20insights/the%20rise%20and%20rise%20of%20the%20global%20balance%20sheet%20how%20productively%20are%20we%20using%20our%20wealth/mgi-the-rise-and-rise-of-the-global-balance-sheet-full-report-vf.pdf.
3 See ibid.
4 Cf. The Architects' Council of Europe, *The Architectural Profession in Europe: 2022 Sector Study* (Brussels, 2023), 4.
5 Cf. ibid.
6 See "'Property Entails Obligations': Hans-Jochen Vogel in Conversation with Arno Brandlhuber and Christopher Roth," *ARCH+ The Property Issue: Ground Control and the Commons* (April 2018), 54–59.
7 See "Bedeutung der Immobilienbranche," *ZIA – Die Immobilienwirtschaft*, accessed June 5, 2024, www.zia-deutschland.de/project/bedeutung-der-immobilien-branche.
8 Cf. ACE, *The Architectural Profession in Europe* (see note 4), 54.
9 "WA100 2022: The Big List," *Building Design*, accessed June 5, 2024, www.bdonline.co.uk/wa100-2022-the-big-list/5115702.article.
10 Cf. ACE, *The Architectural Profession in Europe* (see note 4).
11 Cf. ibid., 38.
12 See Statistisches Bundesamt, "Pressemitteilung Nr. N066," press release, November 26, 2022, accessed June 5, 2024, www.destatis.de/DE/Presse/Pressemitteilungen/2022/11/PD22_N066_63.html.
13 See UN Environment Programme, ed., "2020 Global Status Report for Buildings and Construction: Towards a Zero-Emissions, Efficient and Resilient Buildings and Construction Sector," accessed June 5, 2024, 4, globalabc.org/sites/default/files/inline-files/2020%20Buildings%20GSR_FULL%20REPORT.pdf.
14 See Konzeptwerk neue Ökonomie and Fairbindung, eds., "BIP," in *Die zwei Seiten der Medaille: Argumente für und gegen Wirtschaftswachstum*, accessed June 5, 2024, www.endlich-wachstum.de/wpcontent/ uploads/2015/09/Kapitel-1_Medaillen_BIP.pdf.
15 See Hebert, "Glaube. Liebe. Hoffnung." (see note 1).
16 See Anna Yeboah, "No Recourse to Law," *ARCH+ Legislating Architecture* (October 2016), 196–97.
17 European Union Directorate-General for Internal Market, Industry, Entrepreneurship and SMEs, *Renovation Wave: Doubling the Renovation Rate to Cut Emissions, Boost Recovery and Reduce Energy Poverty*, press release, October 14, 2020, accessed June 5, 2024, single-market-economy.ec.europa.eu/news/renovation-wave-doubling-renovation-rate-cut-emissions-boost-recovery-and-reduce-energy-poverty-2020-10-14_en.
18 See "Steward-ownership," purpose-economy.org, accessed June 5, 2024, purpose-economy.org/en/whats-steward-ownership/.

CONTENTS

p. 11

p.166

ARCH+ Team for this Issue:
Nora Dünser (managing editor), Felix Hofmann, Sascha Kellermann (co-project lead for the German-language publication), Victor Lortie (project lead for the English-language publication), Lukas Meyer, Anh-Linh Ngo (editor-in-chief), Jakob Walter (co-project lead for the German-language publication)

s+ Guest Editors:
Arno Brandlhuber, Ludwig Engel, Olaf Grawert (project lead)

Cover DS landschaparchitecten: Detail from *What are we waiting for?*, 2024
Created for *Nature of Hope*, the 2024 edition of the International Architecture Biennale Rotterdam

The statistics presented throughout this issue draw on two key sources, namely *The Architectural Profession in Europe: 2022 Sector Study* by the Architects' Council of Europe, and the report on the 2022 structural survey of salaried registered architects by the Federal Chamber of German Architects. Switzerland and most Western Balkan countries were not surveyed.

OCCUPATION

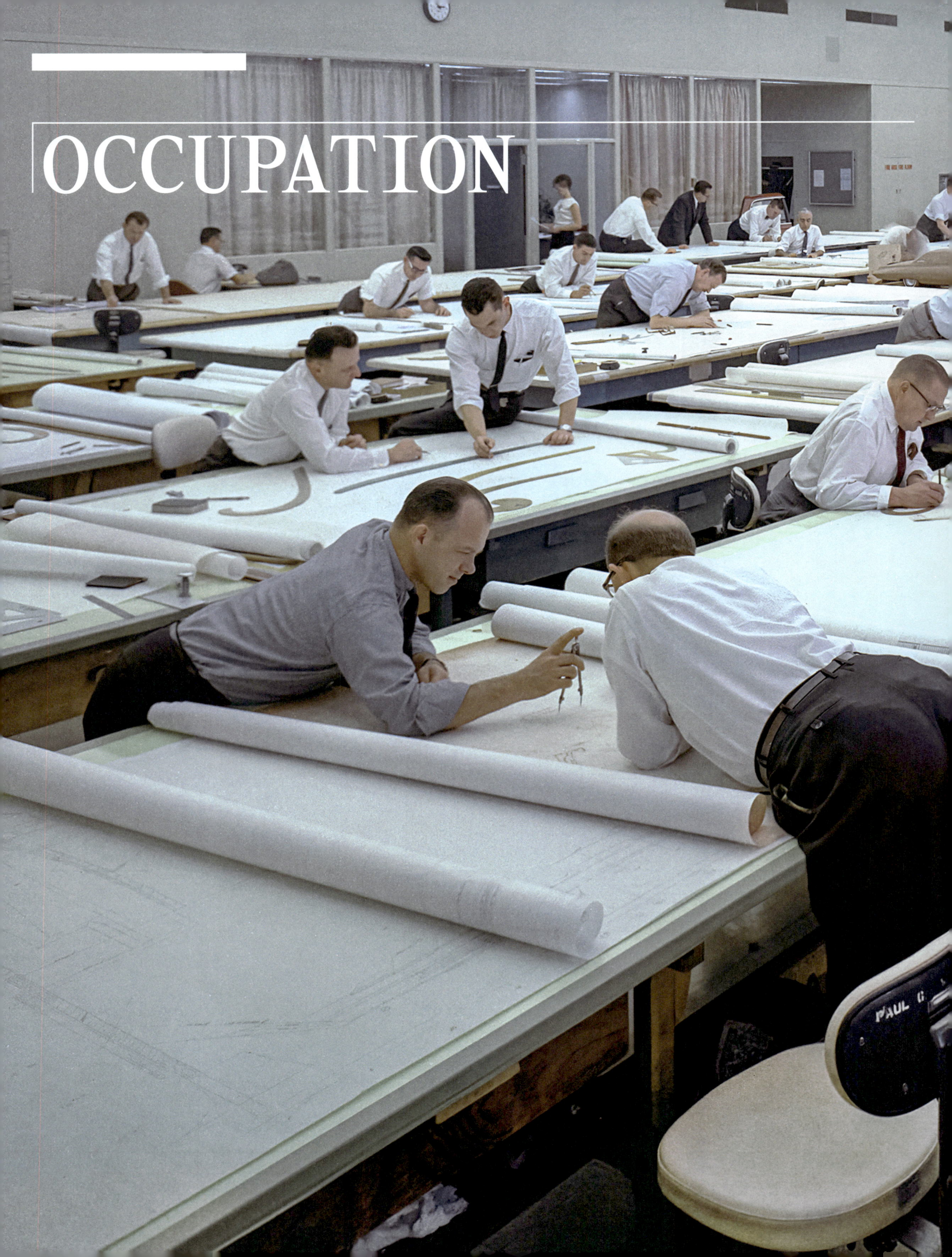

VOCATION

WORK

Text: Peggy Deamer

Fig. 1

Fig. 2

Fig. 3

Fig. 4

According to a survey conducted among members of the Federal Chamber of German Architects, the total gross annual salary of architects employed in the country's architecture and planning offices in 2021 was €58,986 on average, with the median being €53,000. → For members with less than ten years of professional experience, the median total gross annual salary was €48,000. In Germany, nearly one-third of architects are employed in architecture and planning offices with fewer than ten people. → Women in particular are more frequently employed in small offices. → Only 23% of architects work in large offices with 50 or more employees. 47% of European architects are partners, directors, or sole practitioners.

Fig. 1 Alexander Deyneka, *Building Peace*, sketch for a mural mosaic, 1959–60, oil on canvas, 160 × 180 cm.
The lines between work and art—or work and leisure—are dissolved in this sketch for a mosaic commissioned for *The First National Art Exhibition "Soviet Russia"* in Moscow in 1960.

Fig. 2 Christine Hill inside *Volksboutique Small Business*, Choriner Straße, Berlin, 2010, installation
Building on her installation *Volksboutique*, exhibited at documenta X in 1997, Christine Hill—pictured in a recreation of *Volksboutique*—repeatedly explores the notion of labor in art

At a recent symposium, a young audience member asked the distinguished panelists what she could expect from a career in architecture. One of the panelists answered fervently: "Architecture is not a career. It is a calling!"

Prologue: How Did We Get Here?

For a profession that seems to have it all—architects' creativity, unlike artists', is professionally sanctioned; we make things that matter to the world—how could we be victims of the same capitalist ideology which, in the form of Christianity, asks the poor to feel righteous about their poverty?

My first answer is: We don't believe we do work. We go to the office, we get a paycheck, but as a profession architecture produces designs, not mere products or services. We know we are producing an object (indeed, a big one), but we don't like to think that we produce a "commodity." We compare ourselves to doctors and lawyers, but believe our work is too creative and culturally significant to be properly filed under "service sector." Consequently, we fail to conceptualize our work as work.

In comparison to manufacturing jobs, we lack security structures—unions, guilds, or institutionally sanctioned labor laws—that prevent architectural staff from being fired with no cause, working for no pay, or enduring oppressive hours. Considering that the majority of architectural staff are asked to work 70-hour weeks at an average of 55,000 US dollars a year, we earn 15 US dollars an hour, roughly the same as my daughter earns babysitting, and are no better off than factory workers. In comparison to service professionals, the starting salary for architects, with comparable years of education at a top school like Yale, is less than a third of that of lawyers and doctors; six years out, that percentage rises but lingers just above 45 percent.[1]

My second premise is: We have a pathetic notion of design that isolates it from work. Architects design, constructors build; we do art, they do work. This division, which is both conceptual and contractual, keeps architecture from not only achieving the above described financial and monetary rewards, but also social relevance and personal satisfaction. One can't dismiss the similarity between architecture and McDonald's as low-margin industries. How many times have we heard the excuse of the underpaid staff member: "How can I ask for more money when I know the boss isn't paid properly either?"[2] Seeing design as separate from work precludes social relevance because we do not see ourselves in the class of workers. In discussions about minimum wage, in reading about the strikes of non-union food-service providers, in producing designs that are built by indentured labor in Asia and the Middle East—we don't relate. More than this, Marx has made clear that labor is a social issue, not merely because it relates worker to worker, but because it permeates every aspect of our home and psychic life.

Can art and creativity refuse to be divorced from issues of work/labor,[3] value, and money? Art practices are instructive because, if architects think we do art, not work, it's surprising to show that artists *do* think they do work. And why is the idea so pervasive that work in general is inherently not fun, creative, or aesthetic? Theorists, both utopian and practical, who espouse the creative nature of work, offer liberating perspectives on reconstituted and re-managed formulations of work. The implications for architecture are fundamental.

Part I: Art as Work/Labor

I've always held the belief that art is labor that deserves proper compensation. It is often difficult to assert this, in all levels of the art system. I'm sure that all involved would agree that art has "value," but where the work lies, and who is paying for it becomes a very clouded issue. I have issues with the premise that art is its own reward.
Christine Hill[4]

While aesthetics tends to hold itself apart from issues of labor, the two are historically intertwined. The appearance of labor as a concept distinct from feudal obligations in the late fourteenth century depended on the artisans who supplied the goods for export trade; the fact that goods came from "free" work allowed it to be conceptualized as exchange value.[5] Even if artisanal work was not transmitted from workers to employers or exchanged among independent traders, it was central to the mercantile system foreshadowing capitalism.[6] When industrialization broke the hold guilds had on "free" artisans, they became autonomous workers; at the same time their work, like all work, became exchangeable as labor-power. With this shift, the distinction between artists and artisans took hold, as artisans were subsumed by assembly production.

Marx suggests that mental production such as art has the potential to escape capitalist ownership of labor. Indeed, we are all potentially artists, the term "artist" existing only in societies framed/defined by the division of labor. "In a communist society," Marx writes, "there are no painters but only people who engage in painting among other activities."[7] In the ideal society, in which "nobody has one exclusive sphere of activity but each can become accomplished in any branch he wishes, society makes it possible for me to do one thing today and another tomorrow, to hunt in the morning, fish in the afternoon, rear cattle in the evening, criticize after dinner, just as I have a mind, without ever becoming hunter, fisherman, herdsman or critic."[8]

But art work is not free, Marx says, when it plays into the hands of capitalism. "A writer is a productive laborer in so far as he produces ideas, but in so far as he enriches the publisher who publishes his works, he is a wage laborer for the capitalist."[9] While Marx clearly doesn't enjoy this capitalist bracketing of occupations, he nevertheless points to its inevitability.

In the early twentieth century, Russian constructivists added another spin, pressing to prove that art was labor. Given the political atmosphere, they had to prove that art was proletarian, not bourgeois, and did so by emphasizing its kinship to manufacturing. Vladimir Mayakovsky, in a 1928 issue of the journal *Sovremennaia Arkhitektura* (Contemporary Architecture), lists the necessary requirements for poetry, among which the first: "Poetry is manufacture. A difficult, very complex kind, but a manufacture."[10] Later, he adds, "Only by approaching art as manufacture can you eliminate chance, arbitrariness of taste and individual judgment … instead of mystically pondering a poetic theme you will have the power to tackle any pressing problem accurately with full poetic qualifications."[11] Likewise, Alexander Malinovsky, aka Bogdanov, wrote, "Creation, whether technological, socio-economic, political, domestic, scientific, or artistic, represents a kind of labour … whose product is not the repetition of a ready-made stereotype but is something 'new.' There is not and cannot be a strict demarcation between creation and ordinary labour; not only are there all the points of interchange, but it is even impossible often to say which of the two designations is more applicable."[12]

These inspiring pronouncements, while forced by communist conformism, demonstrate a commitment not only to art as labor, but also to coexistence within a work-defined social fabric. This attitude was shared by German Marxists of the same period, although they, unlike Russian artists, were looking at socialism from the outside. Certain members of the Frankfurt School, Walter Benjamin principal among them, picked up on the idea that work could be the model for art. His essay "The Work of Art in the Age of Mechanical Reproduction" links mental, artistic production to material, technical production.[13] In this he followed Bertolt Brecht's instructions for Epic Theatre which negated the divisions between author and actors, actors and stage-hands, and actors/stage-hands and audience; all were seen as creative workers.

Like the constructivists, certain art practices in the late 1960s and 1970s explored the infiltration of work into art practice. To escape any effete notions of art, the Artist Placement Group (APG) staged events that were equally performance and financial negotiation.[14] Making sure that art was not held apart from systems of value, labor, and social change, they put union representatives on their "board," placed their artists in industry, and sought and achieved positions in the government.

More recently, in this same tradition, "Relational Aesthetics," the name given to a particular trend in art of the 1990s by the French art critic Nicolas Bourriaud, has promoted art that, as he writes, "presents itself as an editing console that manipulates social forms, reorganizes them and incorporates them in original scenarios, deconstructing the script on which their illusory legitimacy was grounded. The artist de-programmes in order to re-programme, suggesting that there are other possible usages for the techniques, tools and spaces at our disposition."[15]

In her 1996–97 "Volksboutique" in Berlin, Christine Hill, who "always held the belief that art is labor that deserves proper compensation,"[16] and who is associated with Relational Aesthetics, managed a thrift shop/sculpture where tea was served, inexpensive clothes were available, and discussions were encouraged. When she franchised her boutique in 1997 for documenta X in Kassel, she ascribed the role of thrift shop salesgirl to stand-ins. Rirkrit Tiravanija cooked and served food to the visitors in his 2002 exhibition *Untitled*—a work bought by the Guggenheim Museum with the aid of American Express who handled its programming in its PR department and created subsequent programs and events.[17]

Bourriaud's Relational Aesthetics has been criticized by artists who operate outside the museum/gallery system for its pseudo-social engagement with a rarefied audience. Nevertheless, the Relational Aesthetics artists operate with complete confidence that their work functions within a system of value that can be toyed with. However, an alternate view of that value-cum-art relationship is offered by Jacques Rancière. Rancière stresses that work is shaped by the logic of art, not the other way around. In his *The Politics of Aesthetics: The Distribution of the Sensible* (2004), the "aesthetic regime" of art (in contrast to the more trivial "ethical regime" or "poetic regime"), being "formal" and "sensuous,"[18] shapes our political identities and with it our attitude about work.[19] In *The Nights of Labor: The Workers' Dream in Nineteenth-Century France*, Rancière contends that workers in the 1830 French Revolution were not fighting against the hardships they experienced, but against the constricted nature of their lives.[20] At night, instead of recuperating for the next day's work, they read the works of poets and writers who spent their nights producing a language of liberation. After appropriating this other language and performing these other lives, the workers had the strategies needed for rebellion. Art practice "anticipates work because it carries out its principle: the transformation of sensible matter into the community's self-representation."[21]

Whether art precedes its connection to labor or succeeds it, artists and aestheticians have historically probed the thin line between the two. Why has architecture not listened? Not noticed?

Part II: Work as Art/Play

A spider conducts operations that resemble those of a weaver, and a bee puts to shame many an architect in the construction of her cells. But what distinguishes the worst architect from the best of bees is this, that the architect raises his structure in imagination before he erects it in reality.
Karl Marx[22]

Just as the tradition of art-as-labor suggests that architecture as a profession should consider "labor value," the tradition that sees human work as inherently imaginative, creative, and self-realizing should be equally embraced by architects. Creativity in architecture rests not on an ever-expanding categorical inclusion of form-making but rather on an imaginative approach to problem-solving.

The essential writing for nearly all who explore the liberating, play-structured aspects of work is Friedrich Schiller's *Letters Upon the Aesthetic Education of Man* (1794). Schiller himself does not address "work," but he does examine play/art's essential role in civil society. Civilization, Schiller posits, has suppressed the "sensuous impulse" to serve the "form impulse," such that when the sensuous emerges out of its repressed state, it is destructive. Art and play, Schiller argues, overcome this negative eruption by transcending the false dichotomy between sense and form.[23] In a defense against the possible attack that art, in being aligned with "mere" play, is degraded, Schiller writes, "But what is meant by a mere play, when we know ... that it is play which makes man complete and develops simultaneously his twofold nature? What you style limitation ... I name enlargement."[24]

Working from Schiller, Gottfried Semper justified his aesthetic position in his "Prolegomena" to *Style in the Technical and Tectonic Arts, or Practical Aesthetics* (1860) by appeal to pleasure and play. As he writes, "On a more exalted plane, what we mean by terms like 'sense of beauty,' 'delight in beauty,' 'enjoyment of art,' and 'artistic instinct' is analogous to those instincts, pleasures, and gratifications that govern the way in which we maintain our telluric existence ... Surrounded by a world full of wonder and forces whose laws we may divine ... we conjure up in play the perfection that is lacking ... In such play we satisfy our cosmogonic instinct."[25]

As has been described, Marx's ideal socialist society, shaped by his readings of Schiller and other German Romantic philosophers,[26] envisions all workers as creative and everyone as an artist, whereas when work serves capital, "freedom" is only found outside of work. Marx, in other words, sets out the negative image of labor imposed by capitalism that subsequent, more optimistic theorists have striven to revise.

Utopians go back and forth between espousing Marx's negative view of industrial production and endorsing a hoped-for society where all work is imaginative. For example, where American socialist Edward Bellamy, in his utopian novel *Looking Backward: 2000–1887* (1888), describes a regime dictating the strict division of work tasks and the division between work and leisure,[27] English textile designer and Marxist/socialist William Morris, in his *News from Nowhere* (1890) rebuttal to *Looking Backward*, describes how people in his ideal community live out Marx's vision to "hunt in the morning, fish in the afternoon, rear cattle in the evening, criticize after dinner,"[28] changing jobs for the pleasure of edification.[29] Ebenezer Howard's precise division of private work and public pleasure in his Garden City was countered by Frank Lloyd Wright's insistence, in "Broadacre City," that "our leisure, our culture and our work will be our own and as nearly as possible, One."[30] Le Corbusier, insisting on the essential value of (real) play, says, "Only those who play are serious types ... The mountain climbers, the rugby players and the card players, and the gamblers, are frauds, for they do not play."[31]

If these utopians, in giving a picture of ideal work, only underscore its actual unpleasantness, twentieth-century philosophers of work, who fall into one of two camps—neo-Marxists and pragmatists—look at creative aspects of work within capitalism. Herbert Marcuse picks up on Marx's philosophic probing of Schiller's emphasis on the role of play in a civil society. Equating Schiller's dichotomy of the sensuous versus formal instincts with Freud's pleasure versus reality principles, work is elevated by Marcuse to the pleasure principle. In *Eros and Civilization: A Philosophical Inquiry into Freud* (1955), he writes, "The abolition of toil, the amelioration of the environment ... flow directly from the pleasure principle, and, at the same time, they constitute *work* which associates individuals to 'greater unities'; no longer confined within the mutilating domination of the performance principle, they modify the impulse without deflecting it from its aim. There is sublimation and, consequently, culture; but this sublimation proceeds in a system of expanding and enduring libidinal relations, which are in themselves work relations."[32]

Recent neo-Marxists emphasize the communal, cooperative, and collaborative nature of contemporary work. Antonio Negri and Michael Hardt's *The Labor of Dionysus* (1977 Italian; 1994 English) and Maurizio Lazzarato's essay "Immaterial Labor" (1996) analyze "labor that produces the informational and cultural content of the commodity." In the transition from a service to an information economy, Antonio Negri and Michael Hardt say, "cooperation is completely immanent in the laboring process itself."[33] As Lazzarato puts it, work is now the domain of "mass intellectuality" and workers "are expected to become 'active subjects' in the coordination of the various functions of production, instead of being subjected to it as simple command. We arrive at a point where a collective learning process becomes the heart of productivity, because it is no longer a matter of finding different ways of composing or organizing already existing job functions, but of looking for new ones."[34]

Because the old model for describing production and consumption is no longer useful, one should turn to the aesthetic model involving "author, reproduction, and reception": if "author" loses its individuality, "reproduction" becomes organization, and "reception" is also communication. Lazzarato insists that this is not "utopian" because this form of work still describes capitalism's operations, as the subjects need still to conform to the demands of "production for production's sake." Critics of immaterial labor point out that labor has always had an immaterial side—Marx's argument was never to stress the physical nature of work but rather the social and subjective construct in which work operates—and immaterial labor always will have a material side—sweating through our time in front of the computer, the kitchen sink, or the shopping counter.

Alexander R. Galloway, speculating about post-capitalism, sees play—the ultimate goal—as already embedded in our capitalist production structures: "After trying to understand how to imagine a life after capitalism ... what one sees is how two of the hitherto most useful tropes for communicating a life after or outside capitalism—networks and play—are slowly shifting ... What is clear is that the possibility of life after capitalism is often articulated today through a utilization of the very essence of capitalism. Play is work and networks are sovereigns.[35]

Peter Drucker, "the man who invented corporate society"[36] and who was the guru of corporate management from the 1950s through the 1980s, forecasted capitalism's decentralization, privatization, and marketing. But in his *Post-Capitalist Society*, Drucker goes further in describing the nature of work in late capitalism. In the eighteenth century, Drucker says, the worker's knowledge was applied to tools; in the nineteenth and early twentieth centuries, it was applied to productivity (Taylorization); today, he says, it is being applied to knowledge itself.[37] Today, "knowledge workers" *own* the means of production, that is, knowledge. Because the skills held by these workers—research, product design, fabrication, marketing, advertising, customer consulting, financing, contracting—allow technical insights to be linked to marketing strategy and financial acumen, the traditional distinction between goods and services breaks down. Emphasizing that organizations have been "too thing focused" and produced too *many* things, he advocates "systematic abandonment," non-infatuation with yesterday's successes, streamlining, and embracing destabilization.[38] In addition, the goal of organizational management is to recognize that the most valuable resource is the worker (the most flexible and intelligent component of the system); to construct alternative, specialist-based models of

Fig. 3 Hans Hollein, *Just Landed: Hans Hollein in His Mobile Office*, 1969
Hans Hollein's mobile office consisted of a pneumatic construction that enables its users to work from virtually anywhere. In view of current processes of globalization and digitalization as well as phenomena like digital nomads and the gig economy, this artistic exploration seems to anticipate debates about the locus and transparency of work.

organizations; and to acknowledge that the real business of business is "not how to do things right but how to find the right thing to do."

Work of this sort, which architecture epitomizes—not because it makes form but because it organizes itself so fluidly—sounds pretty fun.

Part III: Architecture

The two trajectories followed here yield remarkably similar projections for post-Fordist work: creativity applied not to object-making but to process; destabilization; organizational flexibility; planned obsolescence; empowering the autonomy of the worker. Architecture increasingly operates this way even if its overt structures do not yet reflect it. Design today is not merely the conjuring of an object, but a problem-defining, problem-solving, information-structuring activity that, on the basis of understood conditions and rules, defines a specific course of action.[39] Instead of it being done by "an architect," architectural work is the creative manipulation of specialized design developed by a socially diverse panoply of contributors. Increasingly, architectural work is distributed and dispersed, collaborative and entrepreneurial, knowledge-based and open-sourced, specialized and flexible.

The benefit for architects—if we endorse the idea that our knowledge/service is spatial, material, and organizational innovation—is a reconception of our compensation and our place in the social fabric.

A reconception of compensation begins with the elimination of percentage-of-construction fees that reinforce the disastrous idea that our value resides in the object we produce and not in the knowledge that produced it. It not only wrongly places value on the one-offness of the object but also, as piece-work, aligns us with the most degrading form of compensation. Marx is clear on this: "Piece-wages therefore form the basis for … a hierarchically organized system of exploitation and oppression."[40] Further, he adds that, "given the system of piece-wages, it is naturally in the personal interest of the worker that he should strain his labour-power as intensely as possible; this in turn enables the capitalist to raise the normal degree of intensity of labour more easily. Moreover, the lengthening of the working day is now in the personal interest of the worker, since with it his daily or weekly wages rise."[41]

If you are an architect, this likely sounds familiar. If this scenario only seems to speak to the architectural firm partner in relationship to the client/owner and not to the salaried worker that makes up the bulk of the profession, Marx covers that, too. As he continues: "[The hierarchically organized system of exploitation and oppression] has two fundamental forms. On the one hand piece-wages … giv[e] rise to the 'sub-letting of labour.' … On the other hand, piece-wages allow the capitalist to make a contract for so much per piece with the most important labourer … at a price for which this man himself undertakes the enlisting and payment of his assistants. Here the exploitation of the worker by capital takes place through the medium of the exploitation of one worker by another."[42] The initial problem swims downstream.

Alternatives to this not only resist the piece-work model of compensation but also its architect-as-subordinate-to-owner framework. The most obvious option is to be the developer-owner. But more crafty and less financially demanding approaches exist. In the Integrated Project Delivery use of the Special Purpose Entity, a type of limited liability company, the owner puts aside an agreed-upon amount of money determined to be the project's worth; the architect and the contractors (and others) provide services at cost so they, in any case, do not lose money. It is agreed that there can be no lawsuits. If and when

Fig. 4 Wang Qingsong, *Work! Work! Work!*, 2012, C-print, 180 × 300 cm
The elaborately staged works of photographer Wang Qingsong are a commentary on the economic constraints and imponderable future of an increasingly capitalist Chinese society. This photo was taken in the Beijing office of architect Ole Scheeren.

the work costs are lower than the target cost, there is a three-way split of savings. Likewise, pay by percentage-of-profit, a calculation used to pay independent project managers, would identify the value added by architectural intervention, a figure that would not be difficult to identify if records were sought.

Models of compensation other than the existing hourly or yearly salary present themselves for architectural staff as well. Knowledge-based organizations compete for the best and the brightest and hence consistently refine their modes of compensation to balance appeal to and retention of top prospects with firm profitability. That architecture firms sadly do not yet approach their hiring and compensation in this manner is surely related to the fact that architecture school graduates, despite seven years of expensive education, present themselves as cheap labor. Be that as it may, in lieu of flat compensation rates, incentive-driven wages should be considered. Co-ownership, performance-based compensation, "pay-at-risk," employee stock options, or other firm owner–employee contracts sharing value creation and profit are common in new-economy, knowledge-work compensation models.

In *Capital*, Marx adds this footnote in his discussion about piece-work: "Even the apologist [John] Watts remarks: 'It would be a great improvement to the system of piece-work, if all the men employed on a job were partners in the contract, each according to his abilities, instead of one man being interested in overworking his fellows for his own benefit.'"[43]

If we never again want to hear a potential architectural employee say that they understand why they will get paid next to nothing since they know the firm they hope to work for earns next to nothing, we also need to look to unions and works councils. Unions—the modern incarnation of the guild system so admired by architecture for its designer/maker integration but totally overlooked as a human resource apparatus for the profession—have traditionally served creative organizations. These unions, traditionally militant organizations whose members have been willing to strike, are today less anti-management and more communities of support and promotion. These alternate forms of compensation and security operating in the heart of capitalism should not be held as perfect solutions for humanist, aesthetic production. But the discomfort we surely feel when trying on these other models of organization indicates the inexcusable conceptual distance between architectural work and other labor structures. The scary thing is not the unfamiliarity of these structures; it is our righteous ignorance of them.

The social benefit of labor lessons for architecture is being socially identified *at all*. Workers identify with workers. While many of the artists associated with Relational Aesthetics refused to have their work exhibited at the Guggenheim Museum in Abu Dhabi—a building built by indentured labor—architects remain unmoved. Pleas by Human Rights Watch for architects designing buildings in the Emirates and China to pressure their clients to reform bad construction practices have fallen on deaf ears. Architects rightly claim that they are not at the negotiating table, but sadly refuse to reflect on how their disengagement impacts this tragedy. Architecture needs to shed its work-aphasia and identify as an organization of workers. Only then will its cultural cachet have real social value.

At this transitional moment in the profession, when design responsibility and financial savvy are shared among various players, the constitution of a new model for architectural practice is entirely open. Now is the time to think expansively about what we want this new practice to look like and how its organization might be linked to larger social, political, and economic formations. As newly enlightened players in the labor game, architects are free to move directly toward an imagined ideal.

This contribution is the abridged version of an article originally published in Perspecta 47: Money *(2014), pages 27–39. Reprinted with kind permission of* Perspecta, *Yale School of Architecture.*

1 See Phil Bernstein, “Money, Value, Architects, Buildings,” *Perspecta* 47 (2014), 14–20. I am indebted to him for sharing and expanding on the indignation expressed here about the profession of architecture.
2 James Surowiecki, “The Pay Is Too Damn Low,” *New Yorker*, August 12, 2013, accessed May 28, 2024, www.newyorker.com/magazine/2013/08/12/the-pay-is-too-damn-low.
3 If the term “labor” has a negative connotation—work indicates use-value, labor indicates exchange value; work is distinctly human while labor is bestial, never-ending, animal-like—it also correctly insists that production is organized by a system of value that is socially constructed.
4 Régine Debatty, “Interview with Christine Hill,” *We Make Money Not Art Blog*, July 4, 2007, accessed May 28, 2024, we-make-money-not-art.com/interview_with_20/; see also Lucy Lippard and Barbara Steiner, eds., *Inventory: The Work of Christine Hill and Volksboutique* (Ostfildern: Hatje Cantz, 2004).
5 Richard Biernacki, *The Fabrication of Labor: Germany and Britain 1640–1914* (Berkeley: University of California Press, 1997), 215.
6 Ibid, 235.
7 Karl Marx and Friedrich Engels, *The German Ideology* (Amherst: Prometheus Books, 1998), 418.
8 Ibid., 53.
9 Karl Marx, *Theories of Surplus Value*, vol. 1 (London: Lawrence and Wishart, 1969), 401.
10 Vladimir Mayakovsky, *Sovremennaia Arkhitektura* 6 (1928), 160–66, trans. and cited by Catherine Cooke in *Russian Avant-Garde* (London: Academy Editions, 1995), 100.
11 Ibid.
12 Alexander Bogdanov, “Puti Proletarskogo Tvorchestva” (Paths of Proletarian Creative Work), *Proletarskaia Kui’tura* 15/16 (1920), 50–52; translated and then cited by John E. Bowlt (as an editor) in *Russian Art of the Avant-Garde: Theory and Criticism 1902–1934* (London: The Viking Press, 1976), 178–82.
13 Walter Benjamin, “The Work of Art in the Age of Mechanical Reproduction” (1935), trans. Harry Zohn, in *Illuminations: Essays and Reflections* (New York: Schocken Books, 1968), 217–51.
14 Founded in 1966, this artist-run organization in London redirected art away from the gallery and toward business and government.
15 Nicolas Bourriaud, “Precarious Constructions: Answers to Jacques Rancière on Art and Politics,” *Open* 17 (2009), 20–37.
16 Debatty, “Interview with Christine Hill” (see note 4).
17 See Walead Beshty, “Neo-Avantgarde and Service Industry: Notes on the Brave New World of Relational Aesthetics,” *Texte Zur Kunst* 59 (September 2005), 119–32.
18 These are Friedrich Schiller’s terms. In the second part of this chapter, Schiller’s view of art is elaborated. Rancière should be seen in the long lineage of aestheticians reworking Schiller’s view of art in civil society. Jacques Rancière, “Artistic Regimes and the Shortcomings of the Notion of Modernity,” in *The Politics of Aesthetics: The Distribution of the Sensible*, trans. Gabriel Rockhill (London: Continuum, 2004), 20–23.
19 Ibid., 23.
20 Cf. Rancière, *The Nights of Labor: The Workers’ Dream in Nineteenth-Century France*, trans. John Drury (Philadelphia: Temple University Press, 1989).
21 Rancière, *The Politics of Aesthetics*, 44 (see note 18).
22 Karl Marx, *Capital*, vol. 1 (New York: New World Paperbacks, 1967), 178; cit. David Graeber, *Toward an Anthropological Theory of Value* (New York: Palgrave, 2001), 58.
23 Cf. J. C. Friedrich Schiller, Letter 25, *The Harvard Classics, Vol. 32: Literary and Philosophical Essays* (New York: P. F. Collier & Son, 1909–14).
24 Ibid., Letter 15, 30.
25 Gottfried Semper, *Style in the Technical and Tectonic Arts, or Practical Aesthetics*, trans. Harry Francis Mallgrave and Michael Robinson (Santa Monica: Getty Publications, 2004), 81–82.
26 For a description of Marx’s faith in the classical imaginary, see George E. McCarthy, *Classical Horizons: The Origins of Sociology in Ancient Greece* (Albany: SUNY Press, 2003).
27 Cf. Edward Bellamy, *Looking Backward: 2000–1887* (1888; London: Penguin Classics, 1982).
28 Marx and Engels, *German Ideology*, 53 (see note 7).
29 Cf. William Morris, *News from Nowhere* (1890; London: Penguin Classics, 1984).
30 Frank Lloyd Wright, *When Democracy Builds* (Chicago: University of Chicago Press, 1945), cit. Robert Fishman, *Urban Utopias in the Twentieth Century* (Cambridge: MIT Press, 1982), 129.
31 Le Corbusier, *Last Works* (London: Thames and Hudson, 1970), 174, cit. Vikramaditya Prakash, *Chandigarh’s Le Corbusier* (Seattle: University of Washington Press, 2002), 20.
32 Herbert Marcuse, *Eros and Civilization: A Philosophical Inquiry into Freud* (Boston: Beacon Press, 1974), 212, emphasis Marcuse’s; see also Marcuse, *An Essay on Liberation* (Boston: Beacon Press, 1969); Marcuse, *Counterrevolution and Revolt* (Boston: Beacon Press, 1972); see also Larry Hartwick, “On the Aesthetic Dimension: A Conversation with Herbert Marcuse,” *Contemporary Literature* 22 (Madison: University of Wisconsin, 1981), 417–24.
33 Michael Hardt and Antonio Negri, *Empire* (Cambridge: Harvard University Press, 2000), 294.
34 Maurizio Lazzarato, “Immaterial Labor,” in Paolo Virno and Michael Hardt, eds., *Radical Thought in Italy: A Potential Politics* (Minneapolis: University of Minnesota Press, 1996), 134.
35 Alexander R. Galloway, “*Warcraft* and Utopia,” *ctheory.net: 1000 Days of Theory*, accessed May 28, 2024, journals.uvic.ca/index.php/ctheory/article/download/14501/5342?inline=1.
36 See John J. Tarrant, *Drucker: The Man Who Invented the Corporate Society* (Boston: Cahners Books, 1976).
37 Cf. Peter Drucker, *Post-Capitalist Society* (Oxford: Butterworth–Heinemann, 1993), 17–18.
38 Cf. ibid., 51.
39 For an excellent discussion on architecture’s confusion over its labor practices, see Paolo Tombesi, “On the Cultural Separation of Design Labor,” in Peggy Deamer and Phillip G. Bernstein, eds., *Building (in) the Future: Recasting Labor in Architecture* (New York: Princeton Architectural Press, 2010), 117–36.
40 Karl Marx, *Capital: A Critique of Political Economy*, vol. 1, chap. 21, trans. Ben Fowkes (New York: Penguin Books, 1976), 695.
41 Ibid., 695–6.
42 Ibid., 695.
43 Marx, *Capital*, 695 (see note 40).

LABOR, PRODUCTION, AND THE ENDS OF ARCHITECTURE

Text: Douglas Spencer

Fig. 1

Fig. 2

Fig. 3

Fig. 4

Directors and partners at architecture firms in Europe earn an average of €46,800 annually. Sole practitioners earn slightly less, with an average annual income of €40,000. Salaried architects earn an average annual salary of €33,000 (rounded, average gross pre-tax earnings, adjusted for purchasing power parity). German architects are among the top earners in their profession in Europe: €80,000 for directors and partners, €69,000 for sole practitioners, €50,000 for salaried architects, €56,000 for freelance architects, and €63,000 for government employees and civil servants (rounded, average gross pre-tax annual income, adjusted for purchasing power parity).

The dynastic families of fifteenth-century Florence, enriched by trade in luxury products, textiles, sugar, and African slaves, as well as by the city's rapidly expanding international network of banking services, invested much of their wealth in architecture. Urban palaces built for private patrons were designed to set moneyed families apart from the masses. Adorned with patrimonial emblems and distinguished from the medieval fabric of the city by their classical elevations, these palaces were designed by a new class of professional architects owing its very existence to the massive concentrations of wealth to which it lent form and expression. Architecture historian Isabelle Hyman, in her analysis of the construction of the Palazzo Medici designed by Michelozzo di Bartolomeo, notes that by the mid-fifteenth century, "it would be possible for a private citizen like Cosimo de' Medici to demolish twenty-two old houses in order to build one new one."[1] Space for a piazza in front of the church of San Lorenzo, designed by Filippo Brunelleschi, observes Hyman, "was to be provided by the destruction of buildings that the governing body of Florence wished to eliminate anyway for they were inhabited by prostitutes and other 'low types' who they believed should not have been living near the church."[2] The building boom in *palazzi*, notes historian Samuel Kline Cohn Jr., was undertaken at the expense of the Florentine working and artisanal classes: "The reverse side of the Renaissance palace construction on Via Maggio and Via Larga, the new hospitals, churches, and monuments to private families," he argues, "was displacement and demographic redistribution."[3] In a contemporaneous report, Filippo di Cino Rinuccini describes the effect of the city's building frenzy on its inhabitants: "Because of the construction of so many and such large houses by the noble and powerful, the masses suffered from a lack of housing."[4] Florence's governing commune attempted to address the housing shortage through legislative means, offering up tax relief in exchange for private housing construction in the city. As Goldthwaite goes on to note, however, "the tax advantage held out by the commune … would have been attractive only to real estate developers, men who wanted to build rental properties, for houses used as residences for their owners had long been exempt from taxation."[5] By the early sixteenth century Florence's core had become a site for speculative building development. "In 1512," writes Goldthwaite, "the mason's guild itself began to work on an apartment over its hall as an investment, and the place was rented on a three-year-long lease long before it was finished."[6]

The architecture of the Renaissance, commonly hailed as a crowning achievement of Western humanism, instead reveals itself as an accessory to capitalism in one of its founding moments. Architecture, in its modern sense, comes into being to serve the interests of a nascent capitalism whose features are all too familiar: social cleansing, housing crises, real estate speculation, and an exploitative rental market. Whatever else might have changed, the profession and practice of architecture appear from a present-day perspective not to have strayed too far from their point of origin. Capitalism and the profession of architecture are functionally conjoined at birth, and in ways that continue to serve and structure their relationship.

Today's big-name architects carry on much like their Renaissance forbears, reaping the rewards of their integral relations to capitalism—only at the infinitely vaster scale and complexity of a globalized planet ruled almost entirely by the imperatives of the latter. Their employees, meanwhile, increasingly find themselves proletarianized, alienated, and disempowered. The contemporary architectural worker is ever more removed from any capacity to respond directly to the social and environmental issues which they might have hoped, or imagined, their profession was supposed to address. As vectors of value extraction, architectural workers are pushed to function as opportunistic and self-serving actors while the products of their own labor are put to work against their interests, raising real estate values and making living in the cities where they work extortionately expensive. In response, the idea of architecture as labor has in recent years been advanced through both academic and activist channels, with a particular focus on the proletarianization and precarization of architectural workers. Exploitative practices—unsalaried internships, unpaid overtime—have been exposed. The self-sacrificial culture of architecture, premised on the idea of "the calling," has been called out and contested in practice and in architectural education.[7] Some architectural workers have sought—and sometimes even succeeded—to unionize their firms. Internationally, various groups and organizations have been formed in recent years to advocate for architectural workers' rights and interests.

All of this, however, leaves open to question the ends to which these initiatives are directed. If the recognition of architecture as labor is supposed to be a wake-up call, then what goals is the architect, now alert to the real nature of their social position, to pursue? Beginning in the Renaissance, the modern profession's own modes and relations of production have, after all, been developed precisely in relation to—and largely in the service of—those of capitalism. These relations, and their effects, cannot be overturned by the simple act of categorizing architecture as labor. The much more complex act of unionization is not guaranteed to achieve these results either. If taken simply as ends in themselves, both might be a little short-sighted.

Architecture as Immaterial Labor

By far the most substantial and widely known engagement with the relations between architecture, labor, and capital is to be found in the work of Peggy Deamer.[8] Deamer and the Architecture Lobby, an advocacy group she cofounded in 2013, have consistently argued that the practice of architecture needs to be recognized as a form of labor, as opposed to a "calling": "We compare ourselves to doctors and lawyers," argues Deamer, "but believe our work is too creative and culturally significant to be properly filed under 'service sector.' Consequently, we fail to conceptualize our work as work."[9] This failure, claims Deamer, leaves architects prone to exploitation, to the acceptance of poor conditions of employment, and to receiving salaries rendering them "no better off than factory workers."[10]

While Deamer wants to dispel the illusion of architecture as a "calling," she argues that counting it as work doesn't deprive it of its status as a creative enterprise. Drawing on precedents derived from the Soviet avant-garde, where art was subsumed under the category of labor to conform it to the demands of the revolution, as well as from Nicholas Bourriaud's theory of "relational aesthetics," wherein artists assume everyday roles—such as retail managers or museum docents—in their practice, Deamer argues that art and, by extension, architecture can be construed as labor without relinquishing their claims to creativity.[11] On this basis Deamer and the Architecture Lobby have promoted the unionization of architectural firms and the creation of worker cooperatives or workers' councils to contest the exploitation of architectural labor. If, as Deamer claims, the failure to identify labor as such serves the interests of capital—"no more organised complaining about how profit is (not) distributed fairly amongst owners, managers, and actual producers!"[12]—then its recognition allows for the conditions of that labor to be contested.

But there are, for Deamer, other advantages that fall to architects in rethinking their activity as labor, insofar as architecture is read as a practice of "immaterial labor": In an essay titled "Architectural Work: Immaterial Labour," Deamer writes: "The immaterial labour/material labour distinction isn't merely a relabelling of the existing one between designer and constructor; rather, it clearly identifies the fact that there is immaterial labour (knowledge work) in all forms of production once we leave behind the manufacturing model of work."[13]

Deamer derives the idea of "immaterial labor" from Italian autonomist Marxism. Maurizio Lazzarato, among its chief theorists, defines immaterial labor as "the labor that produces the informational

Fig. 1 Wilhelm von Kaulbach, *The Artists Entrusted with the Implementation of Monumental Buildings by King Ludwig I*, ca. 1850, oil on canvas, 82 × 168 cm

The composition of this allegorical painting exemplifies the separation between manual construction labor and immaterial design work.

Fig. 2 Jacopo da Empoli, *Michelangelo presenta a papa Leone X i progetti per la fabbrica di San Lorenzo a Firenze* (Michelangelo presenting Pope Leo II with the plans for the basilica of San Lorenzo in Florence), 1617–19, oil on canvas, 236 × 141 cm

and cultural content of the commodity."[14] Alongside other thinkers of this current, notably Michael Hardt and Antonio Negri, Lazzarato conceives of immaterial labor as an essentially post-industrial mode of work toward which capitalism is now oriented, and in which a premium is increasingly placed on knowledge, ideas, and information.[15] For Deamer, the labor of the architect appears—however anachronistically, given the age of the profession—to exemplify these criteria. The subcontractor she watches plastering the walls of a house she and her partner have designed is engaged in a "material labor of construction," while they, the architects, are practicing an "immaterial labor of thinking, drawing and model-making."[16] Both, though, are engaged in labor.

Divisions of Labor

Deamer seeks to equalize different types of activity—material and immaterial, manual and intellectual—and the social values typically attributed to them by invoking the general category of labor. Yet this equalization leaves unquestioned how such divisions of labor have been produced in the first place. That architects practice "thinking, drawing and model-making" is not the result of a natural predisposition to certain activities for which the profession then provides a suitable outlet. Such practices and their attribution to architects as a professional class are the product of capitalist development operating under concrete historical circumstances.

Brazilian architect and activist Sérgio Ferro, in his *History of Architecture Seen from the Building Site*, explicitly frames this separation of architecture from building as implicated in a formative moment in the history of the class struggle between labor and capital. Ferro conveys how Brunelleschi was commissioned by the Florentine guild of fabric manufacturers to design the cupola of the Santa Maria del Fiore cathedral, a project intended to mark the guild's victory over the infamous 1378–82 uprising of workers known as the Ciompi Revolt. In organizing the construction of the cupola, notes Ferro, Brunelleschi "hired workers from a neighbouring city in order to break a local strike for higher salaries—only allowing the locals to return once they accepted even lower wages (thus increasing absolute surplus value). In addition, observing that the workers spent a significant amount of time lunching and drinking wine, Brunelleschi installed a canteen right up on top of the scaffolding and abolished wine, which made them sluggish … And he did not stop there: Brunelleschi hid his designs and models … All the workers were unfamiliar with the project and worked on it ignorant of its objective, which meant they were less resistant to submission."[17]

Divisions of labor are produced by and serve the interests of capitalism. Crucially, they do so in ways that materially and socially advantage certain forms of labor over others, creating class distinctions in the process. Architects have historically been advantaged by the class position afforded them within capitalism. Their profession is constitutively founded on its capacity to distance and distinguish itself from craft and industry in order to assume command and control over these on behalf of capital. Elizabeth Merrill, in her essay "The *Professione di Architetto* in Renaissance Italy," notes that a "profusion of architectural literature in the fifteenth and sixteenth centuries … sought to provide a programmatic foundation for architecture."[18] Treatises such as Leon Battista Alberti's *De re aedificatoria* "argued that architecture was a discipline of the creative mind."[19] The figure of the architect, she continues, "was distinguished from the craftsman, granted a significant salary, and often called upon for his expertise in matters of politics, business, and diplomacy."[20] Goldthwaite, likewise remarking on the significance of Alberti's treatise, writes that "since the architect served all mankind as the complete designer, working on everything from simple houses to great cities, Alberti had a sense of the higher purpose of architecture as something socially necessary and useful and of the architect as a kind of universal man."[21]

Distinctions between architects and craftspeople were not only fashioned from writings such as those of Alberti. Goldthwaite argues that the "complex medium of communication" newly employed by the professional architect—models, drawings, and blueprints—was developed in relation to the specific demands of inter- and intra-urban competition for prestige among newly wealthy patrons. Architecture had, up until the Renaissance, been largely dependent on tradition and imitation, enabling masons and builders to work from their own knowledge. During the Renaissance, with a premium now placed on innovation, invention, and competitive displays of wealth and magnificence, this was no longer the case. Effectively deskilled, those responsible for construction found their labor remotely directed through newly invented techniques of "thinking, drawing and model-making," by a professional class assuming superior status over them. The subjectification of architects as "creative minds" and "universal men" is therefore a product of and for the needs of capitalist development.

The notion that capitalism, beyond producing objects, also generates the subjects that produce such objects—in this case the professional architect—can be found in Marxian accounts of labor. As Marx notes in the *Grundrisse*, production in capitalism "not only creates an object for the subject, but also a subject for the object."[22] Objectification and subjectification presuppose and depend upon one another. Not only do architects produce architecture in the interests of capitalism, but architects are themselves produced, under conditions historically and materially determined by capitalism, to make architecture. In this respect, Peggy Deamer's resort to the thesis of immaterial labor is unfortunate, since it depends on the fiction of a producer autonomous from the conditions of production. The propositions drawn from this interpretation are as questionable as the assumptions that lead to it.[23]

In his essay "Immaterial Labor" Lazzarato writes that "the cycle of immaterial labor takes as its starting point a social labor power that is independent and able to organize both its own work and its relations with business entities. Industry does not form or create this new labor power, but simply takes it on board and adapts it."[24] This type of reasoning leads Deamer to argue that "the worker exists as a person prior to her insertion into a labor context. The architectural worker should therefore play in the system, but use it to her own ends."[25] She goes on to quote a further passage from Lazzarato in support of the idea that architects, as immaterial laborers in a position of independence, are able to challenge the larger structures of capitalism in which their labor is situated: "Industry's control over this new labor power presupposes the independent organization and 'free entrepreneurial activity' of the labor power."[26]

Deamer therefore arrives, via the thesis of immaterial labor, at the conclusion that the architect is free to act according to their own ethical directives on the basis that they recognize their work *as* work, and that all work, as such, is "free entrepreneurial activity." If we understand, however, that labor is not "free," but conditioned by the ends it is supposed to serve, this proposition is untenable. Architects, even as workers, will for the most part continue to assume exactly the kind of agency they have been exercising beginning with the Renaissance: servility to capitalist development while claiming to be representatives of a universal humanism. The "creative mind" attributed by Alberti to the fifteenth-century architect is embodied today by Bjarke Ingels, problem-solving at the planetary scale in his Masterplanet project.[27] The distance between the creative mind and those assigned to perform the manual labor to bring its visions about has only been intensified and exacerbated since the Renaissance. Millionaire architects today design projects to glorify dictators, built by immigrant labor subjected to systemic human rights abuses. This situation is not amenable to correction by the architect alone precisely because it is integral to the functioning of capitalism. The notion of immaterial labor—a supposed special capacity of the architect for "thinking, drawing and model-making"—is an obstacle rather than a means to challenge the political, economic, and environmental injustices in which architecture, as an accessory to capital, is implicated.

Even where ethical choices might be possible—and the opportunities for these will be scarce, given the economic realities to which architectural firms are ultimately subject—the capacity to make such decisions will not be evenly distributed within the architectural firm, especially in its larger instantiations. Choices will fall to the few still positioned to organize and direct the labor of others and able to burnish their own creative credentials in the process. Worse still is the "architectural imagination," a last resort of the ethical architect exercised in an effort to salvage some dignity and purpose for the profession, to persuade of some capacity to which it alone is peculiarly suited; an ability to creatively conjure up visions of a better world.

As long as the architectural profession lays claim to a special aptitude for creativity, the appeal of "the calling" will hold sway. To argue that creativity is but one form of labor, given to some and not to others, does little to deflate the mystique of architecture on which the exploitation of its students and workers thrives. Overcoming this mystique and its larger consequences requires the recognition that it is capitalism that divides and unevenly distributes labor under categories of activity forged through its own historical development. It is not given, as either calling or condemnation, that the labor of some is immaterial, intellectual, creative, while that of others is material, manual, physical. These are artificial schisms inflicted by capitalism on the capacities of human activity.

Fig. 3 A 2020 meeting between Danish architect Bjarke Ingels (BIG) and far-right former Brazilian President Jair Bolsonaro drew international criticism. The reason for the meeting was a tourism master plan for northeast Brazil, which BIG is drafting for hotel developer Nômade Group.

Labor Militancy and the Prospects of Unionization

Turning to the possibilities for collective action by architects, the immediate prospect for any union of architectural workers being capable of—or even invested in—addressing the issues raised here appears limited. The profession of architecture, such as it has been constituted in and for capitalist development since the Renaissance, and the class privileges afforded it as a form on intellectual production cannot be transformed solely through the economic struggles with which unions are conventionally engaged. The September 2022 unionization of Bernheimer Architects, a small firm in Brooklyn, and the formation of SINTARQ, a national union of Portuguese architects, that same year do represent significant and promising gains in advancing the material interests of architectural workers. Unionized struggles against the economic exploitation of architectural workers are both meaningful and essential, especially where the architectural firm operates as capitalism writ large, with vast wage differences between owners and employees, and with the latter often subject to precarious and exhausting conditions of work. The architectural union can function as an effective instrument of economic struggle over the distribution of the surplus value produced by capitalism on more equitable terms. Outside of it being allied to other parties, organizations, or platforms of direct political struggle *against* ongoing capitalist exploitation of labor, land, people, and environment, however, unionization will leave intact architecture's functioning *for* capitalism and the fracturing of human capacities on which it thrives. And while the conditions of architectural production may be improved, its products and the ends to which these are put will remain largely directed and determined by external imperatives. Only a militant project of unionization, explicit in its antagonism toward capital in general, as well as to the bosses of larger architectural firms, may have the capacity to act politically and to address questions of what—and for whom—architects do or do not produce and look beyond the conditions in which production occurs.

The prospects for a militant project of unionization encompassing a political as well as an economic agenda may at present be slight, but they are an emergent potential. As Marianela D'Aprile and I, in our essay "Notes on Tafuri, Militancy, and Unionization," write, "once organized and willing to wield their power as workers, architectural workers could begin to realize a better world, instead of merely imagining one. They could, for example, negotiate contracts that exclude work on prisons or detention centers."[28]

Such prospects have recently been pulled into sharper focus around the AECOM-partnered development The Line, a 170-kilometer-long, 200-meter-wide linear smart city project designed by Morphosis Architects currently under construction as part of Saudi Arabia's NEOM megaproject. The Line, boasts the project website, "is a civilizational revolution that puts humans first, providing an unprecedented urban living experience while preserving the surrounding nature."[29] The humans of the Huwaitat tribe occupying the Tabuk region of Saudi Arabia in which the The Line is being built, however, are being violently displaced from their homes to make way for the project. Abdul Rahim al-Huwaiti was reportedly executed by Saudi Arabian security forces in 2020 after opposing the project's development on social media.[30] Subsequently three further members of the Huwaitat tribe have been sentenced to death for protesting forced evictions from their homes.[31] In response to the revelation of these events The Architecture Lobby posted on its X—formerly Twitter—account the following message: "The most power you have as an architect over an unethical project is that of withholding your labor. No architect should work on this meat grinder of human misery."[32] Responding to Zaha Hadid Architects' work on another project for NEOM—a design for the 2029 Asian Winter Games in Saudi Arabia's Trojena resort—the union United Voices of the World—Section of Architectural workers posted on X: "We always talk about organising for better working standards, which can overshadow the fact you can fight to take an ethical stand too! A unionised [Zaha Hadid Architects] could strike and stop the firm from working on this monstrosity once and for all."[33]

Such sentiments signal the willingness of many involved in architecture's labor movement to act politically as well as economically. They also mark a point of departure in which architects identify themselves not only as workers or with the categories of labor historically assigned to them in the development of capitalism, but with the common interests of a humanity conceived of beyond its instrumentalization in the production of value as an end in itself. Through a politically motivated refusal of labor, the ends of building activity may at last start to be disentangled from the ends of capitalism, even if this were to spell the end of the architectural profession as we know it.

Fig. 4 Poster of the National Association of Local Government Workers / National Union of Public Employees, Great Britain, 1982

1 Isabelle Hyman, *Fifteenth Century Florentine Studies: The Palazzo Medici and a Ledger for the Church of San Lorenzo* (New York: Garland, 1977), 42, cit. Samuel Kline Cohn Jr., *The Laboring Classes in Renaissance Florence* (New York: Harcourt Brace Jovanovich, 1980), 121, note 3.
2 Ibid., 115, cit. ibid.
3 Cohn, *Renaissance Florence*, 124 (see note 1).
4 Filippo di Cino Rinuccini: *Ricordi storici di Filippo di Cino Rinuccini dal 1282 al 1460 colla continuazione di Alamanno e Neri, suoi figli, fino al 1506* (Florence: Piatti, 1840), xc, trans. ARCH+.
5 Richard A. Goldthwaite, *The Building of Renaissance Florence: An Economic and Social History* (Baltimore: Johns Hopkins University Press, 1980), 17.
6 Ibid.
7 Peggy Deamer addresses the problematic implications of architecture being conceived as a "calling" in her essay "Work," (pages 10–17). See also Marisa Cortright, "Death to the Calling: A Job in Architecture Is Still a Job," *Failed Architecture* (August 15, 2019), accessed May 27, 2024, failedarchitecture.com/death-to-the-calling-a-job-in-architecture-is-still-a-job; Cortright, "It Could Always Be Worse," (pages 48–51).
8 See Peggy Deamer, *Architecture and Labor* (London: Routledge, 2020); Deamer, ed., *The Architect as Worker: Immaterial Labor, the Creative Class, and the Politics of Design* (London: Bloomsbury Academic, 2015); Deamer, ed., *Architecture and Capitalism: 1845 to the Present* (London: Routledge, 2014).
9 Deamer, *The Architect as Worker* (see note 8), 61.
10 Ibid.
11 Cf. ibid., 63–66.
12 Deamer, "Architectural Work: Immaterial Labour" in Katie Lloyd Thomas et al., eds., *Industries of Architecture* (London: Routledge, 2016), 137.
13 Ibid., 146.
14 Maurizio Lazzarato, "Immaterial Labor," in Paolo Virno and Michael Hardt, eds., *Radical Thought in Italy: A Potential Politics* (Minneapolis: University of Minnesota Press, 1996), 132.
15 See Michael Hardt and Antonio Negri, *Empire* (Cambridge: Harvard University Press, 2000), and *Multitude: War and Democracy in the Age of Empire* (London and New York: Penguin, 2004).
16 Deamer, *The Architect as Worker* (see note 8), xxvii.
17 Sérgio Ferro, "From Strasbourg to Paris," trans. Ellen Hayward and Ana Naomi de Sousa, in Silke Kappe and Marina Moura, eds., *Sérgio Ferro: Architecture From Below* (London: Mack, 2024), 57–58.
18 Elizabeth Merrill, "The *Professione di Architetto* in Renaissance Italy," *Journal of the Society of Architectural Historians* 76, no. 1 (March 2017), 13, doi.org/10.1525/jsah.2017.76.1.13.
19 Ibid.
20 Ibid., 14.
21 Goldthwaite, *Renaissance Florence* (see note 5), 366.
22 Karl Marx, *Grundrisse: Foundations of the Critique of Political Economy*, trans. Martin Nicolaus (Harmondsworth: Penguin Books, 1973), 26.
23 For a particularly compelling critique of the thesis of immaterial labor, pertinent to the issues raised here, see Sean Sayers, "The Concept of Labour" in *Marx and Alienation: Essays on Hegelian Themes* (London: Palgrave Macmillan, 2011), 32–47.
24 Lazzarato, "Immaterial Labor" (see note 14), 137.
25 Deamer, "Architectural Work" (see note 12), 144.
26 Lazzarato, "Immaterial Labor" cit. ibid. (see note 14).
27 See Ciara Nugent, "The Climate is Breaking Down: Architect Bjarke Ingels Has a Masterplan for That," *Time* (October 21, 2020), accessed May 27, 2024, time.com/collection/great-reset/5900743/bjarke-ingels-climate-change-architecture.
28 Marianela D'Aprile and Douglas Spencer, "Notes on Tafuri, Militancy, and Unionization," *Avery Review* (February 2022), accessed May 27, 2024, averyreview.com/issues/56/notes-on-tafuri.
29 NEOM, "The Line: New Wonders for the World," accessed May 27, 2024, www.neom.com/en-us/regions/theline.
30 See Ali Younes, "Saudi Forces Kill Man Who Refused to Give Up Property: Activists," *Al Jazeera* (April 15, 2020), accessed May 27, 2024, www.aljazeera.com/news/2020/4/15/saudi-forces-kill-man-who-refused-to-give-up-property-activists.
31 See Mohammed Rasool, "Saudi Arabia Sentences 3 Men to Death For Refusing to Vacate NEOM Development Site," *Vice* (October 11, 2022), accessed May 27, 2024, www.vice.com/en/article/5d3kkd/neom-saudi-arabia-howeitat-tribe.
32 The Architecture Lobby (@Arch_Lobby), X (October 23, 2022), accessed May 27, 2024, x.com/Arch_Lobby/status/1584372577279299584.
33 UVW – Section of Architectural Workers, (@saw_unite), X (October 24, 2022), accessed May 27, 2024, x.com/saw_unite/status/1584492187500544000.

ARCHITECTURE WITHOUT A LOBBY

Ruth Schagemann, Andrea Gebhard, and Susanne Wartzeck in conversation with Olaf Grawert and Arno Brandlhuber

Architecture is deeply intertwined with economic and political issues, as made exceedingly clear by today's pressing ecological and societal challenges. However, unlike the construction industry, architecture seems to lack a lobby to advocate for alternatives to the prevailing "growth and construction" mentality in politics. What conditions are needed to establish new systems of economic value creation, and what role do interest groups play in this process? Ruth Schagemann, President of the Architects' Council of Europe (ACE), Andrea Gebhard, President of the Federal Chamber of German Architects (BAK), and Susanne Wartzeck, President of the Association of German Architects (BDA), discuss this topic with Arno Brandlhuber and Olaf Grawert.

Over 50% of the total value of the European construction market is generated by four countries: Germany (€402 billion), France (€386 billion), the UK (€363 billion), and Italy (€301 billion). → Luxembourg (€16 billion), Norway (€16 billion), and Austria (€13 billion) generate the highest output per architect in the construction market. Just over €2.5 trillion is the estimated total value of the European construction market in 2022, including civil engineering and infrastructure work. The architecture market remains largely national in scope: on average, 97.5% of an office's revenue is generated within its country of registration. → Norwegian (70%) and Danish (80%) architects work most frequently on projects abroad.

Olaf Grawert: This publication is driven by two questions. First, how can architects and planners regain more agency? Second, how can they organize more effectively and be more involved? The institutions you represent as their respective presidents have committed to restructuring the discipline, from the European scale with the Architects' Council of Europe (ACE), to the national representation of the Federal Chamber of German Architects (BAK), to the independent advocacy of the Association of German Architects (BDA), a professional interest group. What does this transformation imply for our self-image as architects?

Ruth Schagemann: For thirty years, the Architects' Council of Europe has advocated for the quality of the built environment to serve the common good of European societies and has called for favorable working conditions for architects. Previously, this advocacy was limited to an advisory role. National ministers could meet and discuss issues at the European level, but implementation was left to individual countries and sometimes did not occur at all. However, three years ago, the tide turned. With the New European Bauhaus initiative, recommendations were coordinated, and the common good became part of the European Green Deal and the European Climate Law. Integral to this is the so-called Renovation Wave strategy, which now enjoys political majority support and is influencing forthcoming legislation. The next step involves ensuring that the social and cultural dimensions of our work at the European level become legally binding at the national level, moving from being discretionary recommendations to mandatory regulations. This change does not alter the demands on architects but does change the political and legislative landscape in which we practice. We must ensure that our tools are up-to-date and suitable for our tasks. This requires reforms in education, tendering and competition processes, and market conditions to ensure fair compensation.

OG What do the reforms mentioned by Ruth Schagemann and the new understanding of architecture at the European level mean for German architects, who are represented by the Federal Chamber of German Architects?

Andrea Gebhard: We are part of Europe, and Europe is our future! That is why everything Ruth Schagemann said can be applied directly to us at the national level. As the Federal Chamber of German Architects, we represent the interests of German architects before legislators through sixteen state chambers. Climate issues and the building sector's role in them are currently a central focus. The Federal Constitutional Court's 2021 landmark ruling on the need for increased climate protection has reaffirmed that we must limit our resource consumption and ensure that society at large participates in the necessary climate protection efforts. What is new is that this realization is taking hold in political and legislative agendas. What would a development plan—the legal basis for most architects' work—for the common good actually look like? What new tasks and compensation systems need to be developed? We are moving beyond focusing solely on individual buildings to considering the broader picture, especially regarding the existing building stock. How can we calculate a building's carbon footprint, including its existing structure and any modifications? Standards and fees need to be adjusted accordingly. For these and many other issues, urban and regional planning must adopt a holistic approach that transcends state lines. However, we are just at the beginning of this journey. It's about how we want to live together, not just as humans but with all living beings on this planet. Only then can we ensure that our work genuinely serves the common good, which goes beyond providing basic services to individual parties.

Arno Brandlhuber: Until recently, the fees architects could ask for in Germany were bracketed by law. The HOAI (fee regulation for architects and engineers) set minimum and maximum fee levels for every step from planning, to tendering, to completion based on construction costs. This supported the "common good" in competitions and tenders by prioritizing concept over cost. However, after more than fifty years, a decision at the European level has overturned this model. Given the evolution of what actually needs to be built away from new construction toward reuse, other legislative areas will require comprehensive structural reform as well. Can these changes be effectively managed at the national level?

AG In Germany, we have always been involved in the legislative process. The debates occur in parliament, where bills proposed by ministries are voted on. Since the recent reestablishment of an independent Federal Ministry for Housing, Urban Development and Building, we now have a completely different status and access compared to when the Ministry of the Interior handled construction affairs. Currently, there is intense discussion about residential construction in the era of climate change, including innovative building materials, classifications, and reform proposals for the laws regulating architects' fees, which are integrated into expert reports. Everyone is aware that we need to streamline not only our thinking but also our laws.

OG The Association of German Architects celebrated its 120th anniversary last year, making it the oldest professional association in this field. As a professional body independent from the state, it represents the interests of freelance and independent architects. In what areas do you focus your efforts, and how do you complement and work alongside institutions like the Architects' Council of Europe and the Federal Chamber of German Architects?

Susanne Wartzeck: Our primary responsibility is to society and the environment, a point on which we all agree. Although we are the oldest organization, we are relatively small since we represent only freelance and independent architects in Germany. Unlike a chamber, we do not have a legal mandate, so we require less coordination, which allows us to be more agile, address issues quickly, and collaborate to implement them. While we have strong contacts, the chamber, of course, collaborates with the Ministry for Housing, Urban Development and Building more closely. Instead, we focus on actively influencing public opinion and social processes. Our perspective is practical and centered on the role of architects: How is the nature of our work changing in response to current challenges? What values do we uphold? We have these debates both internally and externally, and these are the areas where I see the most significant changes occurring for both built architecture and the profession.

OG With so much consensus, I would like to interrupt and contend that I don't believe your guidelines could gain majority support within your respective associations and chambers. Their members' primary concern is financial self-preservation in a post-growth era. The architect and transformation researcher Saskia Hebert suggests that an economy for the common good would have to be redefined through a new economic logic that could discard or at least completely overhaul the existing fee regulation. What implications does this have for the financial reality of your respective constituencies?

SW Up until the European Court of Justice declared the German fee regulation HOAI to be non-binding in 2019, architects' fees in our country were solely based on construction costs. The situation is currently changing for those involved in processes rather than buildings—like participatory processes, urban planning, etc. Instead of being able to use construction costs as a base line, new baselines have to be negotiated from scratch, resulting in new working and planning approaches. Compensation for these projects is based on the work that is actually performed, independent of whether anything is built. If that work is followed by a building contract, the regulatory fee brackets can still be used for traditional construction tasks. We are currently working on amendments to this regulation to address refurbishments and adaptive reuse, as they will constitute the majority of building activity in the future. The HOAI is still dominated by issues related to new construction, a relic of the building boom in Germany that started in the 1970s.

AG For the Federal Chamber of German Architects, there are currently two key areas of concern. First, outdated land use plans that don't codify current needs are difficult to work with. How are we supposed to effectively address today's problems with a ten-year-old land use plan? Second, the complexity of a project is not adequately reflected in the German fee regulation. The construction costs should no longer be the sole deciding factor. Instead, the goal should be to find the most practical and sustainable solution—and to establish the financial framework to support that outcome.

RS I fully agree that the delivery of quality work must be fairly compensated. At the European level, we face two major challenges: One is the price war in tenders and competitions. Cost often outweighs quality in these processes in many EU member states. We are actively working to address this by educating stakeholders about the higher long-term costs of seemingly low-cost solutions. The second challenge is fees, which vary significantly across Europe. Germany is the only country that has a statutory fee bracket, and where minimum rates tethered to construction costs are still applied unless agreed otherwise—even after the 2019 ruling by the European Court of Justice. All other European countries have had to abandon their fee regulations, often in conjunction with their accession to the EU, over the last ten to fifteen years. On top of this you have to consider the local economic conditions and the varying states of the construction industry in different countries. Spain, for example, has suffered immensely in recent years, and our Spanish colleagues are very closely following developments in Germany. The European Court of Justice's decision sparked a crucial debate across Europe, which we view as a positive development. A legal codification of fee policy at the European level could be feasible if our member organizations do their part to enforce them at the national level. While Cyprus is currently trying to introduce a fee regulation with our help, the Scandinavian countries remain opposed to mandatory fee rates or even guidelines, due to their lack of historical precedent for such measures.

AB This has led to a lot of architects migrating from southern Europe to Germany.

RS Many European architects from countries like Greece, Spain, and Italy have relocated to Germany due to the challenging economic conditions at home. That is an advantage of the European single market and the mutual recognition of professional qualifications. In the early 2000s, it was the other way around, with Germans more likely to move to Spain or the UK. Today, freedom of movement is a crucial aspect of the European Economic Area. That starts with education through programs like Erasmus, which makes students familiar with other cultures early on, preparing them for potential careers abroad.

AB How are salaries addressed at the European level? I'm not talking about fee regulations, which concern executives and freelancers, but the compensation received by employed architects. Have there been any moves toward legal regulations in this area?

RS We have an ethical responsibility to advocate for fair compensation, but ultimately, the actual implementation depends on our member organizations at the national level.

OG The Association of German Architects co-signed an open letter to Federal Minister for Housing, Urban Development and Building, Klara Geywitz, advocating for a "demolition moratorium." Is prioritizing renovation over new construction a goal of yours?

SW Yes, that is our clear objective. However, if you asked me whether all of our 5,000 members agree with this stance, I would have to say no. Nevertheless, I see it as my duty to stand up for what I firmly believe is right and in the best interest of our members, who would be the first to benefit from a significant increase in demand for refurbishing the existing building stock. We are presented a unique opportunity to engage deeply in this field of activity.

AG The Association of German Architects outlined a thoughtful approach to this topic in its 2022 position paper *Vom Wert der Planung* (On the value of planning). It emphasizes the importance of strategic thinking and future-oriented planning. As architects, we bear a crucial responsibility because the building sector accounts for roughly 40 percent of global CO_2 emissions. Maintaining existing buildings is an important lever for achieving climate goals. To make this a core part of our practice, we have to act in solidarity with each other and prioritize our values. This includes involving the public and educating it about the full scope of what architects can and do achieve. Otherwise, clients might opt for general contractors who handle everything from planning to delivering turnkey products. I believe the greatest transformative potential for our profession lies in adaptive reuse. This process is neither quick nor simple; it requires in-depth knowledge and tailored solutions—professional expertise that sets architects apart.

AB This raises a question for me: How can we turn these ideas—which are great opportunities on paper—into tangible incentives so that not only architects but also clients favor conversion over new construction?

RS By including embodied energy in the balance sheet. A revised version of the Energy Performance of Buildings Directive (EPBD), currently working its way through the EU legislative process [and which took effect on May 28, 2024; editor's note], mandates that a building's embodied carbon be tracked. This will improve the inclusion of existing building stock in carbon accounting and enable local architects to calculate their clients' CO_2 emissions in the future. It also represents a decisive paradigm shift at the European level. The previous version of the EBPD focused solely on the energy consumption of new buildings. Now, the emphasis is primarily on the existing building stock, 75 percent of which does not meet European energy standards. This is not just about individual buildings but also the broader built environment in urban and rural areas.

AG It is important to emphasize that the goal is not merely to wrap old buildings in insulation, but to establish a comprehensive sustainability assessment—a holistic view that fully accounts for the carbon already emitted throughout the building's life cycle. For this reason, the Berlin Chamber of Architects supports the demolition moratorium, although we, at the federal level, would not go as far as to ban demolition completely. Initiatives like these are pivotal steps toward a new construction paradigm. We recently introduced the idea of a new building class E (for "experimental") during a chamber meeting and presented it to the Federal Ministers of Construction and Justice. This new building class would allow architects and clients to decide which technical standards they wish to comply with. While building regulations in general and fire safety remain non-negotiable, the regulatory burden needs to be streamlined to enhance sustainability and affordability. Many of the countless mandatory technical standards contradict sustainability goals and public welfare criteria, making construction unnecessarily complicated and expensive without markedly improving quality of life or comfort.

OG As mentioned at the beginning of this conversation, could mandatory criteria for sustainability and the common good become a unique selling point for architects?

RS Absolutely, and this applies to both the European and national levels. The focus is finally shifting from cost to expertise. We have to capture this expertise and ensure we are capable of delivering it. But we shouldn't be naïve: The legislative process is pressured by purely economic interests. It is therefore crucial to reevaluate costs and profitability through the lens of sustainability.

OG Wouldn't you rather agree that we have no lobby at all? The idea of a trade union for architects has been around for a long time, but its legal basis in Germany remains unclear. Anna Yeboah discussed this in her article "No Recourse to Law" in ARCH+ 225 *Legislating Architecture*, writing, "it's normal in Germany for architects' chambers to serve as an extension of the arm of the law. All architects' chambers in the federated states are subject to the supervision of their respective state ministries, and thus have no legal leverage to wield when opposing contentious construction projects."[1] In short, chambers have no standing to sue because the legal system does not allow lawsuits against one's own self-interest. The trade associations, for their part, are unable to bring class-action lawsuits in the public interest because these kinds of lawsuits are limited to nature conservation, animal welfare, and consumer protection in Germany.

Now, one could argue that we have reached a point where the construction industry's actions have become an issue of nature conservation. Susanne Wartzeck, wouldn't it then be the task of the Association of German Architects, with a new self-image as representative for all architects and architectural workers, to advocate for compliance with the criteria of sustainability and the common good as matters of nature conservation?

SW That's an interesting angle. Indeed, the chambers do not have the right to file class-action lawsuits, and this is a major problem. If I, as an individual architect, am dissatisfied with public-sector clients or a specific project, I am unlikely to take on a state on my own. This hesitancy applies to individuals as well as groups of architects. Therefore, we should be granted the right to sue as an association. The Bavarian chapter of the Association of German Architects and the Bavarian Chamber of Architects are currently trying to address this by issuing public warnings if they feel certain procedures are skirting the law. This approach has already shown impressive effects, even without legal action. Of course, it would be preferable if applicable rules could be enforced. But concerning climate action, nature would first have to become a legal subject with enforceable rights.

RS In terms of taking legal action for unmet emission targets, there are precedents at the European level. For example, our counterparts in Turkey have legal options: If a municipality fails to comply with established architectural standards or improperly implements a project, they can initiate legal proceedings. If architecture chambers are seen "as an extension of the arm of the law," they should have a corresponding role. Ultimately, it's about who stands up for a better environment in the name of architecture and who can enforce the related measures. Spain is now the third country in Europe, alongside Sweden and France, to enact a dedicated law on the quality of architecture. It was passed in June 2022 and, among other things, prioritizes quality-based criteria in the awarding of architecture contracts. This law is the first of its kind to grant architects the right to take legal action—a development we should monitor closely, as it will offer valuable lessons.

1 Anna Yeboah, "No Recourse to Law," *ARCH+* 225, *Legislating Architecture* (October 2016), 197.

CHYBIK+KRISTOF

Cofounder Ondřej Chybík in conversation with Olaf Grawert

Fig.1

Fig.2

Fig.3

Fig.4

Fig.5

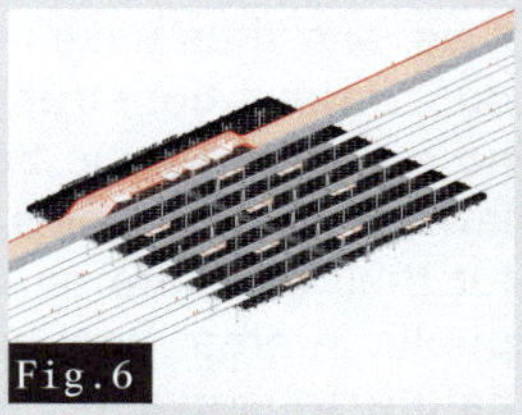
Fig.6

ORGANIZATION

OFFICE

Name	CHYBIK+KRISTOF ASSOCIATED ARCHITECTS S.R.O.
Founded in	2010
Registered in	PRAGUE, BRNO, BRATISLAVA
Legal form	LTD

PROJECTS

Total	462
completed	6%
public	62
private	214
Current	45

TEAM

Total	50
by gender	56% M, 44% F
average age	32.8
nationalities	CZE, SVK, POL, ESP, GBR, HUN, SWE, DEU, FRA, ITA, LTU, MEX
Partners	50% ONDŘEJ CHYBÍK 50% MICHAL KRIŠTOF
Managing Directors	2
Employees	45
Freelancers	0
Working students	0
Interns	3

FINANCES

INCOME PER MONTH / YEAR IN EUROS

Total	291,667 / 3,500,000
Construction projects	
Teaching	
Other external activities	
including lectures	

EXPENSES PER MONTH IN EUROS

Total	
Staff costs	
Average salary (employees / freelancers)	
Average salary (interns)	
Rent and operating costs	
Office supplies	
Insurance, consulting, and legal fees	
Travel expenses	

Olaf Grawert: You and your office partner Michal Krištof are currently building up and running what we might call a "typical" architecture practice: two name partners, steady growth, three locations, fifty-plus employees, roughly four hundred projects—mainly competitions, a decent number of which are completed. That is remarkable, considering that you are both in your mid-thirties. Your practice is young, and so is your team, as well as the Czech and Slovak cultural environment and market you are part of. How did you get to this point?

Ondřej Chybík: We know each other from our studies in Brno and had similar career paths. We participated in the Erasmus exchange program, at first for education: Michal went to Ghent and studied at the Sint-Lucas School of Architecture, I studied at TU Graz. After that, it was for internships: Michal went to intern for BIG in Copenhagen, I went to PPAG in Vienna. The former had around ninety employees at that time, the latter around thirty. We both realized that teaming up is the only way to create a bigger studio. And we also recognized that collaboration works best if you already know each other and have had similar experiences, in addition to being interested in the other's work and sharing a similar way of thinking. So, instead of competing, we decided to join forces for our first competition entry. That was the start of our collaboration.

OG What was your first project as an office, and how did you get the commission?

OC There are two first projects: One was a competition for housing in Bratislava. We took part in it during our diploma project, as we were really interested in the program and site next to the river. To our surprise, we won, which provided us with a small budget—just enough to buy new laptops and software. Within a month, we graduated and opened our studio with a task at hand, which was great. But I don't want to glorify the competition system. Our share of built projects is around 6 percent; the remaining 94 percent are unrealized concepts and designs. In the end, this first competition turned out to be unsuccessful as well: It has never been built.

The second first project—our first built one—was a commission for KOMA, a Czech manufacturer of residential modules. We knew them from our studies because we had won a student competition held by the company every year as an open call for projects. We called them to see if they were interested in collaborating with us, and incidentally, they were looking for someone to design their cafeteria. Beyond that, KOMA was interesting because the market was seeing their products as containers, and not as modular architecture, whose potential was relatively unknown at that time. We started working with them with the aim to promote the system's modularity. The budget was 1 million euros, significantly more than for a single-family house or an apartment.

For us as graduates, this was an unusual amount of money. There's the trope of the three Fs that fund an office's first projects: Friends, Family, and Fools. Instead, we tried to be proactive in finding our own clients with a focus on long-term collaboration. To this day, we have collaborated with KOMA on six projects, among which the Czech Pavilion for the EXPO 2015 in Milan, and have gained a lot of knowledge from their thirty years of experience. Vice versa, they benefited from our fresh look at things to create something new.

OG This kind of expertise, the way you talk about it, is part of your office's tacit knowledge—i.e., knowledge garnered from personal experience and context, and which you can't learn from a textbook. It's hard to describe and measure, and therefore hard to ascribe an exact value to. In that regard, what was your most important project so far? And which was your most profitable one?

OC Michal and I made the conscious decision to stay in the Czech Republic and Slovakia. Therefore, our most important project was one destined for the domestic market, i.e., the EXPO 2015 pavilion with KOMA. We succeed in moving the pavilion back to the Czech Republic afterward, so it was not only an investment for six months in Milan; it will serve a second public function for the next 50 years. That's certainly a nice case in point of transformation and modularity as the basis for a versatile and transferable architectural method. We were also awarded a prize for the pavilion at the EXPO, which translated into recognition from a larger Czech public. This value cannot be expressed in numbers.

The most profitable project is the Jihlava Multipurpose Arena, another public competition we were fortunate to win. Nevertheless, this one-time profit does not make up for all the money spent on competitions we've lost in our office's short history. For sure, competitions are a tool to ensure transparency in public projects, but I don't know if one win can outweigh all the second places, frustrations, and sunken costs.

OG If we look at the 2023 Sector Study commissioned by the Architect's Council of Europe, the eastern European market for

Fig. 1 The bus terminal after the renovation

Fig. 2 The bus terminal before the renovation

Project	ZVONAŘKA CENTRAL BUS TERMINAL
Category	RENOVATION
Use	BUS TERMINAL
Size	10,000 M²
Architecture	CHYBIK+KRISTOF
Client	PS BRNO S.R.O.
Location	BRNO, CZECH REPUBLIC
Team	ONDŘEJ CHYBÍK, MICHAL KRIŠTOF, ONDŘEJ ŠVANCARA, INGRID SPÁČILOVÁ, ADAM JUNG, KRYŠTOF FOLTÝN, MARTIN HOLÝ, LAURA EMILIJA DRUKTENYTĖ
Year	2017–20

Fig. 3 View of the north facade as seen from the street

Fig. 4 View from the east

new construction is still growing, whereas western Europe is shifting towards working with its existing building stock. If we look at your balance sheet, your annual turnover of 3.5 million euros is relatively high, especially when adjusted for purchasing power. Your profitability is that of a commercial firm with over one hundred employees. How do you view your own practice? And do you think your profitability is partially tied to the overall growth of the market you operate in?

OC As I have said, it was a conscious decision to start our office here, in a still-growing market in which we occupy a niche. We are the biggest architecture office not driven by profit in the Czech Republic and in Slovakia, although we do not offer the full range of services. There are bigger firms with up to two hundred employees who offer everything from design, to engineering, to documentation, to construction management. Architects represent a minority in these offices. Our model is different. We solicit most of these services from third parties, sharing the responsibility. This costs us a lot of money but allows us to focus on the parts that should be in an architect's custody. We care greatly about the quality of our work: What are the issues we want to work on? Who are the clients? And under which conditions do we produce architecture? We work for both public and private clients so as not to become full-fledged developers. Therefore, our business can only develop in a quite linear fashion, which we prefer over exponential growth. It comes with less pressure to keep up the workload to hold your staff. Some people are at ease with letting staff go; we are not, and I'm happy that we are able to sustain fifty architects while we focus on the important architectural elements.

OG Still, you felt uncomfortable talking about salaries at your firm in the run-up to this interview. Why?

OC When we received your request, we discussed how transparent we could be. It's certainly a sensitive topic. Let me try and explain why. Generally, I think there is no such culture of transparency or disclosure here. People don't talk about how much they earn—neither in architecture, nor in other professions. We have thought about it, but we haven't yet figured out how to establish such a culture. You don't talk about money here. It's always a private topic, and this omerta is sometimes even formalized in work contracts. Furthermore, many relationships in our office are based on friendship. This sounds contradictory, but it makes it even harder to speak about money. But we are working on it.

OG As you say, it is a question of (company) culture. Initiating discussions about money certainly comes with a lot of consequences, but not all of them are necessarily bad ones. Some employees will feel like they deserve to be paid more, but it also forces you to justify discrepancies in wages, working hours, or perks. I think these conversations have a great potential to make such differences visible and can help understand if advantages are based on hierarchy or competency. Nevertheless, I'm grateful that you speak with such candidness and awareness about the struggles you are facing while building up and running your own practice. In light of the climate crisis and the profession's fatal environmental impact, a younger generation might criticize your growth-driven approach. The promises of a competition-based model of architecture are seldom kept anymore, and the narrative that you will be rewarded with big commissions if you just work hard enough is increasingly eroding. What is your response to this criticism? And, in retrospect, would you have done some things differently?

OC I understand that argument. For the past two to three years, we have been trying to shift the focus of our work away from private developers and toward more public commissions. First, because it makes more sense to build things that are in the public interest. Second, because we don't want to become a business-oriented architecture firm that has to grow quickly to sustain itself. Sadly, a large number of public competitions are organized in a way that spoils the market—mostly due to the lack of remuneration for the conceptual work of architects, i.e., the starting point and the crucial stage of each project. For that reason, we can only afford to participate in a limited number of open competitions per year.

OG But it's also an organizational question: How do you create the time, the framework, and the possibility to work on topics

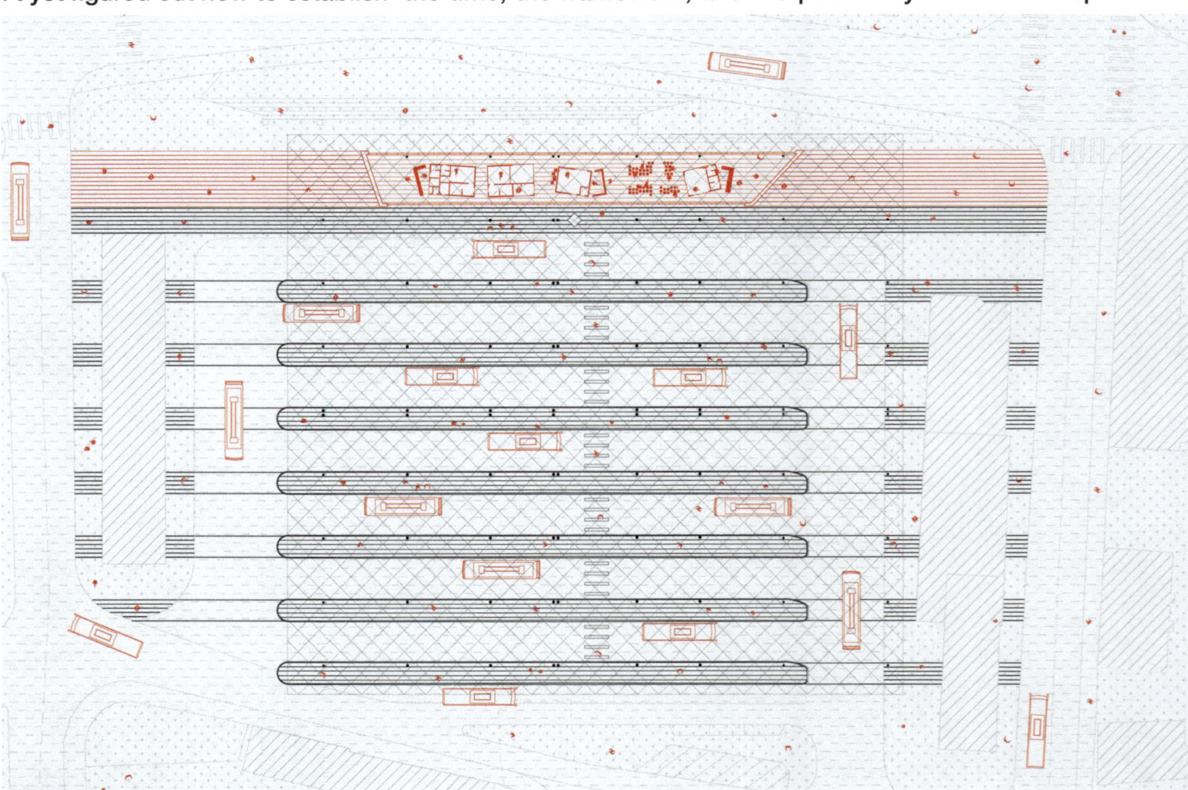

Fig. 5 Floor plan

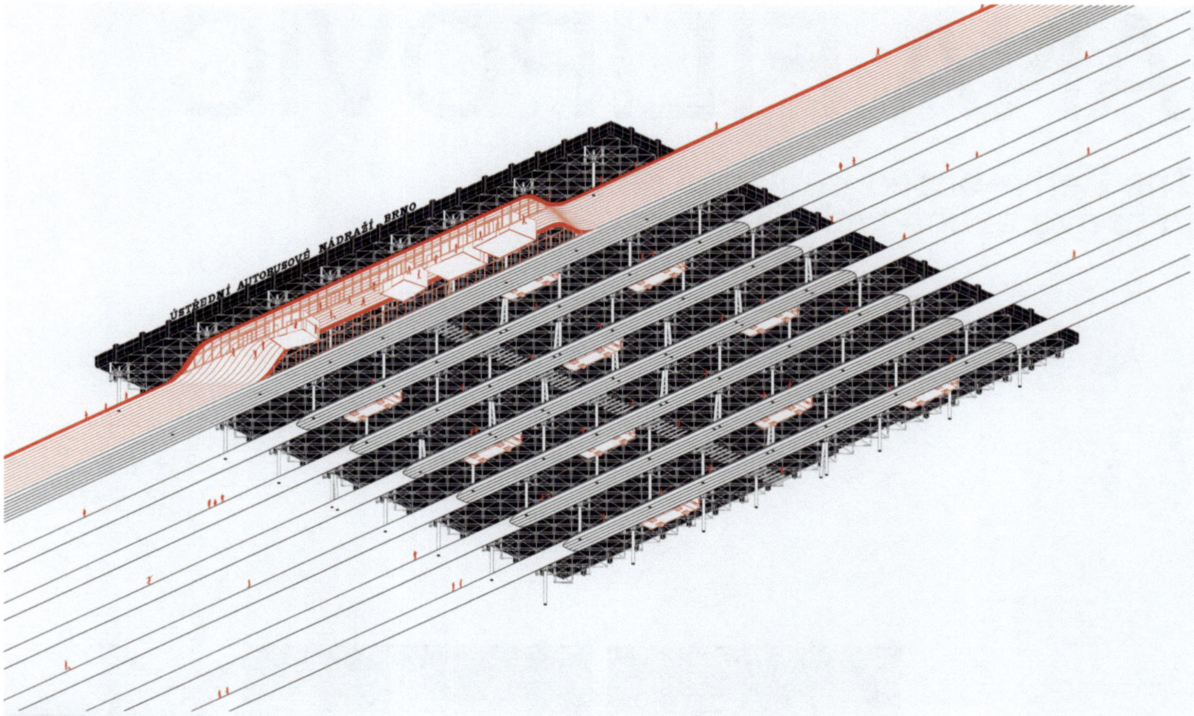

Fig. 6 Isometric view

and projects that are important to you? Again and again, we meet highly motivated, inspired, and outspoken architects who are bogged down by the administrative and organizational grind. How is work organized at your office?

OC Although it is not our priority to make a profit, the practice must be operational. You need money to fuel the machine, but our priorities are clear: Currently, we do twenty design workshops a week—four per day—and only two financial meetings a month. We are keenly aware of how the business is doing, but as long as we earn enough to pay everyone's salary and cover expenses, we are not bothered with the operational aspects. It's very important for my partner and me to free our schedule from as many organizational tasks as possible, such as tenders, contracts, communications—both with clients and the team—so that we can focus on the creative part. Once you employ more than twenty people, managing your team becomes its own task, and suddenly, you're not doing anything else. Not to speak about what happens if you have twenty projects with all the deadlines, responsibilities, and contingencies. You need someone to take care of that. Therefore, we decided to hire a CEO to manage the back office, including business development, controlling and finances, and a public-relations department. This separation allows us to work freely on what really interests us as architects: On the one hand, researching and trying out new things, mainly through competitions; and on the other, establishing *pro bono* work as part of our practice. Currently, we are collaborating with a Czech NGO to support communities in Kashmir in building schools, nurseries, and kindergartens.

OG We already mentioned tacit knowledge and the exchange of expertise. What skills for a viable and future-oriented architectural practice would you pass on to the next generation?

OC My rather practical business advice is: Actively look for topics and opportunities. Look around you; read the newspaper; talk to people. One day I read an article about a winery in Moravia, a region in the eastern Czech Republic. The owner referred to plans for an expansion, so we called and asked them if they might need two young architects for that. We got on board, helped them develop a concept, and got the commission. If you want to effect change, be proactive; don't complain and wait for a brief to fall into your lap.

ANA FILIPOVIĆ

The Berlin-based freelance architect in conversation with Olaf Grawert

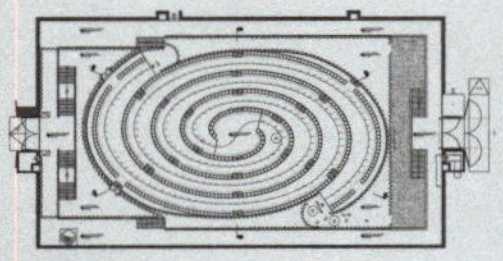
Fig.1

Fig.2

Fig.3

Fig.4

Fig.5

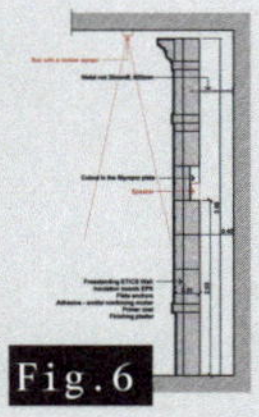
Fig.6

ORGANIZATION

OFFICE

Name	ANA FILIPOVIĆ
Founded in	2019
Registered in	BERLIN, GERMANY
Legal form	FREELANCE ARCHITECT

PROJECTS

Total	20
completed	13
public	13
private	7
Current	3

TEAM

Total	1
by gender	100% F
average age	41
nationalities	SRB
Partners	0
Managing Directors	0
Employees	0
Freelancers	1
Working students	0
Interns	0

FINANCES

INCOME PER MONTH / YEAR IN EUROS

Total	2,750 / 33,000
Construction projects	1,788 / 21,450
Teaching	0
Other external activities including lectures	964 / 11,550

EXPENSES PER MONTH IN EUROS

Total	1,480
Staff costs	
Average salary (employees / freelancers)	
Average salary (interns)	
Rent and operating	1,168
Office supplies	30
Insurance, consulting, and legal fees	251
Travel expenses	30

Olaf Grawert: As an independent freelance architect, you represent the most common type of architecture practice in Europe: 47 percent of offices are individuals or groups of up to four people, working on a project-to-project basis. You work in a lot of formats, collaborating with different people, groups, and collectives. In a way, this reflects the vision of an architectural practice shared by a lot of young architects who, instead of only building, want to work with different media to express themselves. How did you make this happen?

Ana Filipović: I think it is the result of an ongoing search for something that matters enough for me to do it for the rest of my life. I studied architecture in Belgrade because my initial interest, art history, didn't offer many prospects in terms of jobs. After graduation, I was lucky enough to work for a couple of years in offices whose work I found relevant at the time, with colleagues I was interested in. I even managed to get a decent paycheck. This was before the 2008 economic crisis, when the Serbian middle class was still taking out loans to buy apartments and invest in their renovation, creating a certain demand for architects. Still, this work quickly made me realize that catering to private interests—which was the direction in which the entire profession was developing around that time—was not interesting to me, and that I would much rather take part in projects that concern society at large. When I finished my studies in 2007, architecture was all about the form, concerned with finding a signature in proportions and materials. Only the financial crisis managed to radically reshape the premise of how we work today. Ever since, the question has been: How can we navigate our professional lives outside of the dominant economic forces at work in architecture? It is easy to create beautiful things, but there's no point in this unless we make ourselves useful to the community we operate in.

I applied for a scholarship from the German Academic Exchange Service (DAAD) and decided to move abroad and study Architecture & Critical Spatial Practice at Städelschule in Frankfurt am Main, which enabled me to develop a critical view on the built environment's conditions of production.

OG You are from Serbia, a non-EU country. This has a direct effect on your ability to reside in Germany—an ability directly tied to your financial security. How do you deal with that and how do you secure—i.e., finance—your independent practice? What roles do architecture, teaching, and cross-subsidizing play?

AF I hold a Serbian passport, but I don't plan on going back. The political and economic pressure in Serbia is so intense that it is very hard to not become complicit and serve the interests of the ruling elite. And I don't want to be forced into a survival mode that makes me give up on my moral principles. Coming to Germany from a non-EU country meant that I was long obliged to have a well-paid job corresponding to my education, making my visa dependent on my employer's whims and limiting me professionally. After five years of this kind of work, I obtained a residence permit. Now I finance my life through projects: Some of them are architectural, some are not. Working across various formats and scales allows me to cross-subsidize my practice. At the moment, my income is composed of a combination of project grants, direct commissions for exhibition designs or installations, and competitions.

OG What was your most profitable project, and what was your most important one?

AF I believe the project I am embarking on now—a facade design for a large mine drainage pump in western Germany—is going to be the most profitable project to date. The projects I worked on with the Berlin-based studio sub, which is responsible for architectural programming at Balenciaga, were relatively profitable in relation to their workload. In terms of importance, I take into account the degree of freedom and agency I enjoy. This is something I was missing in traditional office hierarchies, where you are often underpaid or voiceless, with little possibility to grow and learn. In this regard, I enjoyed working on Balenciaga's Spring/Summer 2020 show, as much for its playfulness as for the fact that it was carried out by a great production team.

OG How would you describe your professional network? You just spoke about the importance of who you work with, but how that happens—the legal and financial structure—is just as crucial.

AF As I already alluded to, I work across several constellations: independently on smaller, research-based projects and spatial designs; together with my partner on architectural projects; and recently, together with a friend, the three of us established a special kind of non-trading partnership under German civil law, a so-called GbR, for a competition we won. At Soft Agency, I collaborate with five women on projects rooted in feminist methodologies, practices, and formats, without it constituting a legal entity. A general understanding of contracts, pricing, how to set up fees, the mechanisms of self-promotion and marketing

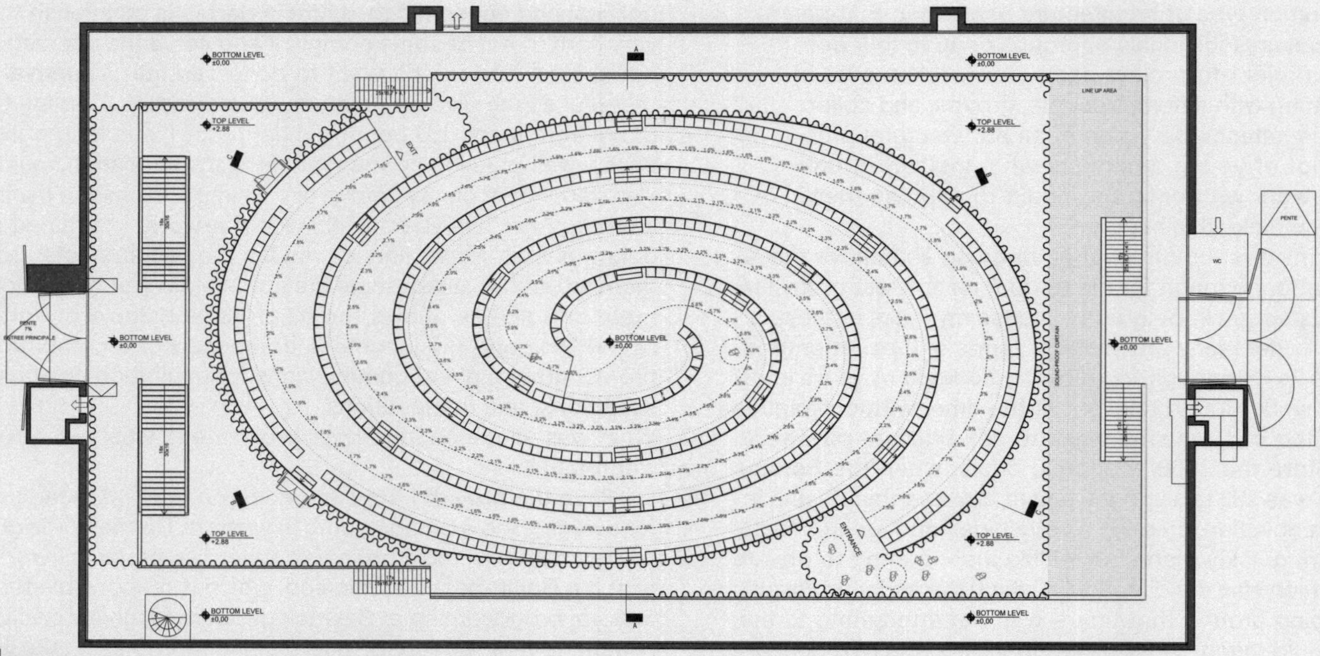

Fig. 1 Floor plan

Project	BALENCIAGA SS20 SHOW
Category	SCENOGRAPHY
Use	RUNWAY
Size	2,000 M²
Architecture	SUB, BERLIN
Client	BALENCIAGA, PARIS
Location	CITÉ DU CINÉMA, SAINT-DENIS, FRANCE
Team	NIKLAS BILDSTEIN ZAAR, ANDREA FARAGUNA, ANA FILIPOVIĆ
Year	2019

Fig.2 The runway for Balenciaga's Spring/Summer 2020 show at Paris Fashion Week was modeled on a plenary hall. The blue color scheme was reminiscent of the flag of the European Union.

Fig.3 The path taken by the models spiraled downwards—and back up again. It was a spatial translation of the collection's underlying theme of power dressing, which reinterpreted classic white-collar workwear such as suits, pantsuits, and shift dresses.

Project	WE STILL WRAP OUR BUILDINGS WITH HAZARDOUS WASTE
Category	INSTALLATION AND AUDIO PIECE
Team	ANA FILIPOVIĆ, PHILIPP MECKE
Text	MIKAEL BRKIC
Sound design	MICHAEL WINTER
Location	KUNSTMUSEUM STUTTGART, GERMANY
Curators	ELKE AUS DEM MOORE, SEBASTIAN SCHNEIDER, SARIE NIJBOER
Year	2020

Fig. 4 For its 30-year anniversary in 2021, the foundation Akademie Schloss Solitude hosted the exhibition *Beyond Walls: Über Grenzen hinaus* at Kunstmuseum Stuttgart with works by former fellowship recipients, including Ana Filipović.

Fig. 5 In Ana Filipović's installation *We Still Wrap Our Buildings with Hazardous Waste*, which she conceived together with Philipp Mecke, she raises ecological questions about the building industry, especially concerning the use of non-recyclable—and therefore eternal—materials.

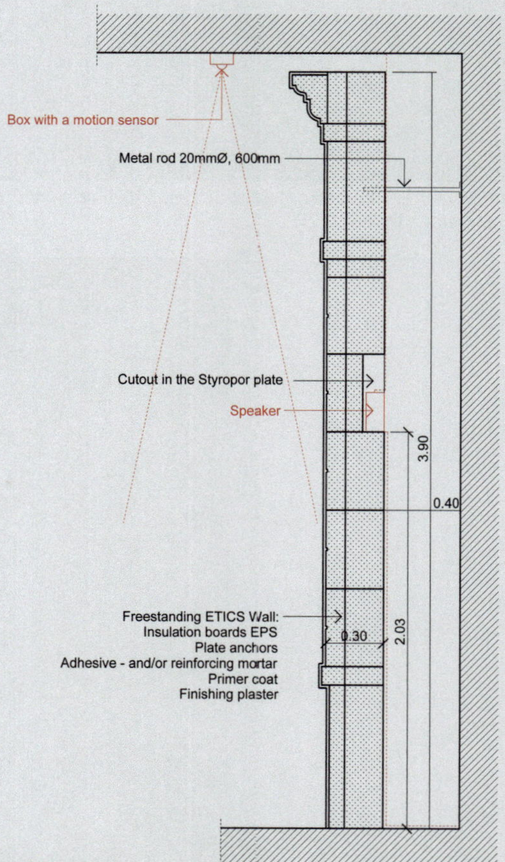

Fig. 6 Section

is mostly the result of an autodidactic process. I am sure there are more profitable ways of practicing architecture. It isn't easy to address such a complex thing as the built environment from a multitude of standpoints, and especially from those disregarded by the logic of the market. Working in such a ramified manner without an institutional affiliation has both upsides and downsides, but it enables me to follow my interests without fearing for my career—because there is no blueprint for it. That is a tremendous amount of freedom.

OG Would you say that you have found a way to follow your values instead of chasing money?

AF I hope so. This is still a rather fragile and precarious construct, and time will tell if it is sustainable enough. I am not against being an employee per se, it just depends on who you work with—if you share values, if there's a good atmosphere, and if you receive fair compensation for what you do.

OG Speaking about fair compensation, several studies highlight the persistent gender pay gap in the European architectural sector. Yet, this gap seems smaller or even nonexistent in formerly socialist countries. Does this square with your own experience?

AF On a professional level, I felt more equal back when I was living in Serbia. This is certainly a legacy of socialism, which saw in the female emancipation a way to make women enter the workforce. Women were still largely responsible for most of the reproductive work, but working mothers were the rule, not the exception, and this led to different modes of societal acceptance and communal support. Gender discrimination surely didn't stop at the former Yugoslavian border, but the omnipresence of female workers created a different culture than in societies shaped by capitalism, whose growth was partially made possible by reducing women to (unpaid) housewives.

OG To decide against economic efficiency, growth, and profitability is also a question of class: Who can afford to practice architecture and to what ends? Practices with different goals than pure economic growth quickly find themselves at a crossroads: Either you can afford to pay your bills or not, which means you have to make concessions. You grew up in a different political system. How do you reflect on that and on the role of architects in the current economic system?

AF The system in which I grew up definitely shaped my worldview, as did my upbringing in a genuinely socialist and atheist family disengaged from the pursuit of worldly possessions. This is an aspect of the socialist ethos I still strive for, just as the aspiration to more collaborative forms of professional engagement. My former university professors had all worked for state companies at some point, which were structured in sub-teams that sparred for the best design solutions but didn't compete economically. Working collaboratively on matters of public interest, such as affordable housing, would still be my ideal scenario, especially against the backdrop of the crisis of neoliberalism and the socioeconomic inequalities that are a result of the waves of privatization in the 1990s.

OG Clearly, growing up in a socialist society wasn't the best preparation for working in deregulated capitalism.

AF No, not at all, and especially not in a society in the throes of a transition from socialism to capitalism. As Serbia was going through a period of sanctions and currency devaluation in the 1990s, my mother at some point demonstratively refused to accept her insultingly low salary. For her, that was her work ethic; she had sworn the Hippocratic oath.

OG Maybe there should be something like a Hippocratic oath for architects?

AF I think the oath is a great idea, but we have to believe in greater societal ideals if we want to be able to keep it. I remember the UK environmental activist group Architects Declare's attempts to raise awareness among architects, which Foster+Partner was initially part of. But they eventually withdrew from the alliance and continued their operations in the Middle Eastern market. It's the work ethic that shapes the oath, not the other way around.

WE JUST BUILD IT OURSELVES

Peter Grundmann in conversation with Anh-Linh Ngo

Fig. 1

Fig. 2

Fig. 3

Fig. 4

Fig. 5

For over twenty years, Peter Grundmann and his Berlin-based office have planned and built low-budget architecture without resorting to standardized solutions, advocating the profession's autonomy. His practice constantly threads the needle between creative freedom and financial constraints.

Average revenue of German architecture firms by staff size, in €:

Staff	Revenue	Staff	Revenue	Staff	Revenue	Staff	Revenue
● 1 Architect	87,259	● 2	153,273	● 3–5	301,210	● 6–10	622,718
● 11–30	1,490,366	● 31–50	3,463,089	● 51+	10,814,250		

66% of all architects in Germany are freelancers / sole practitioners, followed by 12% working in a limited liability company and 14% working in joint ventures with other architects. Alternative business forms like cooperatives or employee-managed trusts make up 8% of the profession's workforce.

Fig. 1 Haus Fügener consists of two structures: a one-story building facing the street, and a three-story building that juts over a quarry lake. The two are connected by an eleven-meter-long bridge made of steel tubes.

Anh-Linh Ngo: You're known for achieving high architectural quality for little money. It seems as though tight budgets are always the starting point for your projects.

Peter Grundmann: For us, a lower budget means more freedom. It puts us in a position to make decisions more independently. When there's little money available, inventiveness becomes all the more important to create good architecture in spite of a small budget. Currently, we're working on the ZK/U – Center for Art and Urbanistics in Berlin. Now that we have reached the construction phase, we're trying to solve the problem of rising costs through ongoing design adjustments. In most of our projects, the design phase continues until the building's completion. This is true at every level, from the materials, to construction and detailing, all the way to floor plans. On the ground floor, for example, we are simply doing away with interior walls. Dividing spaces will only be possible by drawing curtains, or by moving one of a handful of partitions. In Haus Neumann, we also avoided interior walls and instead created spaces by using five-layer, sound-absorbing felt curtains.

Every structure is designed to use as little material as possible, and optimized for the absolutely necessary. Every structural component is designed according to its unique load-bearing capacities, so the result may consist of parts with widely divergent sections. This may seem chaotic, but it's logical and comprehensible structurally. Later on, you'll still be able to read the force flow off of the dimensions of the exposed structural elements. The building reveals how it carries its own load. All materials remain unclad. Different materials clash without mediation, resulting in seemingly aesthetic mistakes, which, of course, are not corrected. For me it's not about perfection, but about complexity and experience. A building must be capable of conveying experiences.

ALN The modernist demand for "honesty" and truth to materials has always had moralizing undertones. Are you also pursuing specific societal ambitions with your approach?

PG The way we design buildings stems, in part, from an insufficient budget, but I wouldn't go so far as to frame low-budget architecture as a political concept or social critique. We see low budgets as a way of evading the constraints of the market. Another aspect of our work, however, can be understood as a critique, namely to what extent our everyday life is influenced—if not determined—by the continuous repetition of practices, actions, and movements—in short, by more or less subconscious habits. Architecture can inspire, but it can also restrict. It determines freedom of action, freedom to decide, freedom of movement. By rearranging different uses and how they relate to each other in space, architecture can break habits and determinations. In Haus für einen Anarchisten (House for an anarchist), the bathroom, kitchen, and bedroom, as irreducible functions, do not claim their own space. Instead, they're shifted into the facade in the form of cuboids, which allows the space in the center of the house to remain vacant. This universally usable space serves no fixed purpose and makes up almost the entire house's footprint. In Haus Neiling II, these same irreducible functions are organized around an old stable. The toilet, shower, and bathtub are lined up one after another in a casual manner. The kitchen, dining, and sleeping areas are also positioned outside the stable walls. The glass facade circumscribes these uses, moving inwards at times, outwards at others, creating spaces between the glass and the old brickwork. When you walk through the house, these objects come to your attention to varying degrees as signs of our everyday practices. Material, structure, and other objects with everyday uses overlap with images from the outside, since the meandering glass facade enables a view of successive spatial layers. The eyes wander outward and, from there, back into the interior space on the other side. The old stable walls render additional inner walls expendable. Haus Mischke-Götzinger likewise has no inner walls. Its uses are only given spatial definition by the glass facade. Scheune Laeven has neither inner walls nor floor slabs. The ceilings rise to six meters at some points, and functions are arranged vertically, suspended from the roof structure.

ALN The conceptual core of your projects always seems to derive from a specific problem. What criteria do you use to determine whether a constraint can be developed into a theme?

PG A building or construction site with problems can be interesting, but only if a *tabula rasa* approach has been ruled out. Even the smallest contextual traces are important and can be used to enrich a design. Old walls—even if they're only remnants—trees, narrow plots that are considered undevelopable, rough terrain, or extreme emissions—noise, soot, etc.—can make a building more complex, and often demand unusual solutions.

We don't go actively looking for clients, and we seldom take part in competitions. In the last few years in particular, we have seen a lot of demand, as have a lot of other architects. And since we are a small firm, we have to turn down certain inquiries. Nevertheless, we welcome commissions in which we have to address certain problems. But we also choose commissions from clients who are open to experiment, who get personally involved, who offer us complete creative freedom, and whom we have good conversations with.

ALN An office oriented toward growth will generally aim for reproducible, standardized solutions in its organization. Otherwise, it's almost impossible to generate a profit. How do you organize your office to preserve the experimental quality of your designs and the indeterminacy in their implementation?

PG We have a solid core of four employees forming an experienced team. On top of that, we generally have two or three interns, who become part of the team very quickly thanks to the mix of office and construction work. An essential feature of our method is that all options are kept open until the completion of a project. Our interns experience this first-hand.

This only works because we often construct parts of the buildings ourselves. Not the parts a construction firm can do, but rather the parts they *won't* do. If an idea requires thinking outside the technical standards, or a bit of detailing seems highly unusual, construction firms will often either refuse to do it altogether, or charge a lot more. So, we have to take matters in our own hands, which comes with many advantages: It allows for the emergence of details that better fit the design and that the client can still afford. Drawing and building, design and practice overlap for us in every possible way.

ALN Do you save money by building things yourself, or is it ultimately a question of design for you?

PG Both. First and foremost, I'm interested in good architecture, in interesting solutions when it comes to construction, material, and function. I'm interested in the result, and less in the creation process. Of course, good design can save you money. Logical, intelligent structures look beautiful and require less material: Raw, authentic materials can be used without cladding, alternative floorplans require fewer walls, and so on. But the structural aspects of a building are essential design elements for me. That's why we always design and plan the structural elements ourselves.

We are currently building two small "twin houses" in the Uckermark region northeast of Berlin, fifty square meters each. The walls will be clad entirely in polycarbonate panels. Compared to the original wood-and-glass design, we'll save 20,000 euros per house. The panels also double as a thermal insulation.

Fig. 2 The section of each steel tube is chosen according to the actual load it has to bear, saving weight, material, and cost.

Project	HAUS FÜGENER
Category	NEW CONSTRUCTION
Use	RESIDENTIAL
Size	130 M^2
Architecture	PETER GRUNDMANN ARCHITECTS
Client	PRIVATE
Location	KAHNSDORF, GERMANY
Year	2015-17

Fig. 3 View of the home's living and dining area

Fig.4 It will take decades before the ecosystem of the quarry lake, which used to be a brown coal mining pit, is fully restored.

Fig.5 The street-facing building occupies the full ten-meter width of the plot, protecting the open space behind it.

To heighten this effect, we will use two layers. Since they are light and easy to handle, we can install the panels ourselves. For the client, the cost savings were an excellent argument for cladding the houses in this way.

Near Leipzig, we recently built a house on a quarry lake. The building's massing is divided in two, with the volumes connected by an eleven-meter-long steel bridge. The bridge's structure consists of steel tubes with twenty-two different sections, each selected according to the actual loads it has to bear. This saves weight, material, and costs. The structure appears confusing, but again, it is thoroughly logical and strictly follows the structural conditions.

ALN When you say that a building's shape only materializes during the construction process, i.e., on-site, you discard typical planning instruments like the German division of the planning and construction process into nine phases as laid out in the fee regulation for architects and engineers. This regulation also specifies how much an architect can charge for each of these phases as a percentage of construction costs. If you apply this model, you are at a disadvantage since you want to keep the budget as low as possible. How do you calculate your fees?

PG For us, design and detailing extend throughout the entire construction process, and therefore take up more time than usual. And low budgets indeed have a negative impact on fees. But our priorities lie elsewhere. We highly value interesting work and our freedom. For clients, it can be difficult that many aspects remain undetermined until their project's completion. Yet some of our former interns seem to appreciate this sort of indeterminacy and uncertainty. In spite of everything, they often reapply for jobs with us after finishing their studies, even though they're aware that they won't make big financial leaps with us.

ALN Let's stop romanticizing this way of working for a while: What do you gain by this approach, and what do you lose?

PG I wouldn't call it romanticizing. It's a conscious decision to practice the profession, and in the process steer clear of routines and constant repetition. In financial terms, we are definitely not the most talented operators. We have a different focus. But it's enough to live on. Often, the most interesting jobs in architecture are paid the worst. You certainly can make good money in larger offices, but you often end up performing the same work over and over, without getting an overview of the entire project. In my view, an architect is a universalist who should not lose sight of the bigger picture.

ALN Using non-industrial solutions and DIY construction methods also involves taking risks, potentially not meeting legal standards, and accepting liability for the consequences. Does one need to choose between creative freedom and economic security?

PG If we sought security, we'd probably work differently. Instead, we are always experimenting. It can go wrong sometimes. But we have never had a civil suit worth mentioning. For over twenty years, we have worked outside of technical standards, but always within what is called the recognized codes of practice. When operating outside of technical standards, we have to provide individual proof to support our claims concerning materials, structure, and detailing. At the end of the day, everything has to function flawlessly. But solutions that don't meet German technical standards can lead to legal difficulties, even if you show all the mathematical evidence and demonstrate that the solutions work seamlessly in practice. The assertion is simply that nothing can function outside of the codified technical standards. But those can lag decades behind practice. Waiting for them to catch up is actually an unreasonable imposition. Technical standards, after all, are industrial standards. They were created by the industry not just to set standards, but also to eliminate competition.

ALN As a rule, how long do you work on a project? And how much extra effort is invested to achieve this sort of experimental architecture?

PG We seldom finish a building within a year. Often it takes longer. Of course, we never work on just one project. We're currently working on about ten simultaneously. As a result, everything takes even longer. Ideally, though, the building will last for one hundred years, so its construction time is negligible in the long run. Sometimes, especially when the cost pressure is high, we need to develop a lot of variants before it works for the client financially. This takes time, of course.

ALN As the project progresses, however, you need to pay your employees, and you have ongoing operating costs. Where does the money come from?

PG Taking longer to build means lower fees, naturally. To keep the office running, we live very modestly. Our workspace is not designed to impress prospective clients. And for nearly every project, we build a portion ourselves, which means that we can reassign a share of the construction costs to run our business. We do this mainly to reduce costs, because things we do ourselves are designed to be cheap. Us being strongly involved in the practice of building means we can advise our clients well. We have grown very knowledgeable about how to build a house.

ALN Is there consensus among your employees on the low prospects for financial success?

PG Maybe we only have idealists working in our office. At least it's never boring. Beyond this, we stress a good working environment. We often have meals together, and we talk nonstop about everything under the sun. Sometimes serious discussions about architecture, too. We have flexible working hours and everyone earns the same salary.

ALN You have mentioned that you have a number of commissions, and you cannot accept them all. How has this developed over the past twenty years?

PG During the 2008 financial crisis, there was a lull. That's when we decided to finish building Haus Neumann, which only stood as a carcass at that time, ourselves. Those were exciting, interesting times. Because work was scarce, we simply worked on the project until it was finished. Another rough patch followed in 2010, so I started working on a film. We spent a whole year shooting *Sie wissen es nicht, aber sie tun es* (They do not know it, but they do it). We gathered 110 hours of footage, of which I screened 40 minutes at the 2011 premiere so I wouldn't have to reimburse the funding. By now the movie is three-and-a-half hours long, which is still too long, so it's not done yet. Next time there is a lull, I will finish it off. Fortunately, the topic is still highly contemporary. Our office is small and we can work flexibly, so hopefully this makes us more resilient in times of crisis. We can build on very little.

ALN Would you recommend your approach to younger architects?

PG No. I think one's way of working is very personal, and it can hardly be recommended to others. I cannot even say for sure whether my approach is worth emulating. It's ultimately about architecture, and there are a many different ways to achieve architectural quality. In the end, everyone has to discover that for themselves.

"IT COULD ALWAYS BE WORSE"

PROFESSIONAL MIGRATION IN THE ARCHITECTURAL SECTOR

Text: Marisa Cortright

With a combined total of 342,500 architects, Italy (151,000), Germany (119,000), and Turkey (72,500) represent more than half of Europe's architectural workforce. → Together with Spain (50,000), the UK (42,000), and France (30,000), these countries account for 464,500 architects, comprising around 75% of Europe's architectural workforce. 21% of Europe's architects studied abroad, especially those from Luxembourg (82%), Greece (50%), and Norway (49%). → Architects from Spain (17%), Italy (15%), and Poland (15%) have the least academic experience abroad. Only 7% of architects in Europe worked abroad in 2022. The primary reasons for staying within their home countries were personal reasons (45%), lack of familiarity with foreign planning and building regulations (32%), and language barriers (31%).

"There are problems; you can't say there are not, even if they are not of the same intensity and type as those in Serbia. When you speak with others—not only other architectural workers, but especially with other professions—you realize how many things are wrong and how, even in Switzerland, it's a really badly paid profession." That is how Jelena, a Montenegrin architectural worker, framed her view on the economic situation of architects living in Switzerland to me. "It's not because it's worse elsewhere that you should accept bad at home," wrote Foreign Architects Switzerland, a campaign with the aim of highlighting the inequalities prevalent in the industry in Switzerland, one of the richest countries in the world, in 2012.[1] Other campaigns like Non-Swiss Architects manage to broadcast the sentiments of foreign architectural workers in Switzerland in such a way that their Swiss colleagues might realize how unfair the situation is for everyone.

As I wrote in *"Can This Be? Surely This Cannot Be?": Architectural Workers Organizing in Europe*, the "crash course in economic citizenship" undertaken by laborers moving toward Northern Europe "forces them to understand themselves as workers … If you don't have to think about yourself as an immigrant, you're less likely to think about yourself as a worker."[2] This interdependence between migration and labor underpins the divide between welcome and unwelcome nationalities across the Northern European labor market. This is what architectural workers native to Northern Europe will have to understand if they want to meaningfully address the exploitation of their own labor in the architectural sector. Toward this end, I have interviewed foreign architectural workers—both from EU and non-EU countries—living in Germany, Austria, and Switzerland. My aim is to make their situation, as Katarina, a Serbian architectural worker in Berlin, put it, "a bit more transparent to people from the EU [so they] can see why their immigrant colleagues easily say yes to things—and [so native workers might] also come to [their colleagues'] defense, because they don't have as much to lose."

Foreign Architects Switzerland's call for immigrant workers to organize—echoing calls across the US and throughout Europe—insists on their refusal of bad working conditions in their new home country—even if the situation might be worse where they came from. If architectural workers should organize—and, indeed, if they should identify as architectural workers in the first place—it is not because they have it worse than any other group of workers. Rather, it comes from the fundamental recognition that individual workers who sell their labor to their bosses below value are structurally disadvantaged. As I argued in an article for *Failed Architecture*, titled "Death to the Calling: A Job in Architecture Is Still a Job," the mystique of architecture being a calling ultimately prevents those practicing it from understanding themselves as workers and recognizing this unequal power relation.[3] The vast majority of architects are *de facto* workers and it would be in their best interest to join forces with other workers across the construction industry to increase their bargaining power and collectively improve their lot.

To succeed, this coalition should explicitly include both non-immigrants and immigrants. Especially in countries where wages seem high when compared to other countries or industries—like in the German-speaking world—architectural workers in general may feel they don't have the right to complain; it could always be worse. However, immigrant architectural workers face multiple disadvantages of a social, economic, and legal nature, preventing them from addressing the very problems they are most impacted by.

The Pitfalls of Emigration

In August 2022, it was reported that "some 67 percent of young people across the Balkans are thinking about leaving their home country and working abroad."[4] As the European Union expands to include the peripheral countries of southeastern Europe, this has become easier for some young people than for others. On a macroeconomic level, unabated emigration from these countries speeds their depopulation: Since Croatia joined the EU in 2013, its population has decreased by nearly 10 percent.[5] Bulgaria and Romania are also facing the same scenario due in part to emigration; the former is expected to lose 22.5 percent of its population by the middle of this century.[6] Among those migrating across the deep intra-European economic divide to Northern Europe are many architectural workers.

In 2018 Eurostat, the European Union's statistics database, reported median hourly wages adjusted for purchasing power standard of around 20 euros in Switzerland, 16 euros in Germany, and 14 euros in Austria. Median wages in the southeastern periphery of Europe pale in comparison: 8 euros in the Czech Republic and Croatia, 7 euros in Romania, and 5 euros in Serbia.[7]

In migrating for economic reasons, architectural workers moving to the German-speaking world reprise the journeys of their compatriots and colleagues working on construction sites as so-called "Gastarbeiter" (guest workers). In contrast to workers from the broader southern European periphery, including Turkey, Portugal, Spain, Italy, and Greece, workers from formerly Yugoslavian countries in the German-speaking world confront the manufactured hierarchical division between design and construction. Born in Skopje, raised in Dubrovnik, and long since living in Leipzig and Berlin, Aleksandr notes that "Yugoslavian 'Gastarbeiter' still make up the biggest share of workers on the construction sites. If I pass by [a construction site] in Berlin, I often hear those languages—and rather seldom in the offices."

Several interviewees initially found themselves in Berlin, Zurich, Graz, or Vienna for their studies. As Ena describes, "I was studying for my bachelor's degree in architecture in Sarajevo, my hometown in Bosnia-Herzegovina. Then I spent a year for my master's studies in Barcelona, which was eye-opening because I saw how different the curriculum and the methodology of learning architecture can be. I came to realize that I could not study [in Bosnia] any further." Yet many more students cannot afford to study abroad for reasons financial, legal, or both. In a manner similar to the European Union's free movement of labor within its borders, the Erasmus program of academic exchange allows students a certain freedom of movement between EU universities. That freedom contrasts sharply with its concomitant restrictions on non-EU citizens. Anamaria remembers how, "in university I tried to do an exchange semester, but because Croatia was not in the EU at the time, you had to pay for it and it was a lot of money that I didn't have."

The feeling of being a foreigner is compounded by social codes and practices. For example, the administrative burden associated with studying weighs heavy on students who come from non-academic backgrounds. Aleksandr describes how, during his studies in Weimar, "some other students would know from their background how to navigate the educational system … I had to find out about these things myself. [My studies were] therefore also a bit longer." The question is not only one of freedom of movement after all, but also one of social mobility.

Insecurity and Social Dumping

The immigration system with its hierarchies based on nation-states, however, makes students and workers alike feel foreign before they ever leave their home countries. "When you try to move to Switzerland [for a job], you kind of have to win a lottery ticket because, of course, Swiss workers will be prioritized [for that job], followed by EU nationals, and then [workers] from outside. You have to show that you [bring] a lot more value added," says Andreea from Romania. This requirement is core to Swiss immigration law, making it far less complicated to hire a person from the two former categories given the reduced administrative burden.[8] Katarina from Serbia interned at Herzog & de Meuron in Basel but "was in Switzerland, unfortunately only for one year." Even though she had already signed a contract for a position as junior architect, "I received a call … telling me that I have to go back home because my visa didn't get approved. So I packed my bags with my contract for a really nice, well-paid job … just because I was [a] non-EU [citizen]."

Non-EU foreigners who manage to gain entry into an educational program, find a job, and learn German still have to prove they can afford to live in the country they're migrating to. In describing her experience in Austria, Ena from Bosnia said: "when you're … from a non-EU country, you need to earn a certain amount of money on a regular basis to be granted a residence permit in Austria. You have this collective agreement for each industry, and architects have their own collective agreement that regulates the minimum wage for every position and level of education for different [parts of] the architectural sector. [But] the minimum wage for architects is actually lower than the minimum wage that you need [for a residence permit]. Bear in mind: I have a master's degree. [This means] you need to find an employer comfortable with giving you more money without knowing you."[9] Thus, the imposition of a minimum wage for non-EU immigrants becomes a curse if it is cheaper for employers to hire EU nationals.

While Austria, as an EU member state, only requires these high minimum wages of non-EU nationals, Switzerland requires certain income levels for all foreigners. For non-EU immigrants, a salary threshold is nonetheless implied since only "highly qualified" people can apply for work permits and their salaries cannot disadvantage Swiss nationals.[10] Andreea from Romania describes how she and her Danish partner, as they moved to Zurich to set up their own businesses, learned that "you have to show proof of sufficient funds. You have to have three clients at the same time to prove that you have a business model, that you have money coming in, and that you won't depend on the unemployment office or [other sources of income]. I [barely had] enough clients and funds. Together with my boyfriend, we had just enough to live in this country. Initially, you're only allowed [entry] on a visitor's permit, like all EU nationals, for three months. But I needed to show that I had more income for … my residence permit. I had to go from one institution to another … for seven or eight months until I ended up finding a full-time job. Once I got the contract and sent it out, I got the permit within a week."

Germany presents yet a third scenario, where important disparities remain even within a single country. Katarina from Serbia describes how, "when applying for a visa in Germany, one needs to [establish proof of] a certain [hourly wage], which is the government's way of ensuring that a worker can live off their salary. For a lot of architecture firms, this is too much to pay … junior architects. So, to fulfill the requirement, a lot of [them] give out fake 30-hour contracts when, in reality, employees work full-time. Unfortunately, the fake 30-hour contracts are well-known among immigrant architects not coming from the EU. And the sad part is that, in a lot of cases, the EU workers … get the same, low salary. Still … I accepted it, because it was the only way for me to enter the market. And a lot of people accept it because it's still better money than they can get in their home countries. But once you get to know the system, it is clear that there is a dissonance between the current state of the market and official labor policies."

When non-EU immigrants work 40-hour weeks (or longer) while getting paid for 30, that devalues not only their labor, but that of all of their co-workers as well. With such a division between workers as a result of cost pressure, fighting together for better wages grows all the more difficult. For this reason, all architectural workers should be concerned with the improvement of working conditions without waging that fight on the backs of immigrants.

Staying informed on one's rights only goes so far in contesting structural forces. As Gracie Mae Bradley and Luke de Noronha write in *Against Borders: The Case for Abolition*, "The suggestion that migrants drive down wages … fails to account for the fact that immigration systems make workers less free and undermine their ability to

1 *Foreign Architects Switzerland* 4 (2012), accessed June 6, 2024, 3, issuu.com/faszine/docs/fas4_all/1?ff.

2 Marisa Cortright, *"Can This Be? Surely This Cannot Be?": Architectural Workers Organizing in Europe* (Prague: Vi Per, 2021), 48–49.

3 Marisa Cortright, "Death to the Calling: A Job in Architecture Is Still a Job," *Failed Architecture*, August 15, 2019, accessed June 6, 2024, failedarchitecture.com/death-to-the-calling-a-job-in-architecture-is-still-a-job.

4 Jovan Ilic et al., "Youth Day Feels Bittersweet to Balkans' Frustrated Youngsters," *Balkan Insight*, August 12, 2022, accessed June 6, 2024, balkaninsight.com/2022/08/12/youth-day-feels-bittersweet-to-balkans-frustrated-youngsters.

5 Associated Press, "Croatia Census Shows Nearly 10% Population Drop in 10 Years," January 14, 2022, accessed June 6, 2024, apnews.com/article/business-europe-census-2020-croatia-european-union-0e5f2012691403f5374b2591a4e02ac9.

6 Slav Okov, "Ever-Shrinking Bulgaria Confronts Worsening Population Crisis," *Bloomberg*, January 25, 2022, accessed June 6, 2024, www.bloomberg.com/news/articles/2022-01-25/ever-shrinking-bulgaria-exports-fertility-as-population-drops; Tim Judah, "Romania's Demographic Tailspin Heralds Social Change," *Balkan Investigative Reporting Network*, November 28, 2019, accessed June 6, 2024, balkaninsight.com/2019/11/28/romanias-demographic-tailspin-heralds-social-change/.

7 Eurostat, "Mittlere Stundenverdienst, Arbeitnehmer (ohne Auszubildende) nach Geschlecht," https://ec.europa.eu/eurostat/databrowser/view/EARN_SES_PUB2S__custom_4004315/default/bar?lang=de.

8 Art. 21, *Bundesgesetz über die Ausländerinnen und Ausländer und über die*

assert their labour rights."[11] It is in fact the immigration systems themselves that drive down wages. For good reason, then, have Foreign Architects Switzerland and Non-Swiss Architects drawn attention to the relatively poor salaries that architectural workers earn. Kateřina confirms that "as anywhere, conditions for architects are hard. You don't get a high salary, and it's the same here in Switzerland. You start with the same salary as the cashier in the supermarket."

Conclusion

Though this sample of accounts is small, it indicates the general contours of that same struggle for foreign architectural workers in German-speaking countries, especially if they're not from the EU. Echoing other interviewees, Ena has "heard so many stories and I know of so many examples which should be brought to light, and which never are because so many of us are not in a position [to talk. Many of us live] in fear of being deported to our home countries. It may sound exaggerated, but I've had so many experiences here which could have resulted in me being deported to my home country, even though I was never in a position to influence it; it was just bureaucracy."

This deportability and the related forms of precarity to which it exposes immigrant workers should worry all workers. As long as any part of the workforce is treated as especially expendable, the potential for workers in general to improve their conditions is weakened. The more precarious the immigrant worker, the more precarious the industry at large. This is why, Bradley and de Noronha argue, "building capacity [for collective resistance] among all workers, including migrants, is critical ... Fighting for the rights and conditions of precarious migrant labourers can improve the lot of all working people."[12]

Integration (Federal Act on Foreign Nationals and Integration), 142.20, Switzerland, 2005.

9 The collective agreement stipulates a gross monthly salary of €2,456 for employed architects with a master's degree or equivalent; see *Kollektivvertrag für Angestellte bei Ziviltechnikern* (collective agreement for employees of civil engineers), January 1, 2022, accessed June 6, 2024, www.arching.at/fileadmin/user_upload/redakteure/Kollektivvertrag/Kollektivvertrag_2022-01-01.pdf. The minimum monthly income to be proven for a so-called Red-White-Red Card, which architects from third countries can apply for as so-called "other key workers," is €2,835 gross and is based on § 12b cl. 1 no. 1, *Ausländerbeschäftigungsgesetz* (Act Governing the Employment of Foreign Nationals), Austria, 1975; § 108 ¶ 3 *Allgemeines Sozialversicherungsgesetz* (General Social Security Act), ibid., 1995.

10 Canton of Zurich Office for Economy and Labour, ed., "Explanatory Notes on Gainful Employment of Third-Country Nationals," January 2024, accessed June 6, 2024, www.zh.ch/content/dam/zhweb/bilder-dokumente/themen/wirtschaft-arbeit/erwerbstaetigkeit-von-auslaendern/drittstaaten-angehörige/explanatory_notes_gainful_employment_third_country_nationals_en.pdf; the median salary for full-time employees (with a master's degree) in architecture firms in 2018 was 6,526 Swiss francs gross (for women) and 7,338 Swiss francs gross (for men), which the Office for Economy and Labour has to use as a guide when issuing permits. Freelancers are subject to further collateral requirements.

11 Gracie Mae Bradley and Luke de Noronha, *Against Borders: The Case for Abolition* (London: Verso, 2022), 57.

12 Ibid., 58.

THE WORKER'S PROJECT, 2021

Photo Essay: Leonhard Clemens

In his 2021 photo series *The Worker's Project*, architect and photographer Leonhard Clemens depicts construction workers on a building site in Berlin. Through portraiture, the very people often overlooked in discussions about architecture are brought into focus. After all, it is still the architect who is generally thought of as the *creator* of a building. The myth of singular authorship stubbornly prevails, although there is no secret around the fact that a multitude of people are involved in the process of producing our built environment. Leonhard Clemens gives visibility to the construction workers while protecting their anonymity—not out of disrespect, but rather out of concern for their precarious employment conditions and volatile immigration status. Respect for and solidarity with *all* participants in the building industry is what Clemens's pictures demand of their viewers. Simultaneously, they remind the architectural profession about its own place in the same system of labor and exploitation.

ARCHITECTURE AS A CLASS SOCIETY

Text: Paola De Martin

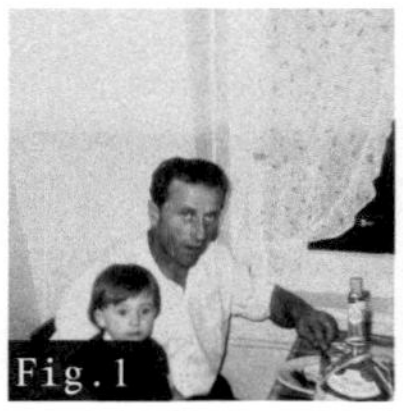

Fig. 1

Fig. 2

Fig. 3

Fig. 4

The widest gender pay gaps between male and female architects are recorded in Cyprus (50%), Romania (43%), and Slovakia (33%). Croatia (8%), Sweden (5%), and Denmark (3%) have the narrowest gender pay gap. €65 is the average hourly rate for partners and directors in Europe. Adjusted for purchasing power parity, the highest hourly rates are found in Luxembourg (€99), Austria (€96), and Denmark (€95), with the lowest in Romania (€35), Poland (€30), and Greece (€17).

By failing to define architecture in relation to society—that is to say, as the spatial reification of social relations—we are doomed to overlook fundamental questions crucial to its understanding: Who gets to study architecture and who ends up practicing it? Whom does architecture design for, and how? Drawing on her own experience, Paola De Martin maps out the social landscape of the design and architecture scene from the 1970s to the present, highlighting how intersectionality shapes the way we experience it.[1]

Fig. 1 Paola De Martin with her uncle in the Zurich apartment where she spent a year as the undocumented child of a seasonal worker, protected from the immigration police.

"I don't stand on the sidelines and nod silently; I talk, and I don't stop."[2] Tupoka Ogette

Locating Perspectives (Not Casting Them in Concrete)

Coming from a working-class family, I became a primary school teacher and later a textile designer. In 2020, I completed my PhD in Design History at ETH Zurich's Department of Architecture. My father was a bricklayer foreman and later a site supervisor. He was a skilled craftsman and adept at reading and executing plans. However, he kept flaws in construction plans secret from his superiors, as he confided to me shortly before his death, because they did not trust him—the *muratore* from Italy—to make competent assessments. My mother performed various roles: wood and water carrier, maid, nanny, laundress, ironer, housewife, factory worker—but above all, I saw her working as a cleaner. She read everything I shared with her; her favorite book was *Orlando* by Virginia Woolf. Throughout their lives, my parents were massively underestimated—including by myself at one point, I admit it openly. Reflexes taught by socialization led to such judgments, side effects of my own educational advancement. My father reacted as one might expect: His acquired hostility toward intellectuals grew proportionally to my acquired disdain. My mother grew resigned. Such experiences of alienation are typical for those ascending the educational ladder, dividing families and influencing their members' actions. They perpetuate and cement social inequalities.

What also shaped our situation—in addition to our class—was the experience of being "migrantized." The impositions we were subjected to as a working-class family without Swiss citizenship extended into the intimate sphere of reproduction. The seasonal worker status limited the duration of any foreign worker's stay to a few months per year, restricted their independence and access to social security benefits, and prohibited family reunification. These racist regulations were enacted in 1934; their repeal only came in 2002.

The interwar period was also the era of the classic modern avant-gardes, such as the CIAM (Congrès Internationaux d'Architecture Moderne) and the SWB (Schweizerischer Werkbund, lit. Swiss association of craftspeople). My research has shown that their avant-gardist habitus of distinction—the reflexive and legitimized demarcation against those perceived as less "developed"—was entangled with colonial racism and eugenics, a connection that remains barely examined.[3] As a working-class family, we, along with hundreds of thousands of others, had to endure the effects of this exclusionary attitude long after the interwar period.

We, the migrant workers, have been taught a lesson without a textbook through the application of violent laws, urban segregation, forced living in barracks, verbal abuse, systematic educational discrimination, contempt for our lifestyle, mockery and amusement at our expense, and tangible violence.[4] Those affected by poverty have no right to exist in this country except as single, working "others" who—as soon as the work is finished or the economy demands it—are expected to discreetly disappear.

Well, I have not disappeared. I am here. I deliberately break the polite silence because dropping out of the "leaky pipeline"—or might we say: "educational mortality"—is the norm for "parvenus" from working-class backgrounds, especially for migrant, working-class daughters. I take an explicit stance and make it transparent in order to avoid the continuous internalization of society's judgment, which has caused irrevocable damage to many people close to me.[5]

Living with the Power of Habit

At some point, the architecture of the social that reflexively divides classes and milieus into high and low becomes second nature—one might say, "common sense." Our lifestyle is the sensual manifestation of this symbolic force of habit. Living, inhabiting, *abitare*, *habitus*. As the term implies, we inhabit historically created inequalities; we settle into them with our innermost being, as we are *habitually* disposed to doing by the practice of our class, rehearsed over decades or even centuries.

My parents always desired a better life for me. When I informed them that I—an experienced primary school teacher with a permanent position—would be resigning to pursue a degree in textile design at an art school, their reaction was an awkward silence; it was a step they could not comprehend. Conversely, one of my most influential lecturers in the textile design program often confided to me, full of ennui, that she had actually aspired to become an architect. However, her wealthy father had vetoed the idea, deeming her wish presumptuous as a woman—end of discussion. The practice of textile design, her second choice, was a dream come true for me. Our perspectives on the same subject differed vastly due to differences in social backgrounds.

Anecdotes like these help us to understand the origins of judgments of taste about what is "beautiful" and "good" that determine our practice. The issue at play is not so much the difference in itself but rather the fact that the perspectives of the heirs to the cultural hegemony are considered legitimate and universal, while others' viewpoints are deemed "particular." It is up to them to explain themselves—a lonely position that can lead to the educational exclusion of the underprivileged, which then appears as if it were a conscious choice. Those who have inherited the self-evident codes of the ruling classes can dispense with self-reflection; they take to the legitimate habitus of any field like a duck to water. From this perspective, it is logically always the "others" who have the problem.

Taking the Invisible Seriously

When "parvenus" fall out of their habitus, silent, habitual ruptures occur. This can be painful, but—if the silence is willingly and collectively broken—these ruptures are an endless source of historical knowledge. It is nothing other than the sudden emergence of erased structural history.

I vividly remember the first painful irritation I felt in the 1990s at Christa de Carouge's fashion boutique at Mühle Tiefenbrunnen in Zurich's Seefeld district—once the working-class neighborhood where I had to live in hiding (though no longer separated from my family) in my father's employer's apartment at just three years old—in hiding from the hands of the immigration police.

Christa de Carouge's chic store, with its formwork panels, rusty scaffolding, and raw concrete, were all the rage in the 1990s. But when I read the store's name, my mind immediately turned to Switzerland's largest barrack settlement on the outskirts of Geneva, in, well, Carouge. These slums of the 1960s and 1970s, *baraccopoli*, as they're called in Italian, ceased to exist when the oil crises hit. Today, nothing in Carouge reminds us of this chapter in Swiss architectural history. The neighborhood and the space it occupied in our minds has been thoroughly gentrified. One might argue that this is simply the natural course of things. But shouldn't we fundamentally take an interest in those who run things and how they run—and ruin—them?

I was irritated by the surrounding discourse's strange obliviousness to history, lacking any architectural-historical analysis to counterbalance the marketing-speak. There were no objections to her romanticizing terms like "the leitmotif is the construction site," or the "ascetic" lifestyle where everything she needed could "fit into a suitcase."[6] Or to her fascination with the "southern flair" in Carouge, the sublimated, exoticizing, meridional Blackness of her fashion. Dealing with the incomprehensible feeling triggered by this postmodern appropriation of working-class aesthetics was far more challenging for me than coping with explicit acts of violence and discrimination. Historical consciousness becomes all the more urgent in the postmodern age. As Stuart Hall puts it, "it is exactly the term 'postmodernism' itself which tells you of the tension of having to recognize what is new, and of struggling to mobilize some historical understanding of how it came to be produced. Postmodernism attempts to close off the past by saying that history is finished, therefore you needn't go back to it."[7]

Quality of Life: Accounting, Counting, Recounting

In hindsight, these examples are embedded within the context of profound structural economic transformations that have taken place since the early 1970s. Zurich has seen its cultural elite grow notably over recent decades. In 1970, only 9 percent of Zurich's adult population held a university degree; by 2017, that number was 47 percent, the highest anywhere in the country. Since the abolition of border controls with the EU in 2002, 80 percent of all migrants who have relocated to Zurich possess a university degree, with 10 percent even having completed a dissertation. In 1970, 33 percent of Zurich's population had not completed secondary school; by 2010, that share had dropped to 19 percent, trending further downward.[8] The new migratory movement is therefore accelerating the structural changes that the old migration—which included my parents—had somewhat held in check.

As for the social makeup of the architectural field, there are no statistics on long-term trends. However, data from the neighboring field of design can serve as proxy variables for architecture. The situation at Zurich University of the Arts (ZHdK), for instance, is essentially the opposite of what we observe in Swiss society overall. Among students in the design department, only 6 percent have parents with less than a secondary school diploma (compared to 14 percent of the overall Swiss population). Additionally, 28 percent have parents who completed high school, a vocational diploma, or an apprenticeship (compared to 42 percent of the overall Swiss population). In contrast, 60 percent have at least one parent with a university degree (compared to 29 percent of the overall Swiss population). The minority of students from educationally disadvantaged backgrounds consists almost entirely of the post-migrant second generation. Their numbers are dwindling in the face of the growing majority of international students who come to Zurich specifically to study design. The latter primarily hail from EU countries and are well-equipped with cultural heritage.[9]

Concurrently, the growth of the creative sector as a whole is striking. In the three years prior to the 2008 financial crisis, the number of people working in the creative industry in the Zurich metropolitan region grew by 8 percent.[10] Starting in the mid-2010s, the architectural profession represented the highest share in terms of employees in the entire Swiss creative industry at 20 percent.[11] In 2016, 15,404 companies were registered in the sector, with a total of 44,168 employees (converted into full-time equivalents), as the most recent creative industries report indicated. Part-time employment in this field is notably lower when compared to other sub-categories of the creative industry, such as music or graphics. The gross value added in the architecture sector amounted to 5.8 billion Swiss francs, with total sales reaching 11 billion Swiss francs.[12] The pace of development demonstrates a robust upward trend across companies, employees, gross value added, and sales.[13]

Working on the Social Fabric: A Web of Relationships

The remarkable growth of the creative industry is often celebrated as part of an enthusiastic discourse that distracts from the precarity faced by most of those working in the field. Only a small minority of designers is able to make a living over the long term without cross-subsidizing their practice with another job or an inherited financial cushion. And what about architects? How societal inequalities are perpetuated within the field of architecture remains largely unknown; our insights are limited to qualitative observations. The response from a sociologist with the Institute for Architecture at the University of Applied Sciences and Arts Northwestern Switzerland (FHNW) to my inquiry about the various social backgrounds of architecture students at ETH and FHNW is characteristic in this regard: there is no data. This source had a hunch that students from educationally disadvantaged backgrounds seemed to be overrepresented at FHNW—where the subject can also be taken as part of a vocational baccalaureate—and underrepresented at ETH, though the sociologist found the topic all too delicate and did not want to inquire specifically about their social backgrounds.

An internal inquiry conducted at ETH Zurich's Department of Architecture revealed widespread unease regarding the lack of socio-economic diversity within the department. "It was mentioned that the professors mainly come from affluent backgrounds, have financial security, or belong to families with historical ties to architecture. Students or assistants who do not share similar backgrounds often feel intimidated, out of place, and pressured to feign assimilation and conform. … Trying to blend in and hide one's non-privileged background, dealing with recurring financial stress, or having to work full-time while studying pose significant risks to both mental and physical well-being and impede academic success."[14]

Current discussions on classism overlook the field of architecture with disturbing consistency.[15] Architectural sociology, which developed starting in the 1970s, focuses on what happens outside the field and is predominantly a sociology *for* architects.[16] The sole book explicitly addressing classism within the field of architecture is Garry Stevens's *The Favored Circle: The Social Foundations of Architectural Distinction*.[17] Drawing on Pierre Bourdieu's conceptual framework, Stevens delves into the distinctions that are part of a class habitus and the mastery of cultural codes within the architecture scene. He describes the workings of an invisible selection process that operates unbeknownst to the actors involved. Recent studies from the UK reveal that the field of architecture indeed constitutes a "favored circle" as one of the most privileged and exclusive domains within cultural production.[18]

Other accounts, such as Douglas Spencer and Marianela D'Aprile's "Notes on Tafuri, Militancy, and Unionization," a contemporary rereading of Manfredo Tafuri's *Architecture and Utopia*, make precisely the opposite argument.[19] They lament the powerlessness of creative architects in the face of economic and bureaucratic forces. Recent studies on the unionization efforts of architectural workers in the US also paint a grim picture of a scene in which exploitation and self-exploitation are the order of the day.[20] However, architectural practice, at least in Switzerland, maintains a certain level of dignity, with a definition of precarity that might sound like a first-world problem to other creatives.[21] While ETH Zurich—which, in principle, is accessible to all, irrespective of an ability to pay for tuition—may seem only moderately exclusive when compared to elite universities in the USA, that perception is misleading. Factors like early academic selection in primary school, self-censorship influenced by one's environment, and internalized feelings of exclusion take effect long before individuals contemplate university studies. The perception that ETH is not for them—too ambitious, too difficult, too pretentious—is especially prevalent among children from economically and educationally disadvantaged families.[22]

The power of distinction also manifests itself in the relationship between sub-disciplines. As someone who commutes between Zurich University of the Arts and the Department of Architecture at ETH, I can attest to the prevalent impression shared by many colleagues in the design field: Architecture is more powerful than design; the former holds sway over aesthetic discourses that span both domains. An architect-turned-design theorist whom I interviewed for my research remarked that only those who can't study architecture opt to study design instead—but only as a second choice. From what I gather from the participants in my seminar at the Department of Architecture, ETH students are encouraged to see themselves as generalists, capable

Fig. 2 Until the mid-1970s, thousands of seasonal workers endured squalid conditions in the barracks of Carouge on the outskirts of Geneva.

Fig. 3 In 1978, fashion designer Christa Furrer adopted the artist name Christa de Carouge—the name of the Geneva suburb where one of Switzerland's largest barrack settlements once stood, and where she opened her first boutique, contributing to its gentrification and, simultaneously, to the erasure of its history.

Fig. 4 Zaha Hadid as a child in front of the Trevi Fountain in Rome, circa 1958

of addressing a wide range of topics with eloquence and wit. Examining self-assured "starchitects," architectural theorist Philip Ursprung contextualizes this phenomenon sociologically, situating it within the context of late capitalism, which fosters the rise of this type of person[23]—or rather, which *once again* fosters the rise of such figures, because ever since Giorgio Vasari's *The Lives of the Most Excellent Painters, Sculptors, and Architects*, i.e., for nearly half a millennium, a common narrative has been to portray (mostly male) architects as iconic figures, akin to secular saints. Even their struggles are sometimes meticulously documented.[24]

In other words, you are not born an architect, much less a star; you are made into one by the material conditions of your time—and today, those are the material conditions of neoliberalism. Cultural sociologist Franz Schultheis calls this the winner-takes-all principle,[25] while Swiss inequality sociologist Ueli Mäder invokes the biblical Matthew effect: To those who have, will be given. In theory, talented and driven children from working-class backgrounds can also reach the top by overcoming both external and internal barriers.[26] However, unlike in past years of economic prosperity when many ambitious individuals from humble origins could achieve success in cultural fields—at least in industrialized, Western countries—today, they're the proverbial needle in the haystack. Cultural theorist Mark Fisher, in an afterword to the German version of his *Capitalist Realism: Is There No Alternative?* suggests that neoliberalism intertwines fate with social class. Fisher notes that individuals can still "rise from the working class, but not along with it."[27] But for children and young people from impoverished backgrounds and "developing countries," no amount of talent or ambition seems to offer a viable pathway. Moreover, refugees face significant hurdles in overcoming the systematic declassification imposed by current refugee policies.[28] Successful architects of color, such as Zaha Hadid, Wang Shu, and Balkrishna Doshi, predominantly hail from families with substantial inherited economic, social, and cultural capital—a fact that aligns with sociological observations. Diversity has a class bias.

How can we reconcile the reliance on big money in the fiercely competitive world of architecture with its profound cultural influence? Overall, one might say, using Bourdieu's terms, that practicing architects hold the highest intermediate position within the cultural production sphere. Yet, in a way perhaps rivaled only by the great intellectuals, they ultimately remain the ruled among the ruling.[29]

Conclusion: Collective Dream Work

Those who make it into esteemed architectural institutions arguably start out their career with the most advantageous capital: cutting-edge technical know-how, cultural sophistication, influential networks, and legitimate charisma. That, at least, it what we might preliminarily conclude. But what happens next? In order to sustain success in the architectural field, one must endure periods of hardship, which can be more severe than those faced by designers, who can often bridge financial gaps relatively easily. Architects, therefore, face greater risks. On the flip side, aspiring architects can look forward to better financial prospects in the long run. However, inherited predispositions are a different matter altogether.[30] They tap into deep emotions, giving rise to boundless dreams. Boris Blank, the son of a working-class father and one half of the successful music duo Yello—alongside Dieter Meier, a multifaceted figure from Zurich's bourgeoisie—expressed this sentiment in an interview with *ZEIT Magazin*:

"My dreams often feature stairs that lead a long way up. In one, a staircase ascends along the side of a house, higher and higher, but it only begins a few meters above the ground. I have to jump to reach it. In another dream, I am sitting in an airplane taxiing up a mountain meadow, attempting to take off. But it doesn't manage to take off. I leave my seat and go to the front. The cockpit is empty. Turning back, I see that the cabin is also empty. I am the sole person aboard the plane … In these dreams, it's always important for me to show others that I can levitate. Coming from a working-class background, I was never encouraged to draw attention to myself as a child."[31]

While working on my dissertation, I often dreamed of letters and words floating in space, wielding them as instruments shaping my destiny. In these dreams, I beckoned others to join me, eager to share the game with them, but did they hear me? The outcome of these dreams remained open-ended. Dreams are concrete emotional work toward a different future. A dream comes true when we begin challenging the boundaries of expectation. In my waking hours, I yearn for rigorous research scrutinizing architecture *as* a class society, addressing previously untold—and unheard—realities. I've often found this to be more than just a solemn endeavor. Discussing architecture, design, art, theater, and literature through the lens of class, without social shame, hasty judgments, or inhibitions, I often feel like I'm part of a group of enthusiastic dilettantes learning a new language together. *Dilettare*, in Italian, means to inspire, to bring pleasure. Creativity means more than shaping the built environment; creativity is a social practice. Today's dilettantes are tomorrow's experts. *We* don't just stand on the sidelines and nod silently; *we* talk, and *we* don't stop.

1 Paola De Martin, *Give us a Break! Arbeitermilieu und Designszene im Aufbruch* (Zurich: Diaphanes, 2022).
2 Tupoka Ogette, "Ich stehe nicht am Rand und nicke stumm, sondern ich rede, und ich höre nicht mehr auf," *ZEIT Magazin* 27, June 25, 2020.
3 See Christina Cogdell, *Eugenic Design: Streamlining America in the 1930s* (Philadelphia: University of Pennsylvania Press, 2004); Patricia Purtschert, "Weiße Waren: Die Erfindung der Schweizer Hausfrau," in Patricia Purtschert, ed., *Kolonialität und Geschlecht im 20. Jahrhundert: Eine Geschichte der weißen Schweiz* (Bielefeld: transcript, 2019), 71–183.
4 Recently, a formerly undocumented child of a migrant laborer told me that his father, who worked on the construction of the runways at Zurich Airport in the 1950s, faced insults and frequent beatings with sticks from Swiss supervisors who had been specifically recruited from the italophone Swiss region of Ticino.
5 See *Schwarzenbach Komplex*, accessed June 5, 2024, schwarzenbach-komplex.ch/cms; *Tesoro e.V.*, accessed June 5, 2024, tesoro2021.ch.
6 Jenny Keller, "Ein Leben lang," interview with Christa de Carouge, *swiss-architects.com*, accessed June 5, 2024, www.swiss-architects.com/de/architecture-news/meldungen/ein-leben-lang.
7 Lawrence Grossberg, "On Postmodernism and Articulation: An Interview with Stuart Hall," *Journal of Communication Inquiry* 10(2), 50.
8 Cf. Daniel Fritzsche, "Zürich, die gebildete Stadt," *Neue Zürcher Zeitung*, February 1, 2017.
9 Cf. Catrin Seefranz and Philippe Saner, *Making Differences: Schweizer Kunsthochschulen* (Zurich: ZHdK, 2012), 38–45, accessed June 5, 2024, blog.zhdk.ch/artschooldifferences/en/preliminary-study; Philippe Saner et al., *Art.School.Differences: Researching Inequalities and Normativities in the Field of Higher Education* (Zurich: Institute for Art Education, ZHdK, 2016), 150–63, accessed June 5, 2024, blog.zhdk.ch/artschooldifferences/schlussbericht.
10 Christoph Weckerle and Hubert Theler, eds., *Dritter Kreativwirtschaftsbericht Zürich. Die Bedeutung der Kultur- und Kreativwirtschaft für den Standort Zürich 2010* (Zurich: ZHdK, 2010), 6.
11 Christoph Weckerle et al., eds., *Von der Kreativwirtschaft zu den Creative Economies: Kreativwirtschaftsbericht Schweiz 2016* (Zurich: ZHdK, 2016), 7.
12 Ibid, 9.
13 Ibid, 40.
14 Department of Architecture, ETH Zurich, "Class: The Elephant in the Room," in *Engage Parity Report*, internal PDF, 57.
15 See also Andrea Kempers and Heike Weinbach, *Klassismus: Eine Einführung* (Munster: Unrast, 2007); bell hooks, *Where We Stand: Class Matters* (New York: Routledge, 2000).
16 For a typical example of a detached view of society from the perspective of architecture, see Heike Delitz, *Architektursoziologie* (Bielefeld: transcript, 2009).
17 Garry Stevens, *The Favored Circle: The Social Foundations of Architectural Distinction* (Cambridge: MIT University Press, 1998).
18 Lizzie Crook, "Architectural Professions Top List of Elite Occupations in the UK," *Dezeen*, October 6, 2021, accessed June 5, 2024, www.dezeen.com/2021/10/06/architecture-privileged-creative-industry-report/.
19 Marianela D'Aprile and Douglas Spencer, "Notes on Tafuri, Militancy, and Unionization," *Avery Review* 56, April 2022, accessed June 5, 2024, www.averyreview.com/issues/56/notes-on-tafuri; see also Manfredo Tafuri, *Architecture and Utopia: Design and Capitalist Development*, trans. Barbara Luigia La Penta (Cambridge: MIT University Press, 1976).
20 See Marisa Cortright, "Death to the Calling: A Job in Architecture Is Still a Job," *Failed Architecture*, August 15, 2019, accessed June 5, 2024, failedarchitecture.com/death-to-the-calling-a-job-in-architecture-is-still-a-job.
21 See Franz Schultheis, "Prekär auf hohem Niveau," in *Gesellschaft mit begrenzter Haftung: Zumutungen und Leiden im deutschen Alltag*, (Konstanz: UVK, 2005), 375–78.
22 See Margrit Stamm, *Arbeiterkinder an die Hochschulen! Hintergründe ihrer Aufstiegsangst*, Dossier 18/1, 2018. Hans-Rudolf Fierz, an ETH student and son of a working-class father, provides unique insight into how exclusionary mechanisms can be internalized and passed on in the documentary *Die Früchte der Arbeit: Arbeit und Arbeiter in der Schweiz 1914–1974*, dir. Alexander J. Seiler, Switzerland, 1977.
23 Cf. Philip Ursprung, "Von der Rezession zur Stararchitektur und zurück: Der Architektenberuf seit den frühen 1970er Jahren," in Winfried Nerdinger, ed., *Der Architekt: Geschichte und Gegenwart eines Berufsstandes*, vol. 1 (Munich: Prestel, 2012), 229–41.
24 See Elahe Haschemi Yekani, *Privilege of Crisis: Narratives of Masculinities in Colonial and Postcolonial Literature, Photography and Film* (Frankfurt a. M.: Campus, 2011).
25 Cf. Franz Schultheis, "Kollektive Heuchelei: Tobias Timm im Gespräch mit Franz Schultheis," *ZEIT ONLINE*, June 25, 2015, accessed June 5, 2024, www.zeit.de/2015/26/art-basel-kunstmarktpreise-franz-schultheis; Sighard Neckel, *Flucht nach vorn: Die Erfolgskultur der Marktgesellschaft* (Frankfurt a. M.: Campus, 2008).
26 Cf. Ueli Mäder, "Der Soziologe entzaubert den Mythos der Tellerwäscher-Karriere. Sein Schluss: Wer hat, dem wird gegeben," *SRF-Club*, July 23, 2013, accessed June 5, 2024, www.srf.ch/play/tv/club/video/ueli-maeder?urn=urn:srf:video:d3fa1c59-febc-4d4f-a284-657227ac9b63.
27 Mark Fisher, afterword to *Kapitalistischer Realismus ohne Alternative? Eine Flugschrift* (orig. *Capitalist Realism: Is There No Alternative?*), trans. Christian Werthschulte et al. (Hamburg: VSA, 2013), 103.
28 Rami Msallam, "Dystopie im Provisorium, Utopie im Erinnern," *trans* 41 (October 2022), 27–31.
29 Eva Barlösius, "Der engagierte Intellektuelle und seine Soziologie der Intellektuellen," in *Pierre Bourdieu* (Frankfurt a. M.: Campus, 2011), 158–71.
30 A particularly apt fictional example of this can be found in Jackie Thomae, *Brüder* (Berlin: Hanser, 2019).
31 Boris Blank, "Es gelingt mir, vom Boden abzuheben—Zuerst nur wenige Zentimeter, dann höher," *ZEIT Magazin* 44, November 12, 2016.

VALUE

VALUES

CRISIS-PROOF

Oana Bogdan in conversation with Olaf Grawert and Felix Hofmann

Fig. 1

Fig. 2

Fig. 3

Fig. 4

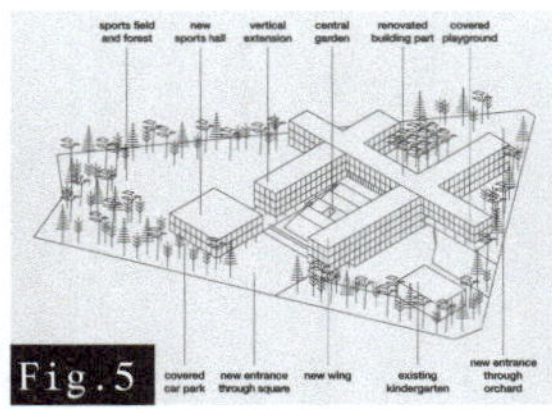
Fig. 5

Fig. 6

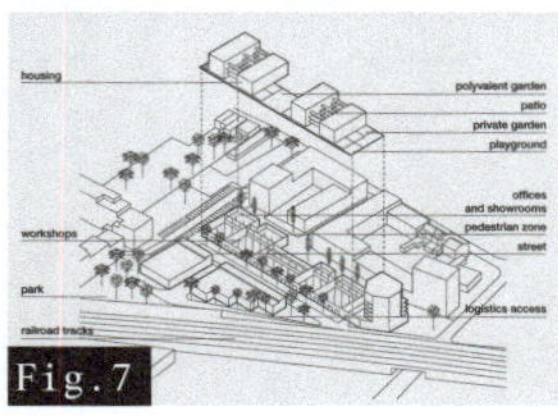
Fig. 7

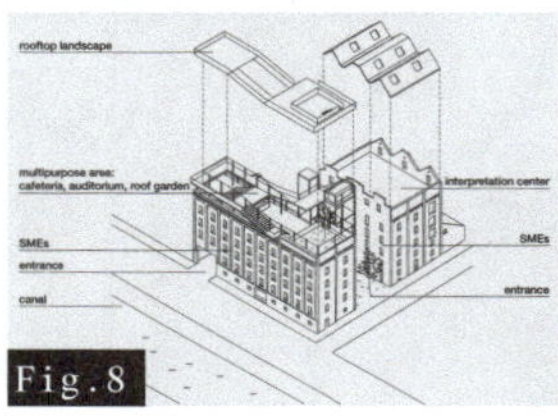
Fig. 8

Fig. 9

Fig. 10

16% of European architecture practices participated in a competition in 2022. → Belgian firms work an average of 1,903 hours each year on competitions, while Danish firms invest just 95 hours. → Austrian firms invest an average of €214,261 (incl. staff costs) in competitions per year; Italian firms invest just €4,154 (incl. staff costs). → The average prize money is €120,960 in Norway and €1,756 in the Czech Republic.

Fig. 1 The building (fig. 2) in its original condition

Fig. 2 Bogdan & Van Broeck, The Cosmopolitan, Brussels, 2014–19
The 12-story high-rise, built in the 1960s based on a design by Charles Verhelle and Henry Profiter for the insurance company Assubel (fig. 1), was converted into a residential tower.

The usual magazine profile of an architect and their office is a string of success stories. Rare is the practitioner ready to talk candidly about failures, hard times, unsuccessful project acquisitions, unpaid invoices. For Oana Bogdan, the former Secretary of State responsible for cultural heritage at the Romanian Ministry of Culture and founding partner of the Brussels-based office Bogdan & Van Broeck, which she has been leading as a sole principal under the name &bogdan since 2022, a near-total failure right after the firm's incorporation provided her with an opportunity to reassess her perception of her own job and the profession in general. In this interview, she talks about the many roles—manager, marketing expert, politician—she has had to adopt in crises and how they in turn have shaped her thinking as an architect.

Olaf Grawert: Right after starting your own business in 2007 you saw yourself confronted with a collapsing market. Your architecture office Bogdan & Van Broeck, newly founded at the time, went through serious economic difficulties. You are an exception among architects, because you talk openly about challenging situations like this one. What happened?

Oana Bogdan: My associate Leo Van Broeck and I founded our practice in Brussels in 2007. I was 30 years old and extremely relaxed, thinking: "I'm starting a business with a guy twenty years my senior and with lots of working experience. So I don't have to care about the business aspect. I just need to have great architectural ideas."

Reality taught me better: We started working right before Christmas 2007. The following year we started to gradually take notice of what was happening overseas with Lehman Brothers and by the turn of the year 2009–10 we started to feel the effects of the global financial crisis here in Belgium. By 2011 we realized that if we didn't win at least two out of the four competitions we were participating in at the time, we would go bankrupt. We literally ran out of cash.

There is a lot of money in the Belgian real estate market. Belgium is rich, but Belgians are risk-averse. As soon as economic uncertainty appears on the horizon, the whole system grinds to a halt. Everyone wants to wait until the situation is under control. Consequently, our projects were delayed, the contracts had to be renegotiated, and the payments were put on hold. You can have a healthy business on paper, including future projects and binding contracts, but if you don't have cash flow to pay your employees and running costs, you go bankrupt. Cash flow is as important as turnover or profit. I learned a lot regarding business administration in that period by getting deeply involved in our finances.

We tried everything to save money and, by extension, our business: We bought the cheapest possible products, reused every piece of paper, optimized the use of software. But although we ended up winning the two competitions, we had by then already started letting go most of our team. We went from sixteen people to five: two founders and three young architects. The latter asked us to not hire more experienced and expensive ones, but to train them instead so as to become our project leads. They wanted to run the business with us. It worked out but ultimately, two of them started their own businesses afterwards.

OG You went on to study for an MBA, a Master's in Business Administration, which you obtained in 2015. Was this education essential to rebuilding the office?

OB The crisis taught us to strategize and diversify. We learned to say no. That brings you clarity—and money. It's counterintuitive but by saying yes, you increase your turnover; by saying no, you increase your profit. Refuse as much as possible, even when you are tempted to take just about any job. Learn to evaluate and understand your client. If you don't get along on a personal level and do not share the same values, the result will be unsatisfying and ultimately cost you money. This requires a lot of discipline, especially when the brief is interesting or you sympathize with the client.

Accordingly, we had to raise our fees. This seems just as counterintuitive as refusing work. But what really happens during a crisis? The mid-market price range disappears, and you are left to position yourself as either a budget or a premium option. As we provide a lot of value, we consciously decided to leave the grey zone and step into a fee range we feel is justified. Although we are still underpaid for the services we provide, and although the undervaluation of the architectural profession's work is a general problem, we are now considered an "expensive" office. We always try and explain these contingencies to our clients, who have to agree. And if they don't, we pull out of the negotiations.

Furthermore, we realized that we needed to work on different types of projects at the same time: public as well as private projects with a programmatic diversity and a range of locations and sizes. Up to this day we use a checklist for every potential acquisition, every competition, and every offer that we make. This ensures the diversity of our overall portfolio. For instance, in times of financial turmoil public-sector projects are a more secure source of income than private ones. They might be delayed, but they will be delivered eventually. Private clients, especially investors, withdraw more quickly in times of high uncertainty. The twenty-first century is uncertain by default, but there are periods, such as the current one, when things come to a head. We now also look to get a foothold in different markets beyond Brussels, Flanders, or Wallonia, which is reflected in our team with Dutch-, Flemish-, French-, (Swiss) German-, and, of course, English-speaking members. This diversity allows us to cover a bigger market.

However, the most important decisions we have made are related to the team and the way we work together. Crises make industries and workers adapt and become more agile—or, one could say: polyvalent. We therefore decided to work with people who have a so-called "T-shaped" set of skills. The vertical bar of the T is your in-depth expertise, your most important skill. The horizontal bar of the T is your cross-disciplinary knowledge. The idea behind this is that we all have one particular thing we're very good at, but we usually don't want to be doing that thing all the time; we also want to explore other areas. The horizontal bar is reaching out to other colleagues' areas of specialization, creating a knowledge transfer. In non-commercial architecture offices, the way knowledge is shared is one of the main drivers of profitability.

That is the conclusion I came to in my MBA thesis, which I based on scientific studies, sector-specific statistics, and field research within the profession. This insight allowed us to increase the team's skillset. Its members teach and learn from each other. Additionally, they can step in for each other, which allows us to reorganize teams all the time. In that sense, the MBA was useful, as I learned to find words for what we had already been doing: Empowering self-steering teams.

OG This requirement of agility and flexibility could also be read as exploitative: an expectation towards staff members to constantly adapt. There is a social media phenomenon called "quiet quitting," where users encourage each other to limit their tasks and working hours to those strictly within their job description. Do you see this change in mindset regarding the polyvalence you referred to earlier within the younger generation of architects?

OB I think we have to make a distinction between commercial and non-commercial offices. The main goal of a commercial office is to make money and turn a profit. But that is not our priority. Certainly, we have to make money to function, but we are not commercial in the strict sense.

Knowing this, the hiring process becomes very important and does not start with the job interview. People who apply for a job in our office have already heard of us—from me, my associates, or the team—because we encourage them to spread the word. Applicants might have heard us speaking publicly about societal issues or read our opinions on global challenges in newspapers. That's where the hiring process actually starts; it's called inbound marketing.

We have a multistage, decentralized selection procedure, involving different team members. We also give each other quite

Fig. 3 Bogdan & Van Broeck, Campus Unesco Koekelberg, 2011–18
Extension and transformation of a combined primary and secondary school

Fig. 4 The school in its original condition in 2014

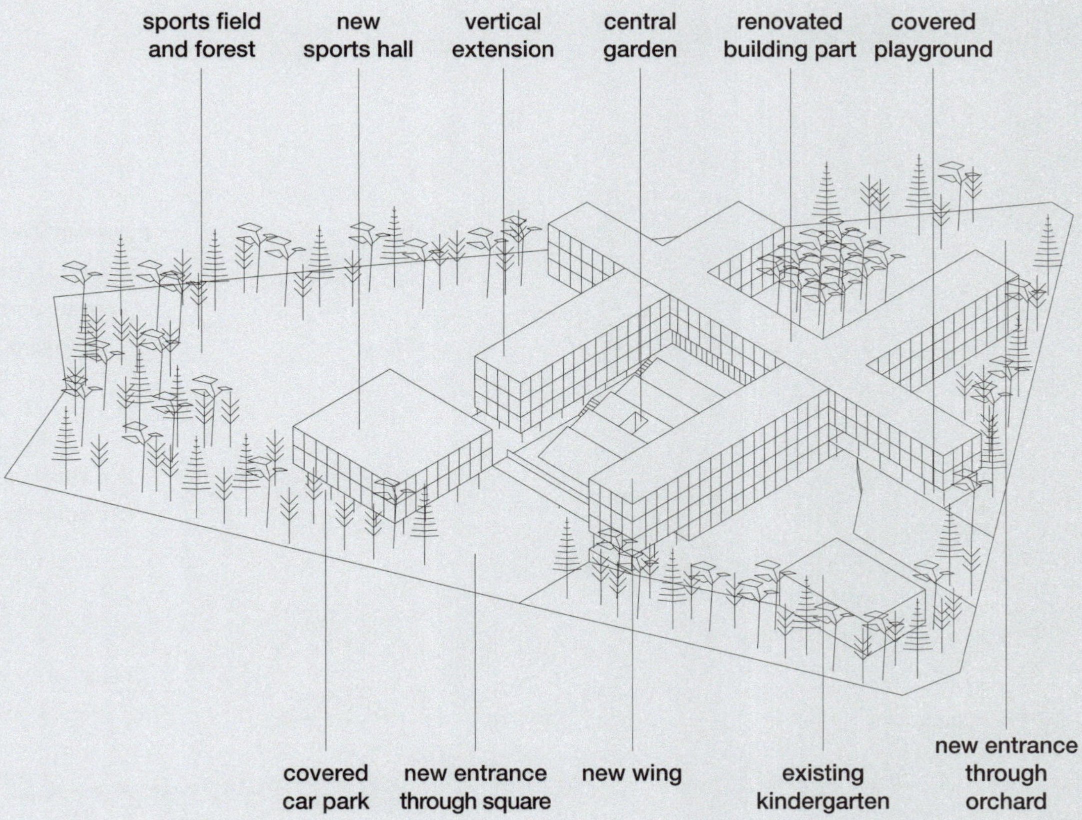

Fig. 5 Isometric view of the school campus

Fig. 6 Bogdan & Van Broeck and DDS+, NovaCity, Anderlecht, 2017–22
New compound including apartments and offices in a mixed-use zone

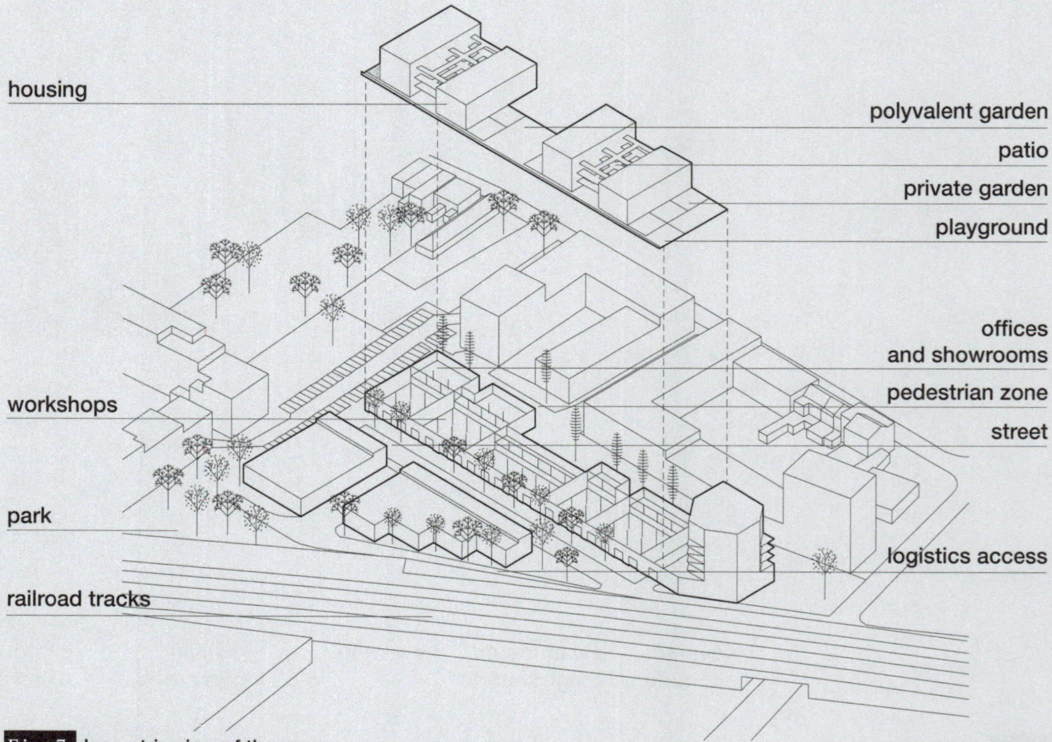

Fig. 7 Isometric view of the area

some time to get to know the other side better. Besides, I think the reason I have never seen any of our team members "quiet quitting" is that we invest a lot in their well-being and empowerment. They have a lot of leeway in their design choices because they know we are going to have their backs and will share the rewards with them if the business is doing well. They are empowered and can work on interesting projects. If they were to start their own businesses, it would take them a lot more time to get to the same point.

We want people to stay with us as long as possible, which is actually another important factor impacting an office's profitability. Things have to be strongly interconnected in a well-functioning business.

OG Are the people working for you employed?

OB No, they are not. For reasons that have to do with the financial system in Belgium, that is not something we can afford. It is a fake system that is nonetheless tolerated by authorities because otherwise we would have to increase our fees. That, however, would not work in a financial system based on cheap real estate as compensation for low pensions. As a consequence, many members of our team are not working with us full-time, but have their own, smaller projects on the side.

OG You spoke about the difference between commercial and non-commercial offices. I would add a third category which is neither commercial nor economically viable because they do not depend on their projects to run the firm; they have other sources of income or wealth. Offices in this group undercut each other's prices and, in doing so, devalue everyone's work. How do your fees bridge the gap between economic security and design freedom?

OB We made the decision to never work for free again. That is our postulate, although we participated in several unpaid competitions and feasibility studies in the beginning. We know that there are many offices out there doing that—we just don't. We try to educate our clients, which is a difficult thing to do. One step that can be easily explained to the client is that we no longer accept to be paid as a percentage of the project costs. Instead, our business relationships are built on trust. If the client thinks that we make certain design decisions purely to increase their project's costs and, by extension, our fees, there is no mutual confidence. Instead, we negotiate a price per square meter; this is better, but still wrong. Both models are based on the time needed to produce the necessary deliverables for the realization of the project and construction supervision. Instead, architects should be paid for the value they generate.

OG On what grounds would you calculate that value added?

OB The evaluation of our activities and the impact of our work is measurable. I don't think it's rocket science. Honest investors and real estate developers will tell you how much value good architecture can generate. We must find a way to put a price tag on the value added, which is the quality of life added to a space by architecture. This sounds abstract, but I want to remind you that there are insurance policies covering celebrities' body parts. If we can assess the value of Jennifer Lopez's butt, how hard can it really be to appraise the value of our work as architects? First, we have to look for it in the built objects, for example in the efficiency of the organization of space on the limited resource of land. But there is a lot more to it than providing the service of planning and building.

In conjunction with reorganizing the firm under its new name &bogdan, we want to redefine the role of the architect as someone who is able to address the great challenges facing us today, someone who can break down and dissect the complexity of these issues systematically. Taming the complexity of our world holds a promise of freedom. Freedom must evolve beyond the narrow interpretation of individual liberty. A fundamental issue for society, therefore, is the reinvention of freedom as commons. We want to return to the social aspiration of architecture and commit ourselves to a common world we all share.

OG Keller Easterling once said that "some of the greatest changes of the globalizing world are being written in the language of architecture and urbanism, so there has to be a chance that we know something about it, more than the 28-year-old McKinsey consultant who is making most of the global decisions."[1] Is architects' failure to create an understanding for the value of what they do beyond building part of the problem?

OB There is significant overlap between our work and that of the consulting-firm oligopoly, the so-called "Big Four" (Deloitte, EY, KPMG, and PwC). I was involved in the reform of the urban-planning regulations of the Brussels capital region and sat across from many stakeholders, among which top consultants who were discussing the city's marketing strategy. Architects may not know much about marketing, but I can tell you those consultants didn't know a thing about the city. Yet their fees will seem astronomical to any architect. We will never be paid as consultants as long as we market ourselves only as architects and not as design thinkers. I've sometimes done the same work as a consultant while being paid an architect's hourly fee.

Consultants are not liable for their actions. It's a lot easier to only provide services without providing plans for a building. Yet I am the one who has to fork over 0.2 percent of total building costs as an insurance premium because I'm liable for ten years for every completed project.

It's about the recognition of what architecture is and what architects do. Society needs architects, there is a constant need to reorganize space. Architects' main task is the organization of the presence of mankind on earth in harmony with nature, be it for the energy transition, to adapt existing buildings in the face of the climate crisis, for the circular economy, etc.

So, why is our work not valued as highly? Let's be realistic: We are part of the real estate market and generate a lot of profit for other people. Buildings are assets and, as tools for value creation, subject to the logic of the real estate industry, which tries to lower construction costs to increase its margins. Our economic system is based on this business model, and even pension funds rely heavily on real estate. To increase the margin, labor costs, including our fees, are kept as low as possible. The privatization of land and entire cities has increasingly become a problem for architects. Building for short-term profit undermines the social mission of architecture and the role of the architect as caretakers of space. This house of cards will fall only if we start asking to be paid for the value that we generate.

OG The profession's self-perception has changed. To consider how we live together or how social relations are organized through the built environment was initially not part of our job description. Still, architects continue to be considered—by some—as "master builders."

OB I think that has to do with our own understanding of the architectural profession. Our education and the complexity of the task make us bad communicators.

It's difficult for non-architects to grasp what we do and are responsible for as architects. We are trained to think in three-dimensional and cross-disciplinary systems, bringing together multiple stakeholders: from city authorities, to engineers, to developers, to users. That, essentially, is what design thinking is. It is not only extremely valuable today, but also very uncommon. Architects just don't know it. As a matter of fact, design thinking has been recognized for decades as an asset in the business world and in business schools. I'm one of *them* now, with all the tricks and buzzwords.

That's why it is interesting to compare the two curricula. To graduate in architecture, you study for five years, during which you address a diverse range of topics in different classes and formats, which prepare you for many situations that may arise during planning and construction. How do you teach that level of design thinking to MBA students in just one or two years? It's impossible! To address this problem, the business world came up with the idea of design leadership, which pairs someone in a managerial position with an artist or designer. This way, two completely different ways of thinking are combined and put in a joint leadership position.

This is what I call the architect's predicament. Architecture actually combines many worlds, especially if you start your own office and you have to be the dreaming artist, the creative designer, the pragmatic engineer, and the rational manager all at once. We are generalists, integrators, and design thinkers. This is what we need to learn to promote.

OG Do you believe design and management in architectural offices should be split into two distinct positions, namely creative director and CEO? Or should architects empower themselves to be both?

OB All these architects that we admire, from BIG to OMA, decided to hire CEOs with experience from outside our field to make their offices function in the current capitalist system. If this is not your objective and you question that system—the growth paradigm, our understanding of nature, resources, and societal responsibility—your idea of success and value will be a different one than theirs. It is my conviction that a good architect needs to be both a design thinker and a manager. I see great value in the struggle of these two sides.

Felix Hofmann: In that regard, you once said that architects need to understand the market to effect change in the city.

OB Not only the market, but also how institutions and politics work. Unlike in private commissions, a special kind of dynamic plays a part in public projects, i.e., legislative terms. Indeed, some of the greatest changes of the globalizing world are being written in the language of architecture and urbanism. That is why we need to understand how this globalized world functions.

If you really want to have an impact as an architect, I don't think it's enough to design great buildings, you have to get involved in politics. In 2019, I was called on to become interim Secretary of State in charge of cultural heritage in Romania. I said yes on the spot. To me it sounded like an opportunity to gather insight into a technocratic government and to actively try to change politics for the better. Back then, I didn't expect that my experience in politics would help me so much with understanding how these systems interconnect and interoperate. Almost four years in politics have made me a better architect.

OG At the same time, in 2016, your partner Leo Van Broeck was appointed to the position of *Bouwmeester* in Flanders.

OB This came as a surprise to all of us. He was named *Bouwmeester* (master builder) only two months after my appointment. An essential position in Flanders, it provides expertise in guiding public and private projects and thereby ensures quality across the industry. He left the office for four years. All of a sudden, we were both gone and our team proved that they could be successful without us. That has made me particularly proud.

OG You spoke about diversifying an office's portfolio to make it more resilient in the face of crises. Is public tender part of that strategy?

OB First of all, we as architects like public projects. They are more complex not only in terms of program, but also because the scarcity of public land makes it necessary to stack multiple uses on small plots of land. That fosters creativity, which is further enhanced by the competitions mandated for all public projects in Belgium. What we learned is that half of our turnover should come from public projects and the other half from private ones. There are two reasons: I already mentioned that public projects will continue even in times of crisis. But you don't make enough money with them, simply because they are more complex than investor projects. Public authorities put everything they need in the little space that is available to them. The architect then has to conjure up spatial solutions, which leads to extraordinary projects, like a two-story childcare center on top of an indoor sports facility. Private developers seldom come up with that kind of program. Additionally, you have to talk to different stakeholders, like authorities and future users. That adds a lot of work, while at the same time public authorities underpay architects. In the end private projects actually end up co-financing public projects, which in turn secure the base.

OG What if you don't have multiple projects running in parallel? Do you have experience taking out short-term loans?

OB In theory we should have a financial buffer covering operations for six months. So far, we have not managed to build up this buffer. We have a 125,000-euro credit line, which allows us to ride out a hard patch for a month. If something were to happen, we'd have to petition our bank, which would be a gamble given the current economic situation.

FH We have talked a lot about your experience and the resilient office that you have built. Are there any other difficulties you see yourself confronted with?

OB The Covid pandemic has turned supply chains and production processes on their head. Coupled with the war in Ukraine and inflation, the price of construction materials has shot up between 25 and 30 percent, at least in Belgium. All our clients, be they private or public, are looking for additional funds, slowing down projects or putting them on hold. Again, we have enough contracts and our business looks amazing on paper; we recently won many competitions. From the outside it looks like we've never been better off. But with these delays, part of our projects have been postponed to next year; this year, it's not enough. While in the past, our projects were smaller but time-consuming, we decided at one point to focus on bigger projects. If one of those slows down, the cash flow dries up.

FH How do you deal with the constant threat of bankruptcy?

OB Differently than fifteen years ago. Most businesses go bankrupt within five years of their incorporation. After that, the probability decreases exponentially. We have no reason to be afraid. In the past fifteen years, we have achieved more than we could ever have dreamed of.

OG I believe this gratefulness is an expression of the highest form of freedom! If we take a step back and take a look at the current situation, what will we learn from these crises and what future are we looking toward?

OB Certainly, our economy needs to shift from quantitative growth to qualitative growth. Economists—like Esther Duflo, Stephanie Kelton, Mariana Mazzucato, Carlota Pérez, and Kate Raworth—strongly agree. They ponder the contours of a new system by questioning concepts such as value, debt, growth, and GDP. Further, government must return to its legitimate role. The latter has become too limited compared to the role of the market, which focuses only on immediate private interest and little on a collective future. This weakness has led to well-known disastrous consequences: increased inequality, environmental collapse, and difficulties with long-term planning. The crisis of democracy further delays our ability to reduce humanity's

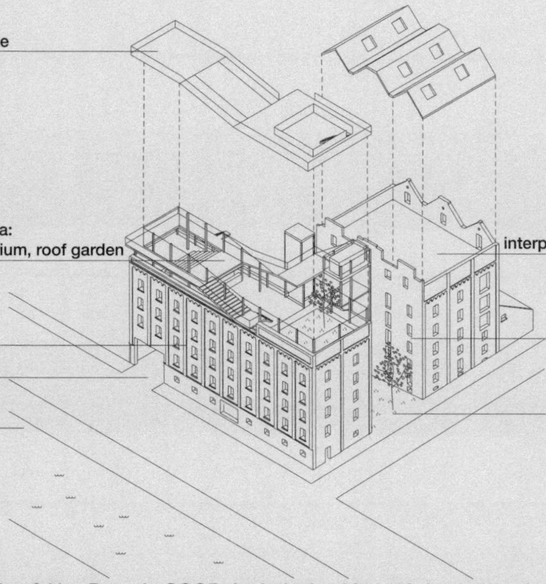

Fig. 8 Bogdan & Van Broeck, COOP, Anderlecht, 2011–16, isometric view of the conversion

Fig. 9 The silo in its original condition

ecological footprint. This reduction, however, is the prerequisite for our health and well-being. We need a new story, a narrative that does not aim at the destruction but at the regeneration of our planet. We need to translate the restrictive definition of sustainability to a broader model of urban development. Cities face the task of not only conserving their natural resources, but also actively regenerating them. If we want to build future-proof cities that bring together the needs of people and nature, we need an inclusive dialogue and an ongoing professional and social debate about the future of cities and their interconnectedness on a global scale: climate crisis, loss of biodiversity, and depletion of natural resources. We want to participate in that discussion.
And that is what we do. As I mentioned earlier, I was involved in the reform of the Brussels capital region's urban planning regulations. The framework, among other radical measures, prescribes that the demolition of existing buildings is only possible in exceptional situations. I believe the future lies in the transformation of what we already have. It is more complicated than building anew, but it values the existing—a notion currently absent from our definition of value creation. As long as the carbon embodied in the existing structure is not part of the financial equation, conversion will always be more expensive than demolition and new construction. Buildings are not stand-alone elements in a city, but contribute regeneratively to the city as a whole. I have great hopes that we can bring about more equality if we change the basis of our calculation, and that the crises we are going through will transform the system—a system that is dying, anyway.

1 *Architecting after Politics*, Olaf Grawert and Christopher Roth, dir., (Germany: Brandlhuber+, prod., 2018).

Fig. 10 Bogdan & Van Broeck, COOP, Anderlecht, 2011–16
Adaptive reuse and vertical extension of a silo built in 1903 (fig. 9) as part of Anderlecht's former industrial harbor

THE MARKETING VALUE OF ARCHITECTURE

HOW TO SELL ARCHITECTURE

Jan Knikker in conversation with Olaf Grawert and Jolene Lee

Fig. 1

Fig. 2

Employment status of architects: → Sole practitioners – Austria 66% / Germany 21% → Directors / partners – Austria 28% / Germany 10% → Salaried architects – Austria 3% / Germany 35% (incl. in-house) → Freelancers – Austria 2% / Germany 2% → Other – Austria 0.5% / Germany 14% → Public sector – Austria 0.5% / Germany 18%

Fig. 1 View of MVRDV's office in Berlin-Kreuzberg, one of the firm's designated "satellites"

In his 2021 book *How to Win Work: The Architect's Guide to Business Development and Marketing*, Jan Knikker examines the financial reality of architects across the globe. In the process, he delves into the economic picture and self-image of various "architectural nations," including the Netherlands, where Knikker has lived since 1992, and where he worked with OMA. He is currently a partner and Director of Strategy at MVRDV.

Olaf Grawert: The following questions come up all the time, both while restructuring our own practice at b+ and in the academic context with students: How do architectural offices finance themselves? What tools facilitate the creation and appreciation of value? And how can architects actively shape their financial environment? How do you approach these issues at MVRDV, and how did you end up in this decision-making role?

Jan Knikker: I started out as a journalist, writing a lot about real estate. This interest led me, somewhat haphazardly, to an introduction with Rem Koolhaas in an attempt to be his secretary. But because of my experience as a journalist, I was brought in as head of PR at his office OMA. In 2008, I joined MVRDV, where I am now a partner and director of the Strategy & Development division, which currently has 35 employees across three teams: public relations, business development, and visual communications. The PR team works on our public image, our reputation, and branding. If they are successful, they generate leads that are pursued by our business development team. That's how acquisition works. We think it's important that most employees on these teams are architects, because we view their expertise as an advantage here. An unusual part of MVRDV's corporate structure is an internal division dedicated to visual communications and visualizations. We are convinced that it's crucial to develop a visual language, a corporate visual identity. Naturally, this works best in-house. This kind of strategic corporate development, of course, is not easily replicable in a smaller office.

I started working at MVRDV exactly three weeks before the 2008 global financial crisis hit. I was worried about my job, and I began actively acquiring clients—with a lot of success. Both at OMA and MVRDV, we started with around 45 employees; when I left, OMA had 260, and currently around 330 people work at MVRDV. I realized how productive the interplay between architecture and marketing can be, and this understanding was ultimately the starting point for my book, *How to Win Work: The Architect's Guide to Business Development and Marketing*. Its target group in particular is small architecture firms who are cautious when it comes to marketing, even though their leaner structures would allow them to operate more flexibly and innovatively—in creative and economic terms.

Jolene Lee: Your book often refers to your own experience. Both public relations and business development are central pillars for you. This is unusual, because architects often balk at participating in the commercial logic of the free market. How did you transition from your PR role to also being involved with business development, and how do you differentiate between the two?

JK For me, the financial crisis of 2008 represented a turning point, biographically as much as professionally. In a few short months, we lost a third of our ongoing projects. We were faced with a question: How do we hold onto our employees, both through the crisis and beyond? In this regard, PR is a passive strategy. Good press on a project can certainly encourage customers with similar projects to get in touch. But this is difficult to control, and only has limited prospects of success during a recession. That's why business development was the more active path forward in this instance. The approach would be, for example, to call up a former customer and ask: "Do you have anything for us?" If you're then in a position to respond promptly to the resulting tenders, you have an opportunity to have some projects in your pocket at relatively short notice. Both approaches—passive and active—are available to architecture firms of every size and organizational structure. On the one hand, you need to go out in the world, to shake hands and get attention, while on the other, you need to actively attract prospective clients.

OG In my own experience both as an architecture student and now as an educator at ETH Zurich, universities don't teach their students that running a business is part of an architect's professional reality, and that the way you structure your business influences not only the way you work but also the work itself. How can the curriculum be expanded so that young professionals become aware of these economic contingencies? Where is the best place for that knowledge transfer to happen?

JK I'm always surprised that so many architects eventually manage to run a business, because having to learn autodidactically takes a lot of time and energy. I think universities should offer some sort of diploma in small- and medium-sized-business administration. How does bookkeeping work? How do you acquire clients? What makes a business run smoothly? How do you organize relationships with employees? Questions like these affect every company, regardless of its size or organizational structure. At a minimum, there should be optional classes on the subject. I have noticed a certain reticence not just in academia but among practicing architects, as well, who seem to see themselves more as artists than as service providers. That's unfortunate because I think reticence toward the business side of architecture hurts more than it helps. If you look at how much German architects with a master's degree earn on average—around 43,000 euros annually as an entry-level salary—it's well below the average for people with the same level of qualification in other fields, which is 47,000 euros per year. Architects spend six years learning conceptual thinking and designing, but afterwards this is precisely what they are *not* paid for. Instead, they are paid to produce drawings, which is considerably less demanding in terms of time and cognitive skills. The ideas, on the other hand, are provided for free.

OG The Belgian architect Oana Bogdan, in our conversation for this issue, has pointed out that good architecture generates value for society, a fact that is neither reflected in the fees nor in the overall economic system. This ideal valuation of "good" versus "bad" architecture plays no role in a system that calculates hourly wages as a function of construction costs. How can this, say, "higher-minded" value added become a measurable part of the architectural fee?

JK At the moment, architecture is often appraised not according to its market value, but according to its marketing value—by which I mean how often it's featured in the press and how often it's discussed. This is always a product of good PR. But a lot of architecture's supposedly difficult-to-measure value added can be quantified. At the moment, we're trying to take a strictly data-based approach to the question, which works comparatively well in the Netherlands, because we have a lot of data available. We are working with the firm Rebel, which analyzes data surrounding transit, urban development, health, and social sustainability. Although we aren't ready to make any definitive statements, some interesting tendencies have already emerged. For example, the rising property costs around MVRDV projects demonstrate the increase in attractiveness of the neighborhoods we design. With projects like Markthal in Rotterdam, the added urban value can also be quantified: The building now has around 8 million visitors per year, even though initially it only aimed to attract 3.5 million. As a consequence, it has changed the city economy and has added tangible value. The positive and negative effects of architecture on its environment is not studied well enough. Fundamental research is overdue at this point, to help us prevent projects which might have a negative impact.

JL I want to go back once again to the tension between values and valuation. The former are based on platonic premises,

while the latter is based on money and growth. In the chapter "Practical Tips for Managing Unpaid Work," you talk about architecture competitions. There might be thirty offices taking part, but only five will receive a symbolic payment, and even that seldom covers the costs. In the worst case, no marketing value ever ends up getting created.
Ultimately, what is the value of communication and PR? How do you determine it? Do you fix a number as part of your overhead as a kind of fixed ratio, skimming a percentage of your income that you reserve for purely PR-oriented marketing or competitions?

JK It's actually quite banal. Every article, every mention, every like on social media has a certain value. You can look at it very unemotionally. It's important, of course, to ensure that the relationship between the time invested and the resulting engagement—measured in interactions or reach—is sensible. At the same time, the business development team is judged by how many tenders and projects it wins. We used to have a success rate of 1 in 20 inquiries, then 1 in 10, and now the ratio is 50-50. This division is demonstrably generating value and contributing to growth. Of course, we now also work with a software that measures the value generated by our PR team.

JL You're describing impressively rapid growth, which sometimes is precisely what leads to problems: When a firm wins a competition, for example, and begins to grow very fast. In a similar situation, BIG decided to hire a CEO to scale the company. This is a move that could be interpreted as serving the self-image of architects as artists, suddenly free to operate as creative directors, concentrating once again on conception and design. It seems that architecture firms who create a special position for economic growth are more successful. What do you think of this business model?

JK When you make targeted hires, you can find specialists who are excellent at business administration rather than people who have studied architecture and are excellent at that. This can have an immediate impact.

JL Yet it's strange that you prefer architects in communications and PR because they have a better grasp of the subject matter, whereas the business side of things can so successfully be outsourced to outsiders, who take responsibility in the office in a completely different way.

JK Only a fraction of the problems that arise in the organization of an architecture firm need a specialist to be solved. For example, an enormous number of mistakes can be made in contracts. Therefore, it's advisable to have lawyers handle your contracts. In the beginning, we didn't do this, and we wound up regretting it. Now we employ three lawyers. Small firms may be tempted to avoid paying for legal advice, but a bad contract can threaten your entire existence. By the same token, I'm convinced that it is a good idea to employ management specialists who excel in their field. There may be architects who can design perfect contracts, perfect corporate structures, *and* perfect buildings—but for the rest of us it's a good idea to rely on specialists who help by using their own conceptual talent as productively as possible. It's beneficial for architects to recognize this. At universities, they are trained to be generalists, but a generalist is not a universal genius.

OG External experts can be brought onto projects, but their fees are often too high for small firms to afford. Models like the one developed by ARGE.CO, a cooperative of fourteen independent architects in Zurich, offer an interesting alternative. All the architects pitch in a share of their revenue to pay an accountant, a legal consultant, and other service providers. In principle, they collectivize their overhead costs. At which scale is this worthwhile? Or, to put it another way, how much support service is necessary per person in your opinion?

JK I'd estimate that 15 percent of our workforce are people who do not perform planning work. Incidentally, we work exactly like ARGE.CO, because at a certain point we decided not to become another big office, because we didn't want the creativity and motivation of our employees to fall by the wayside. So, we divided ourselves into eleven studios. The three service studios—operations, strategy, and finance—can be booked by the eight design studios, each operating as independent units within the larger firm. Each studio is led by a studio manager, and only if there is a problem does it go up to the next level—or the partners might visit the studios, if they're not busy leading one. Only the three founders belong to no studio in particular. They work together with all of them. This level of autonomy allows us to become specialists.

OG When you undertook the reorganization, was the well-being of your employees front of mind, or was it a reaction to the financial crisis? Or was it about competing for talent, in the context of which the concept of new work is becoming increasingly important?

JK When our employee count approached the three-figure realm, I went on a research trip with our managing director and partner Inger Kammeraat. We visited other studios, including Olafur Eliasson's. Our question was: "How can such a huge company stay creative?" The answer: "It can't." That is why we undertook this division into smaller studios where people stay on a permanent basis. What this means is that, if someone is working at DAS Studio, they probably will not take part in any projects at the Studio Americas. The studios have a maximum size of thirty-five employees. Everybody knows each other; everybody comes to the office and leaves at the same time; there is a lot of trust and exchanging of ideas. The individual studios form a closed financial entity, but not a legal entity like a limited liability company. That means they are measured according to their profitability and they are budgeted as individual units, but they do not act individually vis-à-vis the outside world, and they are not individually liable. Of course, regarding younger employees in particular, there is some fluctuation between the teams, but that also ensures potential for innovation. But if someone wants to switch, for example, from DAS Studio to Studio Americas, they have to officially apply like everyone else.

OG Striving for innovation has received a certain amount of criticism from the younger generation. Young people increasingly see their responsibility to the environment—internationally and intergenerationally. Some have even embraced the idea of ceasing to build altogether. Such a stance, of course, leads to conflict with a business model in which fees are determined as a percentage of how much is built. Without a new compensation model that does justice to new aspects of the profession, the younger generation faces an enormous economic challenge. As a globally active firm, do you see a productive way of handling this conflict?

JK This is definitely something we focus on, for example through the analysis I mentioned earlier concerning our buildings and their effects on their surroundings. When it comes to economic sufficiency, however, I think in particular the time *before* starting a project is the most relevant. For example, architects are often involved as advisors in public tenders, where they have an opportunity to ask critical questions. What do we actually need? More critical voices in these rooms would reinforce the perception that not building—or rather adaptive reuse—is the best way forward, or that at least that the balance sheet needs to be even. At the moment, in ecological terms, we are deep in the red.

JL The European Union recently changed the way a building's energy efficiency is calculated across the bloc to a comprehensive life-cycle assessment—just as we don't just pay for clean water, but also for the disposal of greywater. Changing the balance sheet for existing buildings in this way would, in one fell swoop, make demolition unprofitable.

JK We are also noticing a paradigm shift in how architects understand their work, which is increasingly process-oriented instead of results-oriented. In the future, all the conceptual, problem-oriented thinking skills that architects learn while studying will need to be monetized through activities beyond just drawing and building. This means that, like other professionals—doctors, lawyers, etc.—we will need to start charging for our cognitive output again, not just the finished plan. We recently launched a computing division called NEXT – New Experimental Technologies, which is receiving more and more inquiries, such as performing an analysis of Rotterdam's inner city. Where can more density be achieved? Where would it be better to hold off? Since analysis is the product here, not a plan, the architects can evaluate objectively, without a building commission in the back of their minds.

OG At the same time, studios profit from these public-interest projects, don't they? The Czech firm CHYBIK+KRISTOF, for example, takes on a certain percentage of *pro bono* projects that they actively pursue. Paradoxically, this "philanthropy" has economic value, because corporate clients are subsequently willing to pay the studio more than their Czech competitors. The *pro bono* projects they're indirectly supporting can be used for PR.

JK MVRDV also does *pro bono* work, but we seldom publicize it. Maybe that is a mistake, but we avoid it because everyone else involved in these projects is also working for free. And you have to be careful not to give clients who can afford your services the impression that you are willing to work for free. Particularly when it comes to political issues, we believe in getting involved. Our analysis of the housing question in The Netherlands is an example. We would love to solve it with less new construction.

OG When our students look at the biggest firms worldwide, they are often astonished to discover how much money or value is generated in the global architecture sector, while the ten biggest firms are mostly so anonymous they barely have any name recognition within the discourse. Of course, there are different portals, data, and criteria of assessment at play, but in general it seems that the smaller and younger firms defining the discourse are not necessarily the most profitable.

JK It's true, although it's worth being cautious here. People often purchase their spot on these lists. MVRDV did it for the first time in 2020, although we could have managed it much earlier, economically speaking. What happens is, you send in your data, pay a fee, and afterward receive a ranking. At OMA, I did this every year, but at MVRDV the benefit was no longer clear to me. The lists, therefore, are not complete, although their rankings are presumably correct, at least among the top 20.

OG At what point are offices optimally staffed, at least in terms of profitability? In Germany, the data is quite clear: Offices with 150 employees or more suddenly become extremely profitable, partly because individual workers create much more value than in smaller firms. In MVRDV's case, the value creation per employee is around 100,000 US dollars annually, compared to 200,000 at BIG and 70,000 at gmp. Are my estimates correct?

JK I think the first "leap" becomes noticeable at around 100 employees. From 150 employees and up, things become dramatically more efficient, because suddenly you can involve many services and specialists. Especially when it comes to competitions, it's noticeable that a company benefits enormously from experienced employees—one of whom can achieve almost as much as a team of five younger architects. At the same time, you can work on larger projects that bring in more money and incorporate more varied markets, especially in countries where the competition system is lucrative. In Germany, you tend to lose money with competitions, whereas in China the margins are greater, regardless of whether the project is ever built.

JL Is the takeaway from this conversation, and also possibly your book, that firms are profitable above all when they make growth the premise of their practice? This might be a bitter conclusion for firms with non-monetary or post-growth premises.

JK Yes and no. You need good organization, you need to be professional, and you cannot cut corners in the wrong places. But growth doesn't have to be your *raison d'être*. It never was at MVRDV. For the first ten years we were architects mostly on paper, like many others, and we hardly built anything. Maybe this is the better takeaway: To be commercially successful always requires a bit of luck.

Fig. 2 View of the 2,400-square-meter MVRDV House in Rotterdam, located inside a building originally designed by Dutch architect Huig Maaskant in 1952

THE COMPANY AS A PROJECT

TOOLS OF COOPERATION

Text: Elke Doppelbauer

While employees in private German architecture and planning offices were most critical of their salaries, public-sector employees criticized the lack of career opportunities. In Germany, sole practitioners typically work 49.9 hours per week, closely followed by partners and directors (48.8 hours) and salaried architects (39.7 hours). Freelance architects work 38.8 hours per week on average; architects in the public sector work 39.5 hours per week on average. In Germany, 32% of employees in architecture and planning firms are not compensated for overtime

Norms regulate and shape our shared lives and the way we work together. This is especially true of architecture, and particularly in Germany, where the German Building Code (BauGB), technical standards by the German Institute for Standardization (DIN), and ISO standards play a constant role. In fact, the ISO 9000 directive even offers a precise definition of the very term "project", stating that it is a "unique process, consisting of a set of coordinated and controlled activities with start and finish dates, undertaken to achieve an objective conforming to specific requirements, including the constraints of time, cost and resources."[1]

Unlike with projects, the temporality of a company—and therefore an architectural practice—is not finite,[2] but here, too, specific requirements need to be fulfilled to steer a company toward its goals in terms of time, profitability, and staff. The objective of all entrepreneurs is to develop processes to this end: to find or invent tools and procedures that square up to the complex contexts and unforeseeable events of everyday operations, irrespective of whether the company has a payroll of one or of one hundred. Accordingly, every company consciously or unconsciously devises its own value system, which structures and orders these processes and enables the team to collaborate productively. Alongside mathematical values, ethical values also lay the basis of this system and underpin each and every entrepreneurial activity. These decisions constitute the company's ethos and sense of responsibility: Should I gear my company to growth, to functionality, to adding value, and/or to ideals? In the search for the right-fit system, a look at the history of organizational structures, organizational theory, and industrial science as well as sociology can offer countless explanations, with one being Frederic Laloux's 2015 juxtaposition of organizations.[3] He distinguishes between five models:

1. *Impulsive organizations* are characterized by authoritarian power structures and usually with a single leader; they are maintained and held together by fear. This organizational structure has a short-term focus and is highly reactive, and typically based on a division of tasks and a chain of command. Examples are the structures of organized crime or rackets.[4]

2. *Conformist organizations* have highly formalized roles within a hierarchical pyramid. Instructions and control are top-down. The primary premise is stability, with the creation of formal roles (stable and scalable hierarchies) and processes (long-termism) intended to secure continuity. Examples are the Catholic Church, the military, or government agencies.[5]

3. *Achievement-oriented organizations* are geared toward profit. They are premised on expansion, in part through innovation. Management follows performance indicators and uses instruction and control mechanisms to this end. How the targets are achieved is left up to the person in question. Such organizations are shaped by innovation, reliability, and the performance principle. Examples are multinational corporations, business schools, and private (charter) schools.[6]

4. *Pluralistic organizations* rely on outstanding staff motivation to achieve commercial success. They still act within the classic pyramidal structure while focusing on culture and empowerment. Typical features include some level of decentralization, a value-oriented culture, or consideration of different interest groups (stakeholder model). Examples are mainly to be found among non-profit or cultural organizations.[7]

5. *Evolutionary organizations* use new organizational models and tools to achieve the aforementioned operational requirements. The intellectual forebear of evolutionary organizations is Frithjof Bergmann, who back in 1985 coined the term *New Work*. In his pursuit of new systems for handling transformations and changes of human consciousness in professional settings, he has influenced corporations, employees, and management and organization developers ever since, not least owing to the new vocabulary he used to denote the complex requirements and new ways of working. Bergmann insisted that we must sharpen our understanding of the fact that organizations are complex, idiosyncratic, and self-organizing systems that often evade goal-oriented control.[8] Using new tools, their management can succeed in deploying systemic concepts for thought and action that grasp occurrences within projects and corporations as an ongoing process and, with the inclusion of all participants, can continuously and actively shape them.

GLOSSARY

● AGILITY
is a measure of a system's ability to adjust and respond to events. Coping with changes in work and organization requires awareness and engagement. By helping design the process of change, you become the designer of your own organization. Using methods, models, and tools for designing agile organizations, you facilitate addressing dynamism and complexity, enabling gradual development.[9] The more adaptable or agile an organization becomes, the more it can bounce back from or embrace unplanned events.

● CO-CREATION*
describes collaborative working and thinking where new ideas build on one another, emerging through collaboration. For co-creation to succeed, ego-free structures are needed: During the creation process, no one should seek to improve their standing within the organization's hierarchy. Creating open-ended, non-judgmental spaces for experimentation is pivotal.

● COMMONS*
refers to resources used collectively and often self-organized. The concept opposes privatizing resources and appropriating them through patents and copyrights, which restrict use according to the owner's rules.

● COMPLEXITY
arises from feedback loops and self-organization. Organizations tend to be Taylorist (i.e., characterized by standardized, iterative processes) and geared towards efficiency. A complex and dynamic market setting can overtax organizations, making it hard to predict necessary communication and cooperation. Reality forces adaptation to market situations, changing parameters, and technological advances. Managing complexity involves recognizing the necessary leadership forms for specific contexts. Efficiency and performance are supplemented, not replaced, by the ability to adapt and cope with complexity.[10]

● CRADLE-TO-CRADLE*
describes a completely waste-free working and business concept. Raw materials are either returned to a natural cycle (e.g., compostable) or reused in closed technical cycles (e.g., modular). The social aspect of raw material extraction and recycling methodologies needs examination.

● DESIGN SPRINT*
is a time-limited, structured process to develop concepts, products, or services. It consists of five stages: 1. Analyze the problem (Map); 2. Sketch solutions (Sketch); 3. Decide on a solution (Decide); 4. Create a prototype (Prototype); 5. Test the prototype with users (Test). Each sprint forms a loop in an iterative process, with prototypes adjusted and advanced as needed. Design sprints, based on the design thinking method developed by Jake Knapp at Google Ventures, have largely replaced linear development methods in the New Work context due to their suitability for complex challenges.

● DESIGN THINKING*
is an approach that applies product design principles to solving various problems. It focuses on understanding people and their needs, allowing for many ideas and viewpoints, constantly reviewing assumptions, and rejecting them if necessary.

● EMPOWERMENT*
describes the more equal distribution of responsibility in corporations. People are encouraged to discover and utilize their abilities. The term implies a hierarchical relationship: One person shares power with others. Empowerment focused solely on the personal level without addressing structural inequalities is inadequate. Structural empowerment is shown by role-based organizational models where power is inherent in positions and roles distributed across all members based on their competencies, eliminating the need for empowerment by a superior.

● **HIERARCHY**
is a basis for control and management. In the classic sense, responsibility for the big picture is delegated to the top level, with directions running top-down. This simple form of connection constitutes a fixed structure. As complexity increases, control needs adjustment: Mutual dependencies require interaction and cooperation across the system for coordination tasks.[11] Increased connections within a corporation can be achieved by assigning decision-making powers based on competence rather than position or role.

● **LEADERSHIP**
is traditionally understood as a top-down approach. However, the term is evolving towards a more holistic notion where leadership adapts to requirements or situations to achieve optimal results. This process allows management to be led by employees.[12] Leadership is an ongoing process involving interaction, communication, and negotiation. Ideally, it focuses on designing the future rather than maintaining the status quo. The challenge lies in managing the paradox of responsibility for an unpredictable future.

● **POST-GROWTH***
is an economic school of thought rejecting unlimited growth, favoring healthy shrinkage. It advocates reducing consumption and production, focusing on a sustainable economy that preserves ecological balance and promotes peaceful coexistence. Conventional economics views growth as necessary to avoid unemployment and ensure social stability. Critics argue that unlimited growth is impossible in a limited system, a point highlighted by the climate crisis.

● **POST-HEROIC LEADERSHIP***
describes leadership where the executive at the top is not the sole hero. Responsibilities are distributed among many individuals, reducing dependence on decisions by an omniscient leader.

● **SKIN IN THE GAME**
means those making entrepreneurial decisions assume personal risk. The term implies that personal consequences result from decisions, promoting accountability. Originating from Nassim Nicholas Taleb's book, it argues that decisions should not be made by those not directly affected by its consequences.[13] For example, in the climate crisis, key decision-makers often come from wealthy countries and older generations, less impacted by climate change consequences than younger generations and poorer countries.

● **TEAMWORK**
is essential for solving extensive tasks. Successful cooperation depends on team cohesion, individual knowledge, and experience. Understanding team skills allows for optimal positioning within the organization. Continuity in collaboration maintains experience, knowledge, and social stability over time.[14]

● **TOLERANCE FOR AMBIGUITY***
describes the ability to endure ambiguities, uncertainties, and contradictions, vital for navigating complex, changing settings. For example, in a structurally changing organization, executives, tasks, and decision-making powers may be relinquished, with teams increasingly self-organizing. Executives must accept multiple working methods and solutions paths. Teams must handle new responsibilities as management simplifies its role.

● **VALUES**
guide actions and decisions. They often result from unconscious processes, becoming visible through executive behavior. Individuals, groups, and organizations have a value canon, not a clear value system, potentially leading to conflicts. Values direction is determined through a top-down and bottom-up value formation process. Company management prescribes and lives values, but their manifestation in cooperation is the responsibility of individual staff members.[15]

* These concepts are based on the *New Work Glossary* and used with kind permission of *Neue Narrative*: newworkglossar.de.

1 *ISO 9000: Quality Management Systems. Fundamentals and Vocabulary* (Geneva: International Standards Organization, 2015), s.v. 3.4.2 "Project."
2 See Frederic Laloux, *Reinventing Organizations: A Guide to Creating Organizations Inspired by the Next Stage of Human Consciousness*, chap. 1.1 (Brussels: Nelson Parker, 2015), 13–36.
3 Ibid.
4 Ibid., 17–18, 36.
5 Ibid., 18–23, 36.
6 Ibid., 23–30, 36.
7 Ibid., 30–34, 36.
8 Cf. Frithjof Bergmann, *New Work, New Culture: Work We Want and a Culture that Strengthens Us* (Alresford: Zero Books, 2015).
9 See Bernd Oestereich and Claudia Schröder, *Agile Organisationsentwicklung: Handbuch zum Aufbau anpassungsfähiger Organisationen* (Munich: Vahlen, 2019), 6.
10 See ibid.
11 See Rudolf Wimmer, *Organisation und Beratung: Systemtheoretische Perspektiven für die Praxis* (Heidelberg: Carl Auer, 2012), 106–13.
12 See Markus Väth, *Cooldown: Die Zukunft der Arbeit und wie wir sie meistern*, (Offenbach: GABAL, 2013), 234.
13 See Nassim Nicholas Taleb, *Skin in the Game: Hidden Asymmetries in Daily Life* (New York: Random House, 2018).
14 See Wimmer, *Organisation und Beratung* (see note 12), 147–70.
15 Cf. Väth, *Cooldown* (see note 10), 224–25.

L'ATELIER, NOMADIC ARCHITECTURE STUDIO

The founder Pierre Escobar in conversation with Olaf Grawert and Paul Barth

Fig.1

Fig.2

Fig.3

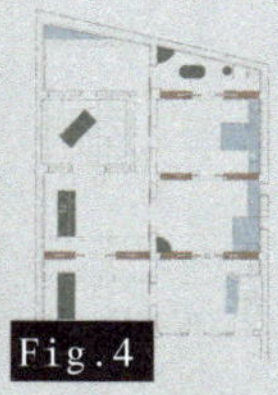
Fig.4

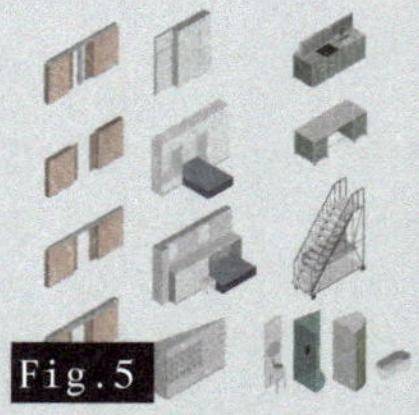
Fig.5

ORGANIZATION

OFFICE

Name	L'ATELIER, NOMADIC ARCHITECTURE STUDIO
Founded in	2018
Registered in	FRANCE

PROJECTS

Total	120
completed	20%
public	10%
private	90%
Current	20

TEAM

Total	9
by gender	33% M, 67% F
average age	30
nationalities	FRA, ESP, ITA, ISR, ARG, CHN, COD, ROU
Partners	100% PIERRE ESCOBAR
Managing Directors	1
Employees	0
Freelancers	8
Working students	0
Interns	0

FINANCES

INCOME PER MONTH / YEAR IN EUROS

Total	20,000 / 240,000
Construction projects	18,333 / 220,000
Teaching	1,667 / 20,000
Other external activities including lectures	0

EXPENSES PER MONTH IN EUROS

Total	20,000
Staff costs	12,000
Average salary (employees / freelancers)	1,000*
Average salary (interns)	
Rent and operating costs	1,000
Office supplies	2,000
Insurance, consulting, and legal fees	2,000
Travel expenses	3,000

* TEAM IN ARGENTINA

Olaf Grawert: l'atelier Nomadic Architecture Studio is, as the name indicates, not sedentary. What are the implications of this for the way you work?

Pierre Escobar: We are nomadic in the sense that we work in a decentralized and completely virtual way, and are not bound to one physical place. Our office consists of twelve people across seven countries on two continents. The tools we use to work together either didn't exist five years ago, or weren't good enough. Platforms like Miro are extremely efficient for designing collaboratively; we use it for everything from plan corrections, to workshops, to office management.

I'm convinced that this is the future of work. In a few years, virtual tools will mean designing virtual buildings for our avatars to meet in. That is the future of the office. I am optimistic about these developments because I think they make sense for the work we do. People prefer to be physically and personally in touch with each other, but the metaverse can serve professional relationships. This way, you can live in a village in the middle of nowhere with your friends and connect to work in cyberspace for eight hours a day.

OG This indicates a clear separation between the personal and the professional, on both a human and a spatial level.

PE I believe in respecting the privacy of my team. Going out with colleagues can create a strong sense of community, but it also mixes up your professional and private life. I would rather everyone have their own space than a strong sense of community. We have guidelines regarding mutual respect, gender balance, and queer-friendliness, but also for working at most eight hours a day and not at all on weekends. This allows us to focus on work when we are together. We don't need to be friends to work well together, but we do need to respect each other.

OG How did you come up with this organizational model? Is it based on professional experience?

PE It's a mix of different things. In retrospect, my education played an important role. I studied at La Cambre in Brussels. The architecture department was in an abandoned building without WiFi, printers, or heating. I even squatted there awhile. It was anarchy, which was great for creativity, but there was no money for anything. We had to create everything out of nothing. It was the exact opposite when I did an exchange at the Academie van Bouwkunst Amsterdam: A professionalizing education with part-time work where everybody was serious and clearly money-driven. I thought of quitting architecture and did an MBA in real estate management. I learned a lot but also realized that I didn't want to go in that direction.

I went to work with some offices: HHF in Basel and 51N4E in Brussels. At HHF the partners really understood my character and strengths. I was hungry for independence and responsibility, so they let me do the master plan for La Défense in Paris alone. This then led to my first teaching position at EPFL in Lausanne, which in turn allowed me to start my first office. It was planned as a partnership with some friends, which seemed perfect on paper, but ultimately didn't work out. That experience taught me more than anything. In theory it should have worked: One of us was intellectual, the other had great technical knowledge, and the third was a conceptual thinker. But it wasn't meant to be. Although our skills complemented each other, our ambitions and values were completely different. I was ready to take risks to move forward, while they were very cautious.

After this experience, I wanted to open a studio but was traumatized by constantly losing votes against partners and not moving at my own pace. I didn't want anything big; I was just on a quest for independence and freedom. I thought that with a few projects here and there on my own, I wouldn't owe anyone anything as long as I earned enough money. My office then grew more or less by chance. Initially, it was difficult to shoulder all of this responsibility, but at least I was making all the decisions myself. Growing the studio enabled me to outsource tasks I don't enjoy, like human resources to an office manager for HR, or structuring CAD drawings to a design aide. I can't do everything on my own. Now, with a modest turnover in the office, I don't need to micromanage everything and can share decision-making since the team works independently, yet well together.

OG How have your projects changed over time, and to what extent is this change influenced by your organizational model?

PE Without our model, we would never have won our most important project: a landscape master plan in Brussels, which we were commissioned for in 2020. Only three offices applied because the deadline was in the first week of the Covid-19 lockdown. Most offices couldn't participate as they were working with fixed computers and local infrastructures, inaccessible from home for security reasons. Also, they had no practical knowledge on how to work together remotely. For us, nothing changed during the pandemic. We had always worked remotely anyway.

With regard to our portfolio, we are aiming to achieve a mix of one-third each: investors, private commissions, and public

Fig.1 The new wooden sliding doors partition the floor plan into a succession of non-hierarchical rooms.

Fig.2 The roof is accessed via repurposed passenger boarding stairs.

Project	GRID HOUSE
Category	EXTENSION AND RENOVATION
Use	RESIDENTIAL
Size	160 M^2
Architecture	L'ATELIER, NOMADIC ARCHITECTURE STUDIO
Client	PRIVATE
Location	LAEKEN, BELGIUM
Team	PIERRE ESCOBAR, LUCIANA TEPER, JULIEN DELOFFRE
Year	2020-21

Fig.3

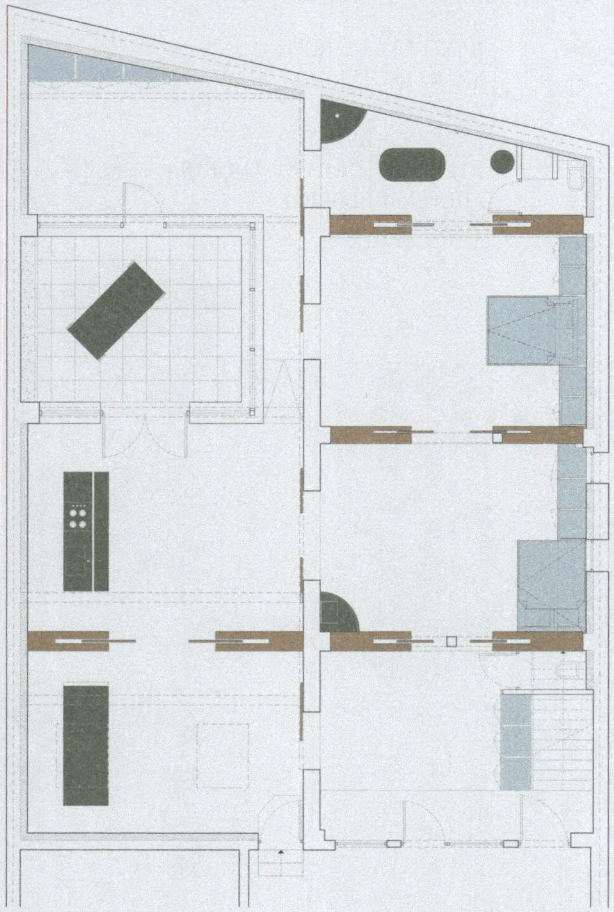

Fig. 4 Floor plan

Fig. 5 Isometric view of sliding doors, built-in furniture (incl. Murphy bed), built-in kitchen, stairs, and bathroom fittings

clients. Investors are slow because they're constantly changing their minds due to the market; private clients have the funds and will see a project through; the public sector works long-term with their financing and, in that sense, is fairly crisis-proof. We enjoy the diversity in design work that this mix gives us, and the financial stability it provides for the studio.

Our biggest source of income, also cross-subsidizing other projects, are large interior renovations that don't need building permits. They move quickly: six weeks for the design, ten weeks for technical documentation, and four months for construction. For the same budget, a roof extension for a property with multiple occupants includes applying to the city for a permit and negotiating with neighbors, which rarely works out the first time. These negotiations mean the project needs to be amended, which is frustrating when the design is already settled and the project risks becoming uneconomical. Right now, we are discussing how we can avoid these hazards by adapting our contracts and by charging for last-minute changes.

Paul Barth: Does working as a nomadic organization limit the types of projects you can take on?

PE We are honest from the very beginning about the fact that we work in a nomadic—and not in a local—way, and we usually attract people with the same mindset. Private clients either love the way we work or they hate it. Investors are interested because they often have the same lifestyle as us—traveling every week for business. Smaller rural municipalities are also interested since locals are excited to work with a young, international firm that sees the potential in their community.

Nomadism involves being interested in the world. We're the opposite of locals living in the valley they grew up in and working with construction workers from the same village. Being nomadic means that the members of my team add to the design by incorporating their own local, contemporary architectural references into their designs.

PB You benefit greatly from globalization. You pay your Argentinian team members a salary of 1,000 euros per month, which is three times the local median salary for architects there. By comparison, the median monthly salary in Germany is 4,000 euros. How do you deal with criticism that this is social dumping?

PE Our first connection to Argentina was established by an architect who had asked to do an internship at our office for 500 euros a month, a proposal I was not comfortable with. I was hoping we would find more money, but in the meantime, he had gone back to Argentina for holidays and got stuck there during the Covid-19 pandemic. We realized that 500 euros was decent money there and decided to take him on as an intern. Today, we pay our Buenos Aires–based architects 1,000 euros, a good salary for Argentina. As a young, conceptual office ready to take risks, we haven't made a profit yet. So, we have not profited off of our international team.

I started the office with 1,000 euros in my bank account, not 100,000. It was impossible to hire an architect for 250 euros a day in Paris to work with me. I don't care if people say that I am stealing jobs. This criticism is nationalist; we, however, are nomadic and not connected to any country in particular. Every human is connected and we're creating a team of interesting people. I don't see why that would be wrong.

OG In other words: The individual mindset and values must be evident not only in the projects, but also in the way we work together. How would education have to change for that to become a reality?

PE While studying, our projects were out scale or without scale at all, and often structurally impossible. Theory is important, but once you transition into practice you discover there are clients, laws, and technical obstacles. I think it is vital to stay conceptual in university because you can't think outside the box if you only have technical knowledge, but conceptual thinking must be rooted in reality. Practical classes could help with the economics of practicing architecture; we have added or changed something in every new contract we've signed, since templates by professional associations don't offer enough protection. Architecture is a labor of love, but it is also necessary to understand the value of your work.

OG What is your entrepreneurial advice?

PE Look at finances in the long run and be aware of risks. Opening a studio is a crazy game riddled with obstacles: potential bankruptcy, lawsuits, and toxic clients bleeding money and trying to blame you for it. A lawsuit might look like the end of your practice, but in truth it's an indicator of how well you are doing, since you're taking risks. With enough hindsight, I can now refuse clients because I can tell their budget doesn't make sense, or that they are emotionally unstable, or that we don't share values.

When architects I look up to reach a certain financial scale, they start taking on clients I would have a problem with, like pharmaceutical companies. These designs would also become more industrial, repeating the same details over and over and simply combining stock products. I love how the scale of our work currently allows us to be contextual and work with custom-made parts. But it remains a balancing act.

SPACE & MATTER

Cofounder Marthijn Pool in conversation with Olaf Grawert

Fig. 1

Fig. 2

Fig. 3

Fig. 4

Fig. 5

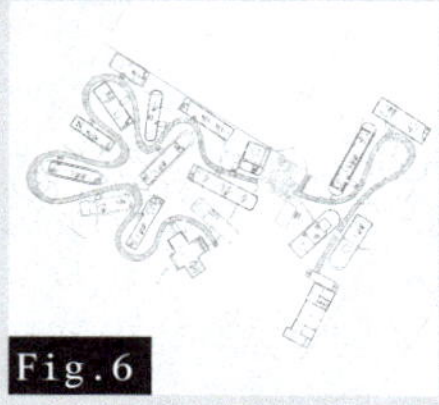
Fig. 6

ORGANIZATION

OFFICE

Name	SPACE & MATTER B.V.
Founded in	2009
Registered in	AMSTERDAM

PROJECTS

Total	<50
completed	20
public	0
private	20
Current	15

TEAM

Total	23
by gender	70% M, 30% F
average age	32.8
nationalities	NLD, POL, ITA, ESP, DEU
Partners	MARTHIJN POOL, TJEERD HACCOU, SASCHA GLASL, 33.3% EACH
Managing Directors	3
Employees	18
Freelancers	0
Working students	0
Interns	2

FINANCES

INCOME PER MONTH / YEAR IN EUROS

Total	100,000 / 1,200,000
Construction projects	90,000 / 1,080,000
Teaching	0
Other external activities including lectures	4,500 / 54,000

EXPENSES PER MONTH IN EUROS

Total	100,000
Staff costs	75,000*
Average salary (employees / freelancers)	3,333
Average salary (interns)	1,500
Rent and operating costs	15,000
Office supplies, insurance, consulting, and legal fees	5,000
Travel expenses	5,000

* GROSS

Olaf Grawert: You run quite a unique architectural practice: Space&Matter acts as a consultant to private and public clients, as a developer, and as a construction company—all at the same time. Can you explain your understanding of architectural practice and, accordingly, your goals as an office?

Marthijn Pool: We believe that architecture is not about an outcome or a building. Instead, architecture is about the systemic approach that eventually results in a building. Therefore, we do a lot of system thinking and research in our practice, which we replicate, refine, and try to scale. The outcome might be different every time. Primarily, we aim for maximum social and environmental impact. These values, or impact parameters, are based on an understanding of architecture that goes beyond the static built environment. We believe it must be dynamic—as opposed to a finished object—to offer more for the future of society. Accordingly, we take on different roles, using architecture as a vessel to reach our goals. Our responsibility is to make something abstract tangible, which builds trust. As architects, we are trained to be creative human beings with a strong capability of explaining a vision, creating an appealing future that you can believe in.

OG As architects we are constantly pitching or, as you describe it, convincing someone to believe in our vision. Ironically, whenever we finish a project and the client is satisfied, we move onto the next project and begin to imagine everything from scratch. Your office has a different approach.

MP I believe architects are taught to feel ashamed to do something twice. If the premise is, "everything has to be original," repetition and adaptation are depreciated. But I strongly believe that if you've found something that works on a systemic level, something authentic and smart, you must repeat it instead of taking risks, which are ultimately borne by the client, be they public or private. Architects should improve their product thinking and understand the potential of repetition: You gain precious time and money that you can spend toward refining your approach with each new project. In our case, that approach is to create architecture with minimum environmental and maximum social impact.

OG You just touched upon rather abstract aspects of architectural work: Intangible values which are not only hard to describe to non-architects, but also hard to put a price on. How do you measure and appraise social impact, for instance?

MP Fighting for socially equitable results is all about how you understand your role in the process. As architects, our designs have a long-lasting impact for fifty to one hundred years. If you additionally consider yourself a developer-investor, like we do, it becomes clear that we hold a lot of responsibility toward society. But responsibility alone is difficult to capitalize on. If we take, for instance, a project's social impact, you can both measure and argue for it, and both private investors and municipality developers will understand its value. Nobody is against positive social impact, but it is our job to put it on the agenda and fight for it, to make it an integral part of the architectural practice. A project with a positive social impact is associated with higher costs. Not because you bill an extra service, but because it increases the complexity of the project and, therefore, the risk profile.

OG Why?

MP Of course, a project in a segregated, quiet, and homogenous area comes with less friction and is therefore easier to market. But we really challenge this logic and try and convince investors to open up the development process and make an effort for different values to be realized. Sure, this means it will be more complicated, but the results will be more valuable in the long run, as the architecture contributes systemically to society. Which brings us to the question of how to measure social impact. Social sciences and anthropology have identified a lot of factors that help define and quantify these values. For example, social inclusivity or a high degree of diversity can be signs of higher social value reciprocity, meaning that people are part of a network in which they feel safe and trusted. This sense of community is something you have to build; it takes time and effort to turn a group of individuals into a group of strongly connected neighbors. We have developed the process of community building to be part of our project development process. The design and development follows the input we gain from the community. Vice versa, the constraints informing the development and design are fed back to the community. We believe our community building approach can tackle issues like anonymity and loneliness

OG Is this something that you were trained for in school or developed in your practice? How did you establish this methodology?

MP We started our office in 2009, in the middle of the economic crisis. Suddenly, developers were not developing, investors were not investing, but people were still in need of housing. If no new houses are built, where do you move to? I, too, had to find

Fig. 2 The 4,600 m² site is an interim lease from the city of Amsterdam for a duration of ten years. It remains to be seen what will happen to the area afterwards.

Fig. 1 Aerial view of the site. The grounds of a former shipyard in Amsterdam-Noord are now home to offices, studios, workshops and conference rooms for activist groups as well as creative and social enterprises. The soil was heavily contaminated with heavy metals and oils from the industrial activities and is gradually being cleaned using plants, a process called phytoremediation.

Project	DE CEUVEL
Category	TEMPORARY REUSE
Use	ECOHUB
Size	902 M² (GFA)
Architecture	SPACE&MATTER
Location	AMSTERDAM
Team	SASCHA GLASL, MARJOLEIN SMEELE, MARTIJN VAN WIJK
Year	2012-14

Fig.3 To avoid touching the contaminated soil, the 17 upcycled houseboats and the wooden walkway meandering through the site stand on plinths and stilts. Underneath is a self-sufficient energy and water infrastructure.

Fig.4 By using discarded houseboats, the project is both sustainable and mobile. The eco-hub can be easily dismantled and relocated.

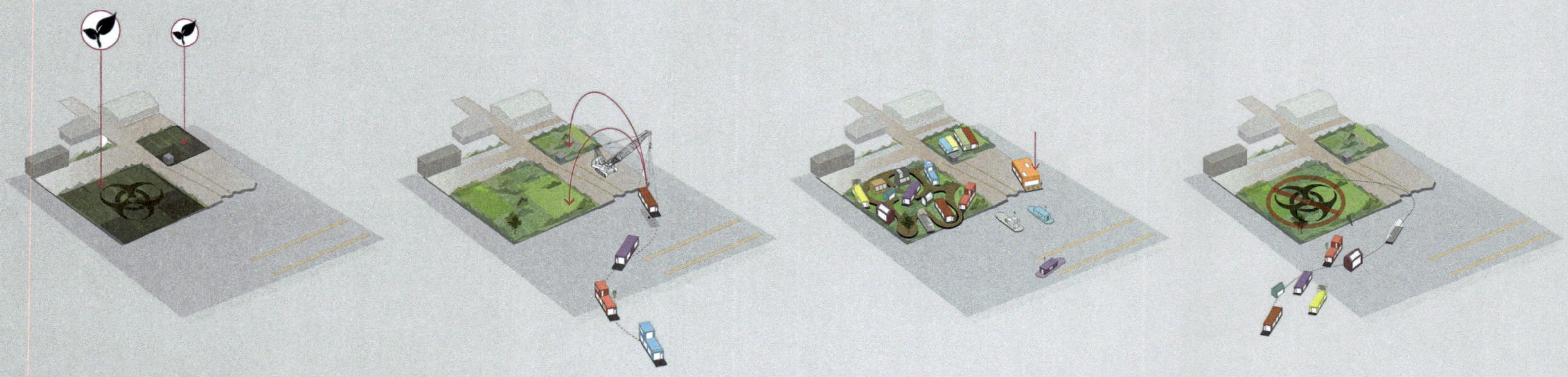

Fig. 5 During the ten-year interim use, the contaminated soil will be completely cleaned using bioremediation technology. DELVA Landscape Architecture planted lush vegetation consisting of willowherb, bulrush, foxglove, yarrow, and various grasses. These plants have the ability to extract pollutants such as heavy metals from the soil.

Fig. 6 Site plan

a home for my family of five during this time of economic uncertainty. And as professional developers were scared to invest and build, and as even municipalities eventually halted new developments, we had to take matters in our own hands. We quickly realized that we were not the only ones looking for housing. This is when we started drafting a plan: How could a group of twenty to thirty people develop their own collective apartment building? Over the years, the system we elaborated for that project has evolved into a model that works and pays off. Even though one crisis is over, the next one is coming, and we believe the only way forward is a decentralized approach to who is making the city. Eventually, it's the people that make the city come to life. The best foundation for a thriving community is to involve future users in the creation of their house, their neighborhood, and their city.

OG This level of participation sounds like a nightmare for the people in charge of coordination.

MP Not if you are very clear from the start about who gets to decide what. In such a process, you have twenty individuals but only one group. It ultimately is about navigating between these two spheres: What has to be decided collectively and what is a personal decision? By now we have become quite skilled when it comes to guiding communication between the two levels. It takes up to four months of speaking on a weekly basis to get a roomful of individuals to start arguing and thinking as a group. You need this time to align on certain premises. When people are willing to trust each other, listen to each other, and respect each other's different positions, a collective emerges from the shared values and the individual becomes ready to compromise.

OG In that regard, what is your most important project?

MP The project with the biggest impact—both on a social and environmental level, and for the most people—would be the forty-six-household floating neighborhood. It's an adaptive floating structure in a former industrial area of Amsterdam that is self-sustaining: Neither does it occupy land, nor is it connected to the city's energy grid. The aim was to minimize its environmental impact, a goal behind which all individuals could rally. This shared purpose created a high sense of belonging and maximized the social impact.

OG You cannot sit down forty-six households around a kitchen table. At which scale does your approach reach its limits and how do you deal with that?

MP Indeed, it is very laborious. You can only meet when others don't work, which means weekday nights—and I cannot do that every week. Reality forced us to look for an alternative. But instead of just focusing on the outcome, complaining about the lack of tools, and waiting for someone to come along and solve our problem, we developed the tools ourselves. This is architecture! As architects, we must be able to design the tools needed for our process. That's how we created the CrowdBuilding platform, which tries to mimic the kitchen-table process online. There, you take on different roles: initiator, activator, ambassador. You can join forces for a cause and search for supporters online. On that platform, people with a very specific lifestyle ambition can start a concept that will attract people if it is appealing. These are the initiators. As soon as the group grows, we detect who is outspoken and actively contributing to the conversation. These people are called the activators and accelerate the community-building process. The people who join and communicate about the project initiative are so-called ambassadors. We often describe it as meeting your neighbors before the neighborhood is built. Social media has helped facilitate the notion that if you put an idea out there, it might resonate with others. Once a critical mass has been found, we join in. Only then do we start translating these ideas of living together into an architectural prototype.

OG You talked a lot about developing design processes and entire systems, and how this approach changes your understanding of architecture. How did you acquire this knowledge and how can it get passed on? Which subjects and skills are missing in architecture studies today?

MP I think it's a combination of personal character and professional interest. When we started working in our twenties, we first had to critically assess the meaning of the economic crisis: What is going on and what is our position as architects in this new reality? Does this intermediate period allow us to regroup and create another system? With that activist attitude, we started our practice, pushing through until it worked. It took us four attempts until it began to look like what we had aimed for in the beginning. It takes a lot of work and keeping the faith—and a willingness to make a lot of mistakes along the way. I would try to teach students an experimental mindset. Don't teach them one method as the gospel truth. Teach them how to build their own tools. They'll figure out the rest themselves.

IFUB*

Founders Bernhard Kurz and Johannes Krohne, and studio manager Verena Limmer-Mahrous, in conversation with Paul Barth and Olaf Grawert

Fig. 1

Fig. 2

Fig. 3

Fig. 4

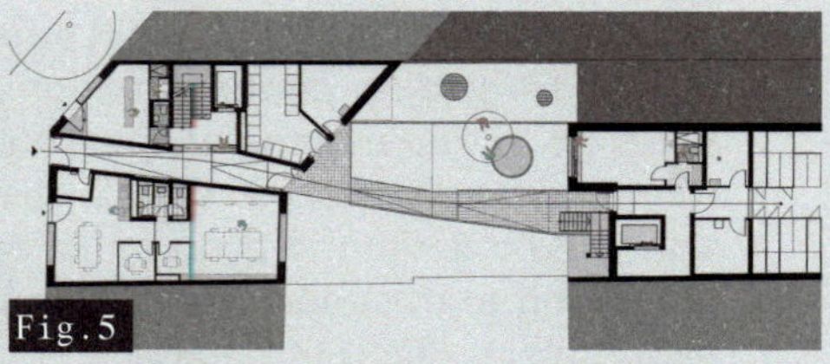
Fig. 5

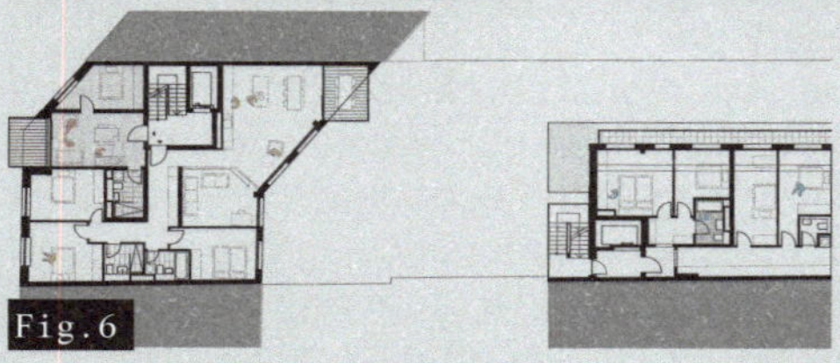
Fig. 6

Fig. 7

ORGANIZATION

OFFICE

Name	IFUB GMBH
Founded in	2012
Registered in	MUNICH, BERLIN

PROJECTS

Total	119
completed	58%
public	4%
private	96% (77% INDIVIDUALS, 33% CORPORATE)
Current	25

TEAM

Total	9
by gender	12% X, 55% M, 33% F
average age	35.4
nationalities	DEU, LVA
Partners	50% JOHANNES KROHNE
	50% BERNHARD KURZ
Managing Directors	2
Employees	4
Freelancers	1
Working students	2
Interns	0

FINANCES

INCOME PER MONTH / YEAR IN EUROS

Total	28,750 / 345,000
Construction projects	28,333 / 340,000
Teaching	0
Other external activities	
including lectures	0

EXPENSES PER MONTH IN EUROS

Total	32,500
Staff costs	28,275*
Average salary (employees / freelancers)	3,500
Average salary (interns)	
Rent and operating costs	975
Office supplies	975
Insurance, consulting, and legal fees	1,625
Travel expenses	325

* GROSS (32H PER WEEK = FULL TIME)

Paul Barth: You're the Institut für u. Baukunst (*Institute for U. Architecture*), or IFUB* for short. What does the "U." stand for?

Bernhard Kurz: Before Johannes and I founded the practice back in 2012, just for fun, we called ourselves the Institute for Unprofitable Architecture. We didn't like the fact that in all the practices where we had worked until then, all the talk was about money and not about people or quality. When we set up our own company, we toned the wording down and abbreviated it to a "U," as we were worried people would think we didn't know how to handle money. Today it stands, among other things, for German words that mean comprehensive (*umfassend*), unburdened (*unbeschwert*), environmentally conscious (*umweltbewusst*), and, for the last couple of years once again, for unprofitable (*unwirtschaftlich*).

Johannes Krohne: Another reason was that we didn't want to be "Bernhard and Johannes Architects," but wanted to keep our options open, including hiring not just architects and doing more than just architecture.

BK Johannes and I are the founders and continue to be the partners, but IFUB* belongs to all the staff. I somewhat regret that when we re-founded the company two years ago, we were not yet aware of the steward-ownership model, in which partners have voting rights but do not participate in the profits; had we known about that form of limited liability company, then I am pretty sure that is the direction we would have gone in. But we are trying to put the idea into practice in our work. We have complete transparency as regards salaries, documents relating to contracts and commissions, and the fees we negotiate with clients; moreover, we lay out the finances every quarter. We don't distribute profits among the partners but decide as a team what the profits should be used for. There are now nine of us: seven architects, two of whom are still in university, a structural engineer, and Verena.

Verena Limmer-Mahrous: I graduated in cultural studies and aesthetic communication from the University of Hildesheim, and at IFUB* I am officially in charge of office management.

Olaf Grawert: In seminars, you tend to get taught that an architectural practice doesn't need office management until it has about fifteen to twenty staff members. If you have fewer people on your payroll, then a partner or managing director should handle the duties in question.

JK A lot of our work does not have much to do with architecture. They're things someone with a different background can possibly even do better.

BK From what I have experienced, architectural practices tend to be incredibly chaotic and waste a lot of time with meaningless activities. A good organizational structure can prevent a lot of frustration and also enable everyone to work fewer hours—for us, full-time means a 32-hour workweek. Engineering offices, even the small ones, always have someone to help with office management. For some reason, architects are the only ones to believe they don't need that. Good office management pays off, even in a small office.

OG Your value added is twenty percent higher per person per year than other practices of a comparable size in Germany. You're actually on a par in this regard with companies with a staff of one hundred people working forty hours a week. How do you go about your work, and how do you structure it?

BK We don't take part in public competitions, only ones we get invited to. Open competitions cause financial imbalances in our profession and are leaving it at risk of collapse. Our business is running so well because our team has been with us for a long time and we share a set of values. You need an awful lot of time and there are a lot of costs involved in onboarding someone new to the office, which is why we prefer to offer permanent employment contracts.

VLM Permanent contracts give a sense of security and stability: Someone trusts me, and I am therefore more willing to dedicate myself all the more.

PB How is it that all your full-time employees only work a 32-hour week?

BK The interesting thing is that all of us could work far less and still cover our basic needs. Virtually everything you need for a good life is at hand. What we all lack today is time—pretty absurd. So, we ask ourselves about the significance of work and the true meaning of prosperity. Imagine a graph representing both GDP and the happiness index: The two variables correlate up to a certain GDP size, and then start to diverge. As soon as the basic needs are covered, other factors are responsible for driving happiness. Unfortunately, we don't focus on those but rather on what is virtually meaningless for us as humans, namely GDP growth. Yet our growth-oriented and growth-dependent economic system is destructive—that much we all know. We need systemic change, and I feel certain that without it there is not going to be a revolution in how we build, either. And to dedicate ourselves to bringing about that change, what we need, once again, is time.

Fig. 1 The condominium project co-developed independently by its future residents without a real-estate investor—a process called *Baugruppe* (building group) in German—was carried out on one of the few remaining empty lots in Berlin's Neukölln district and features a building sitting on a street corner and a second building in the courtyard.

Fig. 2 Open-air emergency staircase on the courtyard building's firewall

Project	BAUGRUPPE D2
Category	NEW CONSTRUCTION
Use	RESIDENTIAL AND OFFICE BUILDING
Size	3,107 M²
Architecture	IFUB*
Project development	WINFRIED HÄRTEL
Client	BAUGRUPPE D2
Location	DONAUSTRASSE 2 12043 BERLIN-NEUKÖLLN
Team	JOHANNES KROHNE, BERNHARD KURZ, MIGUEL LOPEZ, MIKUS DRUVIŅŠ
Year	2018-22

Fig.3 View of the front building from the street

Fig.4 View of a duplex apartment in the courtyard building

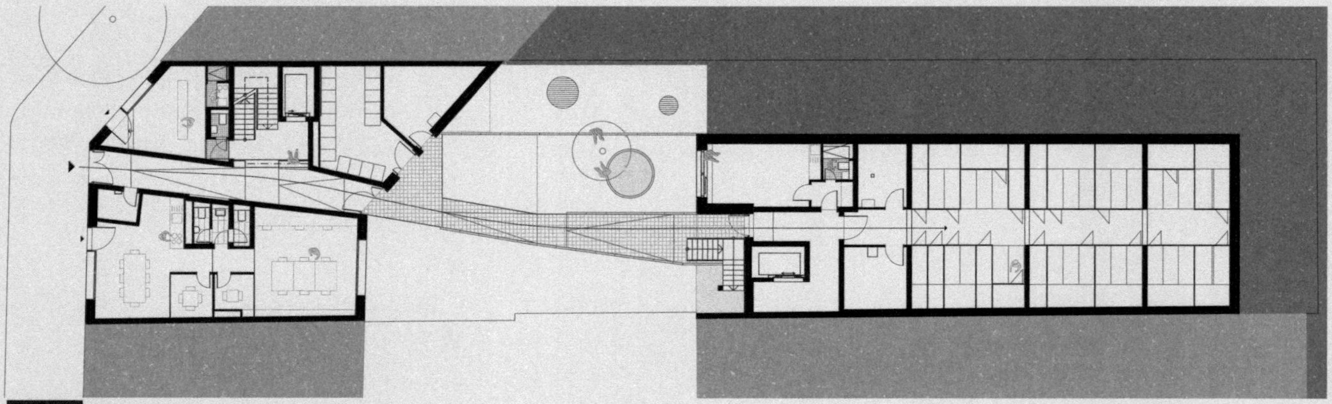

Fig. 5 Ground floor / basement

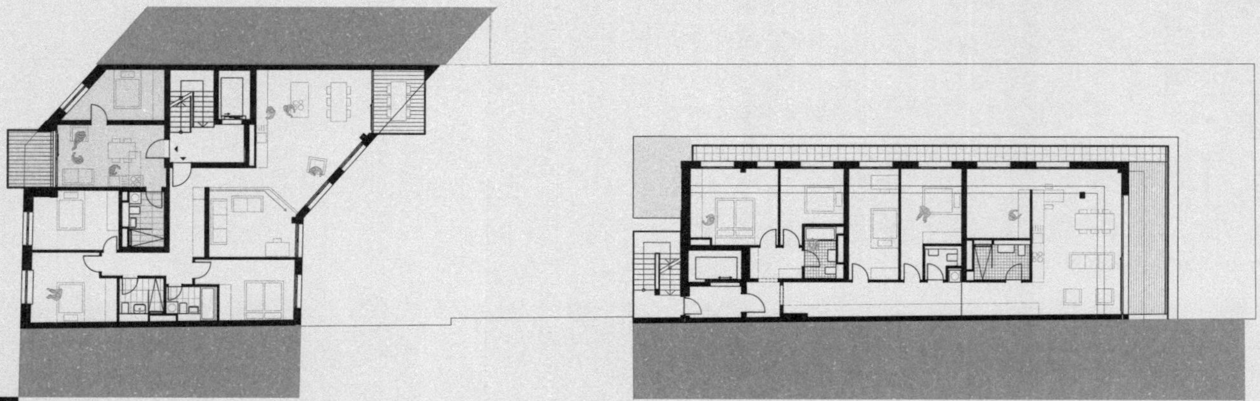

Fig. 6 Second floor

Fig. 7 Longitudinal section

PB You allude to the theory of an Economy for the Common Good, and in your practice, you have compiled a so-called common-good balance sheet. What is that exactly, and what is the purpose behind it?

BK The Economy for the Common Good tries to shift the economic focus away from profit and to adopt a position between capitalism and communism. Humans like their independence and, if only for that reason, it makes little sense to control everything centrally. But we need to shift the emphasis toward the common good. These days, companies are rated in terms of how much money they generate, and every company has to compile a financial balance sheet by law. But why only a financial balance sheet? In the Economy for the Common Good, every company, every local authority, or every community in general prepares a Common Good balance sheet assessing how it interacts with suppliers, owners, and financial partners, staff members, customers, and fellow entrepreneurs. The sheet also covers social aspects to see whether the organization's actions align with the values of human dignity, solidarity and justice, ecological sustainability, transparency, and co-decision-making. The balance sheet can then be used as a simple management tool. Companies that post good figures, in the sense that they work for the common good, could be granted tax breaks, or lower barriers to public contracts, or favorable loan terms. It is a system that is very simple to put into practice.

PB What consequences did the common-good balance sheet have for your practice?

BK The simple act of compiling the balance sheet, even without having a direct incentive to do so, changed our focus on doing business. Preparing it strengthened an awareness of our own influence on the world around us through both our work as architects and our office structure and organization, starting with our choice of bank or insurance company. That led, among other things, to a realignment of future projects. The balance sheet helps trigger internal changes and thus facilitates the transformation process.

OG How is this consciousness reflected in your projects?

BK It was in the context of the common-good balance sheet that we produced our *Handbuch des gemeinwohlorientierten Bauens*, or Manual for Architecture Aligned with the Common Good. In it, our team developed shared guidelines which we take as a reference and can also communicate to clients. This is not a built project of course, but perhaps has more of an impact than any single building could develop on its own.

JK I believe that our "Park Your Park" project—a garden planted at our own initiative on a three-wheeled Piaggio Ape pickup—is a good description of our work. It shows that you don't always have to wait for a contract but can start doing something yourself. And the recently completed D2 condominium project in Berlin is crucial for us, as the project meant renegotiating the architect–client relationship. The clients were not profit-oriented investors, but rather a group who share interests and finances and who participated in discussions about the project's embodied values. This is where the principles of our manual get applied. The Economy for the Common Good and our manual also come up in inquiries we receive from prospective clients, so they are not financial nonsense. We have in fact received commissions where we know that we were not the cheapest option, but the clients shared our values and were, and continue to be, willing to invest accordingly.

OG None of these considerations and strategies really play a role in the architectural curricula in universities. In your opinions, what needs to be changed in the world of teaching to convey these principles and the necessary tools to act on them?

BK Architecture should not primarily be based on a design concept, but on values. It is still difficult to remind ourselves of this in everyday office work. We must also try and get away from the lone-wolf mentality, which universities strongly promote. During your studies, you design your projects mostly on your own. And if you do work in a group, you are not given the tools for managing the process, let alone understanding it. You learn nothing about team structures, nothing about communication, nothing about reflecting on your own actions and thoughts. What are you good at? What brings you joy? Not everyone is the right person for everything, but if you deploy people in line with their abilities, you find the office works better and the staff is more motivated. Lecturers should talk about work process, convey concepts like agile work, or organize communication workshops.

VLM People need to be made aware of these topics and values, and this is a demanding and time-consuming process of self-reflection.

JK Sadly, at university there is no time for reflection.

OG What entrepreneurial advice would you give young architects?

VLM Alongside the substantive values mentioned above, I think it is important to know your own worth. Young graduates should make sure they are offered fair working conditions, in particular regarding pay and working hours. And in my opinion, it is important to cooperate with other people more. The greatest challenge, however, is to take your time. As a graduate, you're thinking of your career, your salary, because that's what you've learned from your parents, or your immediate circle, or the media. But it's advisable to look around a bit and ask yourself what you really want. Only that way can the system itself can be changed. As long as everything keeps on going the way it does because no one dares to speak up, we can't expect anything to change.

CONFLAGRATION
THE (SELF-) IMAGE OF THE ARCHITECT

Text: Nick Beech

Fig. 1

Fig. 2

Fig. 3

Fig. 4

Fig. 5

Fig. 6

Fig. 7

Fig. 8

€21 billion is the estimated total value of Europe's architectural market; it has grown by nearly 50% in the last 10 years. Architecture services account for less than 1% of the European construction market's total revenue. Retail and shop fitting generate 9% of market revenue. By contrast, the public housing sector contributes 7%.

Fig.1 Christopher Wren and Robert Hooke, *Monument to the Great Fire of London*, 1671–79
The relief on the western side of the base was created by Caius Gabriel Cibber.

Just before 1 a.m. on June 14, 2017, a fire broke out in Grenfell Tower, a twenty-four-story residential high-rise in North Kensington, London. Seventy-two people died and scores were injured in the resulting inferno.[1] As the immediate palpable trauma and distress of the residents who survived settled into public consciousness, it soon became clear that large swaths of the UK's building stock—including schools and other public buildings—were at risk of precisely the same event.[2] People continue to live in buildings that may kill them unless substantial—and expensive—measures are taken to reverse developments that have been taking place since the turn of the millennium.

Design for the Grenfell Tower began in 1967; construction was completed in 1974. A simple design approach was taken: a central service core, surrounded by four *in-situ* concrete columns, tied together by precast concrete beams. In 2016 the lead architect for the building, Nigel Whitbread, recalled that the design was a response to the failures of system-built, modular point-blocks—failures dramatically exposed in 1968 when Ronan Point, a twenty-two-story tower in Newham, London, collapsed soon after completion.[3] In addition to the elegant structural solution, Whitbread designed the exterior of Grenfell Tower, placing particular attention on the fenestration to emphasize the building's verticality and height, and to avoid a squat appearance.

This original design assumed an absolute separation between the units, and residents were instructed to shelter in place if a fire were to break out. During renovations carried out in 2012–16, overcladding was applied to the building's facade to improve energy efficiency and the tower's "appearance."[4] It was due to this overcladding system, made of highly flammable materials, that the fire could spread so quickly from one of the apartments to the rest of the tower. Following a disastrous, panicked response from both local and central government—demonstrating neither compassion for the victims nor understanding of the events—a public inquiry into the conflagration was launched.

The client for the refurbishment, Kensington and Chelsea Tenant Management Organisation (KCTMO), was a management committee established by the local council who owned the majority of the flats in the building.[5] Studio E had been tasked with the design for the renovation, which had been contentious with many residents, who initiated the Grenfell Action Group (GAG) in response.[6] Throughout the renovation, the group, alongside other residents, raised concerns about the lack of consultation and information given to the residents as well as Studio E's lack of understanding of the building and the lives led within it. This lack of engagement, their vociferous argument went on, had resulted in a renovation scheme that disregarded the health, well-being, and desires of those who actually used it.

In evidence submitted to the subsequent public inquiry, KCTMO confirmed that the procurement negotiations with the architects had not raised any doubts and that it had further not felt obligated to have the proposed design approved by independent experts.[7] Indeed, it became clear that the actual discussions between Studio E and the clients had exclusively concerned the overcladding's appearance. Its other features—its performance as a thermal insulation, its potential interactions with the facade's existing structural elements, and its flammability—were left aside.

The Grenfell Tower Inquiry is still open: Phase 1, which focused on "the factual narrative of the events," concluded in December 2018 and resulted in a report published a year later. Evidential hearings for Phase 2, examining "the cause of those events," concluded in July

Fig. 2 This detail of the relief by Caius Gabriel Cibber shows Charles II as sovereign, baton in hand.

2022, and closing statements were made in November; the inquiry's final report has not been published at the time of writing, but is due in September 2024.[8] No commentator has seriously suggested that culpability will lie with any one individual, service provider, or product manufacturer. It is widely accepted that the fire was a consequence of systemic flaws in the construction industry that can be traced back to political, economic, regulative, ethical, technical, and epistemological failures.

Petrified Stares

Nearly three-and-a-half centuries ago, architecture did not have to sit in evidentiary hearings, accounting for its role in a deadly conflagration. Quite the opposite. As the relief on the base of the *Monument to the Great Fire of London*, completed in 1677, shows in all the potency and alarming candidness characteristic of early-modern allegorical images, architecture was a knowledge-power exercised by the imperial sovereign over the rebuilding of London: In the image's background, we see buildings engulfed in flames on the left-hand side, another structure in the process of being rebuilt after the fire on the right-hand side. In front of this split image, the sovereign—Charles II—is depicted in Roman imperial garb, wielding his authority—in the shape of a baton of authority—over three allegorical figures.

The three figures are Liberty, waving her hat with the inscription *Libertas*; (artistic or scientific) Imagination, leaning forward, crowned by dancing children, clutching the fecund staff of nature; and, finally, Architecture, the trio's central figure, square and compasses in one hand, a roll of parchment in the other. Liberty looks outward, toward the viewer, a gift of free expression from the sovereign to his citizens. Imagination stares forward at the ruins to be restored, a gift of ingenuity to the industrious city. Architecture, meanwhile, turns her head backward, facing the sovereign. Measure, rule, proportion: These are techniques used by the sovereign to transfer his will onto paper—and in which, in turn, he recognizes himself.

Perhaps the monument's architects, Robert Hooke and Christopher Wren, when they instructed artist Caius Gabriel Cibber for the relief, still had memories of their great plans for London—the grand radial axes and *rond-points*, monuments, churches and cathedrals, parks and squares, at once framing and framed by the spectacle of Wren's vision of the resuscitated baroque city.[9] But by 1677, both Hooke and Wren had been advising the King as part of the Rebuilding Committee for eleven years. Hooke, for his part, was in charge of surveying the City, drawing up a cadaster for London, crafting legislation on building regulations for Parliament, and, as an expert, providing evidence to courts in private disputes following the Great Fire.

While it may seem like individual architects of the early modern period embodied a fusion of many roles, a certain fracturing was simultaneously occurring in the meaning and value of architecture. Imagination, as depicted in the relief, is explicitly free: Anyone might use their inventiveness in the course of industry and communications; the latter are allegorically represented as attributes of the city itself in the shapes of a beehive and a caduceus. While this freedom seems limitless, the imagination as it concerns architecture has become much more specific. It is a reflection of the sovereign and is, therefore, regulative of the commonwealth and of social reproduction.

This reality is highlighted by the text on the monument, which, whilst praising the reconstruction of London in stone as an embellishment made possible by the sovereign through the imposition of a coal tax, emphasizes building regulations as his chief contribution. Architects can no longer rely on their artistry, but must engage with the humdrum tasks of road widening, boundary surveying, fire regulation, and contract supervision; additionally, they have to arbitrate in property disputes and report to Parliament and the city. It is through these tasks that architecture brings peace and prosperity, as alluded to by the olive branch and cornucopia wafting about in a cloud above the scene. It is precisely this mandate which is expressed in the look exchanged between the allegorical figure of Architecture and the sovereign.

At surface level, this initiates a process of embourgeoisement through expansion. On the one hand, urban improvements—bridges, paved streets, urban squares, crescents, parks, and large-scale ensembles sponsored by fractions of propertied interest—required approval by Acts of Parliament. Architects were tasked with ensuring public assent for these decisions. As architect and civil engineer John Gwynn expressed it in 1766:

"In settling a plan of large streets for the dwellings of the rich, it will be found necessary to allot smaller spaces contiguous, for the habitations of useful and laborious people, whose dependence on their superiors requires such a distribution; and by adhering to this principal a political advantage will result to the nation; as this intercourse stimulates their industry, improves their morals by example, and prevents any particular part from being the habitation of the indigent alone, to the great detriment of private property."[10]

Architects served individual patrons—to secure the latter's commercial interests and to discipline the working class—by investing aesthetic principles with moral virtue. This can be read as an extension of the process of accumulation through rural enclosure—as described by Karl Marx in chapter 24 of *Capital*—to the urban center. The sovereign recedes in favor of private interest, from now on tasked with securing the "public good." Architecture's face begins to turn away from the sovereign.

A Battle of Visions

As a consequence, new building typologies and infrastructures proliferated: banks, prisons, galleries, hospitals, ministries, law courts, warehouses, libraries, public theaters, shops, and pleasure gardens; toll roads, canals, embankments, and docks. If some of these can be considered "improvements"—i.e., embellishments—to the city, others—particularly those at the service of material extraction as well as of exploitation and subordination of labor—were more austere and required little additional flourish according to the predominant decorum or taste of the day. And finally, one cannot forgo the private villa. Neither manor house nor palace—which were simultaneously experiencing their own transformations under the influence of Palladianism and picturesque landscaping in the shape of the English Garden—this new typology proliferating along the Thames valley provided the bourgeoisie with a little countryside space of their own for the weekend and off-season, expertly guided (for a fee) by the purveyors of taste: their architects.

Whether their designs were grandiose (William Chambers, John Nash, John Soane) or utilitarian (John Rennie, Thomas Telford), by the 1830s architects were captives of a new structure of relations. However resistant to change they might have been, architects of the early nineteenth century could not stem the rise in general contracting and the competitive tendering that accompanied it. This forced a radical shift in the role of the architect and their deliverables: from establishing the cost of a building after the construction process to determining that process's cost *ex ante*.[11] The rise of the general contractor and competitive tendering placed pressure on the architect to produce specifications that not only included the quantity and quality of material to be employed, but of labor time, too. Katie Lloyd Thomas has defined this development toward a new form of tender as the "process clause."[12] Unlike bookkeeping, the architect was required to symbolically represent for the imagination not what had happened in the production process, but instead that which was yet to come. As a result, the general contractor was provided with a complex and effective instrument for the realization of surplus value. Architecture had now firmly turned its face toward the city. The brickyards flourished.

In navigating the rapidly evolving building industry, as it lurched from speculative boom to bust, architects faced a twin ideological pressure. On the one hand—cognizant of the aesthetic and social costs of industrialized commercial society—a succession of architects and critics suddenly injected stylistic decisions, which had been matters of taste in the eighteenth century, with moral weight: Classicism was associated with post-Reformation commercialism and standardization, indicative of the mechanization of society and decline of the "organic" community; the "Gothic," conversely, was associated with pre-Reformation guild autonomy, the result of an "organic" community forged through stable institutions such as church, guild, and sovereign. The main features of this program of aesthetic discipline mirrored a wider European project to historicize knowledge.[13] On the other hand (though intimately related), individual architects found themselves in conflict with their clients. Architects persisted in treating them as patrons, but the charging of form and appearance ("style") with moral and even political-economic implications resulted in private and just as often public disputes regarding the overall form and sometimes even the finest detail of any design proposal.

Questions of style veiled debates over the relations of production as well as over the relationship between architecture and other institutions of knowledge-power: church, law, politics, civil service, and other emergent professions from civil engineering to medicine. These debates occurred not only in architects' individual practice but within the emergent professional body itself: The Royal Institute of British Architects, or RIBA, gained its Royal charter in 1837.[14] Campaigns for the President's Chair were organized in camps of "Classicists" and "Gothicists," disregarding the pressing questions resulting from a revolution in productive forces, the extension and deepening of the world market, and the architectural interactions between European metropoles and their colonies.[15]

Only the Arts and Crafts movement managed to cut through the babble regarding style to confront the question of architecture's relationship with its underlying labor processes and relations of production. William Morris was able to identify in the organized working class the only wellspring for full autonomy within socialized production. He effectively smashed the architect's self-image as servant and all the trappings presupposed in such a bourgeois imaginary. In its place he proposed a form of solidarity with, not service to, the political working class. As long as class struggle was ongoing, went Morris's argument, architecture as such could not exist, and art would be subordinated to propaganda. Architecture could only exist in any real sense once the destruction of capital and the end to exploitation and violence by one class over another had been achieved.[16]

The ideas of the Arts and Crafts movement, as practiced by Morris's followers—whether for philanthropic patrons, such as the Hampstead Garden Suburb in London commissioned by Henrietta Barnett, or for municipal governments, such as Arnold Circus commissioned by the London County Council—had the distinct advantage of turning Architecture's face back to the sovereign, thereby identifying the regulation and control of building in the interest of the public good as being of utmost importance. But their refusal to confront the more radical elements of Morris's formulation of architecture on the one hand, and their protective attitude toward architecture's monopoly as a quasi-state knowledge-power coupled with an acceptance of the extractive and exploitative logics of power on the other, led to Morris's legacy being appropriated and banalized in the form of controlled vistas and rational treatment of materials indicative of an anti-classicist, so-called "free style."

Modernist (Self-)Images

When the RIBA built its new headquarters, designed by George Grey Wornum, on Portland Place in 1934, it was once again a relief's task to unequivocally portray the practice's change in self-perception. On the Weymouth Street facade, the artist, Bainbridge Copnall, chose to represent five male figures: At the center, we see Christopher Wren, as the representative figure of the architect, staring out toward us, flanked by a painter, a sculptor, an artisan, and a mechanic. The latter are turned towards—i.e., in service to—the architect. Human figures, created by the artist James Woodford, stand atop two pillars framing the main entrance to the building. Typically discussed as the "spirit" of creative "man and woman," each has technical instruments of geometry to hand. They appear to us naked, pulling aside veils as they turn their heads to gaze upward toward a relief depicting Architectural Aspiration. This giant male figure—another of Copnall's—raises its head and its hands toward heaven while striding through a classical city. What is this but Narcissus and Echo? Architecture spellbound by an image that it cannot recognize as of its own making, dependent on the adoration of others, whom it conceives merely as outside, subordinate, and marginal. The interior of these headquarters, as much as the fabric of the building, is further saturated with the iconography and didactic imagery of late-imperial delusional immanence, painful to even the most casual visitor.

It is an irony of history that at the moment of the RIBA's culmination as an imperial institute, a growing minority of its members found themselves in structural conditions completely at odds with the professional conditions for which the RIBA had originally been established. In place of the disinterested middle-class professional materializing the imaginary of a private client, very large numbers of architects found themselves to be, effectively, salaried public servants. The largest architectural practice of the mid-twentieth century in Europe, if not in the world, was the London County Council Architects' Department. Even those architects working not for public offices but for private corporate practices found the figure of the architect presented by the RIBA as wholly unrepresentative of their interests. Not only were questions such as salaries, working conditions, and technical educational requirements left unaddressed by a professional body interested in monopolizing knowledge-power and cultural status, they were actively suppressed. The founding of the Association of Building Technicians (ABT) in 1942 and its merger with other labor unions to eventually become the Union of Construction, Allied Trades and Technicians (UCATT) in 1971 were part of an attempt to redress the conditions of the salaried architect, which also included demands for research funding, qualification and education measures, and alternative ways to control the building process.[17] These demands were consistently rebuffed, however, and the ABT's effectiveness in achieving change is registered in the histories of architecture in Britain: It is barely mentioned at all.

The mid-twentieth century appeared to provide the architect with a moment of perfect fusion for their professional, technical, aesthetic, and ethical roles. The welfare state's expansive duties in

Fig. 3 Gottfried Kneller, *Sir Christopher Wren*, 1711, oil on canvas, 125 × 100 cm

Fig. 4 Mary Beale, *Portrait of a Mathematician*, 1680, oil on canvas, 127 × 101 cm Researchers widely agree that this portrait depicts Robert Hooke.

Fig. 5 Portraits often show architects with attributes such as compasses and plans at hand.

provisioning housing, hospitals, school buildings, cultural centers, and infrastructural projects appeared to resolve the contradictory elements of architecture. Gone was the twisting and turning between private interests and public good: The state was the public, and private interests were realizable only in partnership with the state. This moment of triumph was both short-lived and, in parallel, disguised opposite developments occurring in the building industry.[18] As architects tightened their grip on the profession, they ceded actual knowledge about the building process to contractors, simultaneously generating a wholly artificial hierarchy which reproduced the division of labor within society through the division of labor in the production of buildings.[19] Architectural education was progressively absorbed into the steadily increasing number of universities, where students were presented with a concept of the profession steeped in a particular vision of creative art practice: tacit, speculative, formal, and projective. Students were only occasionally confronted by demands for acknowledgment of technical and social conditions—demands normatively managed as constraints, but explicitly framed as opportunities for further creativity.[20]

By the mid-1970s architecture—among many other things in postwar Britain—was "in crisis," as Malcolm MacEwen starkly put it in the title of his 1974 report to the RIBA.[21] In it, MacEwen identified the institutional, economic, and political structural conditions that had supported the development of modern architecture in Britain before demonstrating both the contradictory effects this produced for the ethical and aesthetic ambitions of architectural practitioners and for the surfeit of democratic control. Modern architecture relied on state power and control to impose large-scale infrastructures and built environments that degraded nature as much as the people living within them, and also depended on massive resource extraction while simultaneously discarding construction workers' contributions to architectural knowledge and practice.

MacEwen further argued that modern architecture was blind to the demands of social groups systematically excluded by the profession. While these groups are not explicitly named in MacEwen's report, it is clear that he was referring to the working-class, feminist, Black political, and gay and lesbian political movements that demanded that the built environment must respond to the needs of the communities that reproduce it. Their contributions to architecture and planning, articulated in various conservation and resistance campaigns, proposals for urban and community infrastructure projects, demands for participatory processes in design, struggles for squatters' rights, and self- and community-build programs throughout the 1970s, were barely registered by the profession's entrenched representatives.

The downfall of the architectural profession in the 1970s and 1980s, as neoliberalism's hegemony took hold, was arguably more profound than that of any other professional group. Gone were the state building programs; gone were the social housing schemes; gone were the municipal architectural offices; the planning offices were decimated, and the architectural profession was stripped of its monopolies: no more national fee setting, no more disinterest—architects could now work directly for a contractor, or act as a developer.[22] The architect was transformed from a private public servant into a public private entrepreneur.

At the same time, building control, which had developed since the nineteenth century into a distinct sub-profession, was itself undergoing radical transformations.[23] In 1965 a set of national building standards, at once detailed and prescriptive, was introduced for England

Fig. 6 The Royal Institute of British Architects (RIBA) headquarters in London by George Grey Wornum, completed in 1934, with a facade relief by Edward Bainbridge Copnall The two columns in front of the main entrance are topped with sculptures of a man and a woman by the artist James Woodford.

Fig. 7 View of the Weymouth Street facade with further relief figures by Edward Bainbridge Copnall

and Wales. This inaugurated a twenty-year period of contestation, as building control officers wrestled with the application of standards for new products, practices, and production processes. The year 1984 saw the abandonment of any attempt to specify exact properties of building design in favor of functional performance standards that are neither prescriptive nor proscriptive. Contrary to technical standards, functional performance standards require demonstration that any aspect of a building—from individual elements, to structures, to services, to environmental impact, to infrastructural operation—perform in compliance with requirements specified in a so-called Approved Document. Although these provide "guidance" on any possible approach to meeting the requirements, it is left to those responsible for the building work to decide on how best to do so. And who is included in "those responsible" is wide indeed: "e.g., agent, designer, builder or installer."[24]

In a parallel process, surveying in building control has been effectively privatized in the UK, so that while it remains the duty of a local authority to ensure compliance with building regulations, they now compete in a marketplace with private "approved inspectors." Further, all actors—including regulators—are tasked with identifying opportunities for value creation: Reducing non-value producing activities (such as time spent on oversight, travel, and interpersonal exchange), but also identifying potentials for financialization (of tangible assets and risks) and value production (through innovation and automation in the procurement process as much as in the production process).[25] Marian Hawkesworth and Rob Imrie, as well as Liam Ross, have argued that these fundamental changes to building control cannot be looked at through the prism of privatization or deregulation alone. Deploying spatial and discursive critiques, they suggest that regulations are better understood as zones, areas, or sites in which competing actors generate risks, rewards, responsibilities, and, ultimately, physical outcomes and knowledge.

Overcoming the Urge to Design?

As a result, architectural practices face increasing pressure to both navigate regimes of regulation and simultaneously generate innovative solutions for precisely the same regimes. This leads to excruciating experiences for individual architects who have to contend with financiers, developers, contractors and sub-contractors, product manufacturers, lawyers, approved inspectors and local authorities, in addition to special interest groups. When the architectural practice itself becomes either an entrepreneurial or corporate entity and therefore behaves competitively in this marketplace for its own interests, then Architecture, as an allegorical figure, is no longer turned toward the sovereign; instead, it looks at the market as if the latter were its own image. Were we to build a monument today—not to the Great Fire of 1666, but to the many fires of which Grenfell was only the worst—the sovereign would be erased from that monument entirely. All other actors—the city, the market, the clients, the citizens—would carry batons of varying strength. And Architecture would look on this crowd and see herself reflected in each and every one of them, her role now to dissimulate her own loss of control.

The pressures of everyday practice, felt particularly by younger members of the profession who face an extraordinary collapse in real income, worsening working conditions, increasing precarization, and entrenched gendered, sexed, ableist, and racialized inequalities, is matched only by the pressure of the climate crisis induced by the very forms of racial capital to which the architectural profession has contributed. Overcoming the present crisis would require a new radicalism of which the profession, with the ideological weight it still places on "design"—is incapable. Design, as the self-definitional purpose of architecture, has been protected by the profession in education and registration as long as possible, even as the value of design itself has shifted within the complex amalgamation of professional, technical, aesthetic, ethical, and political-economic elements which constitute architectural praxis as a whole. All too often, representatives of the profession retreat to the defense of Imagination through design. The result is that it becomes not "easier to imagine the end of the world than the end of capitalism," but easier to imagine the end of capitalism than the end of architecture.[26]

Many practitioners demand that a different set of questions are posed. What social formations and, by extension, what knowledges of the building process and built environment are excluded in the current constitution of architectural practice? Can architects, and their praxis, be represented collectively, not as a profession that serves, but as a union in solidarity with other workers that produce and reproduce the built environment? Can architects shrug off their role as projective bookkeepers? And if not, can architecture overcome the urge to design?

1 Grenfell Tower Inquiry, *Grenfell Tower Inquiry: Phase 1 Report*, October 2019, accessed June 3, 2024, 3, assets.grenfelltowerinquiry.org.uk/GTI%20-%20Phase%201%20full%20report%20-%20volume%201.pdf.
2 Architects for Social Housing, eds., *The Truth About Grenfell Tower*, July 2017, accessed June 3, 2024, 37–54, architectsforsocialhousing.files.wordpress.com/2022/02/19083-the-truth-about-grenfell-tower.pdf.
3 Cf. Constantine Gras, “Lancaster West Estate: An Ideal for Living?,” *grasart.com*, June 3, 2016, accessed June 3, 2024, www.grasart.com/blog/lancaster-west-estate-an-ideal-for-living; see also Matthys Levy and Mario Salvadori, *Why Buildings Fall Down: How Structures Fail* (New York: WW Norton and Co, 1992), 76–89.
4 See Grenfell Tower Inquiry, *Phase 1 Report* (see note 1), 33–37.
5 See Jim Dunton, “Grenfell Inquiry: What We Learned from Project Client KCTMO this Week,” *Building*, October 16, 2020, accessed June 3, 2024, www.building.co.uk/news/grenfell-inquiry-what-we-learned-from-project-client-kctmo-this-week/5108510.article.
6 See Architects for Social Housing, *The Truth About Grenfell Tower* (see note 2), 42–49.
7 Cf. Dunton, “Grenfell Inquiry” (see note 5).
8 Cf. “Final Grenfell Report to Be Released in Autumn,” *BBC*, May 23, 2024, accessed June 2, 2024, www.bbc.com/news/articles/cgee0rlgzkdo#.
9 On the work of Hooke and Wren, see Lisa Jardine, *On a Grander Scale: The Outstanding Career of Sir Christopher Wren* (London: Harper Collins, 2002); Jardine, *The Curious Life of Robert Hooke: The Man Who Measured London* (London: Harper Collins, 2003).
10 John Gwynn, *London and Westminster Improved, Illustrated by Plans: To Which Is Prefixed, a Discourse on Publick Magnificence; With Observations on the State of Arts and Artists in This Kingdom, Wherein the Study of the Polite Arts Is Recommended as Necessary to a Liberal Education: Concluded by Some Proposals Relative to Places Not Laid Down in the Plans* (London, 1766), viii.
11 On the emergence of general contracting, see Richard Price, *Masters Unions and Men: Work Building and the Rise of Labour, 1830–1914* (Cambridge: Cambridge University Press, 1980), 19–33.
12 Katie Lloyd Thomas, *Building Materials: Material Theory and the Architectural Specification* (London: Bloomsbury, 2022).
13 For a condensed summary, see Raymond Williams, *Culture and Society, 1780–1950* (Harmondsworth: Penguin, 1961), 137–65. On the wider European project see Barry Bergdoll, *European Architecture, 1750–1890* (Oxford: Oxford University Press, 2000), 173–205.
14 See Barrington Kaye, *The Development of the Architectural Profession in Britain* (London: George Allen and Unwin, 1960).
15 See David B. Brownlee, *The Law Courts: The Architecture of George Edmund Street* (Cambridge: MIT Press, 1984), 366–69; Irene Cheng, Charles L. Davis, and Mabel O. Wilson, introduction to *Race and Modern Architecture: A Critical History from the Enlightenment to the Present* (Pittsburgh: University of Pittsburgh Press, 2020), 3–20.
16 This reading of Morris follows those of Williams, *Culture and Society* (see note 13); and Edward Palmer Thompson, *William Morris: From Romantic to Revolutionary*, rev. ed. (London: Merlin Press, 1976).
17 There is no official or comprehensive history of the ABT. For some indications as to its policies and efficacy, see Andrew Saint, *Towards a Social Architecture: The Role of School Building in Post-War England* (New Haven: Yale University Press, 1987).
18 See Andrew Saint, *The Image of the Architect* (New Haven: Yale University Press, 1983).
19 See Christine Wall, *An Architecture of Parts: Architects, Building Workers and Industrialisation in Britain, 1940–1970* (London: Routledge, 2013).
20 Historically, different schools have emphasized technical, managerial, or cultural dimensions, but design practice dominates. See Paul Jenkins et al., “Research in UK Architecture Schools: An Institutional Perspective,” *arq*, vol. 9, no. 1 (2005), 33–43.
21 Malcolm MacEwen, *Crisis in Architecture* (London: RIBA, 1974).
22 For a summary of professional changes, see A. Roderick Males, “Architects’ registration,” in Anthony Speaight and Gregory Stone, eds., *Architect’s Legal Handbook: The Law for Architects*, 7th ed. (Oxford: Architectural Press, 2001), 375–76.
23 See Marian Hawkesworth and Rob Imrie, “Organisational Change in Systems of Building Regulation and Control: Illustrations from the English Context,” *Environment and Planning B: Planning and Design*, vol. 36 (2009), 552–67; Frits Meijer and Henk Visscher, “Deregulation and Privatisation of European Building-Control Systems?” *Environment and Planning B: Planning and Design*, vol. 33 (2006), 491–501; Liam Ross, “Regulatory Spaces, Physical and Metaphorical: On the Legal and Spatial Occupation of Fire-Safety Regulation,” in Katie Lloyd Thomas et al., eds., *Industries of Architecture* (London: Routledge, 2016), 235–44; Sarah Wigglesworth, “Unapproved Document O: Design for Ageing,” in ibid., 329–37.
24 *Building Regulations 2010, Approved Document B*, vol. 1, 2019, accessed June 3, 2024, iv, assets.publishing.service.gov.uk/government/uploads/system/uploads/attachment_data/file/937931/ADB_Vol1_Dwellings_2019_edition_inc_2020_amendments.pdf.
25 See Jonathan Massey, “Risk and Regulation in the Financial Architecture of American Houses,” in Aggregate Architectural History Collaborative, ed., *Governing by Design: Architecture, Economy, and Politics in the Twentieth Century* (Pittsburgh: University of Pittsburgh Press, 2012), 21–46.
26 See Fredric Jameson, “Future City,” *New Left Review* 21 (May/June 2003), 65–79.

Fig. 8 The Grenfell Tower fire on June 14, 2017

COMMODITY

COMMUNITY

HOC OPUS, HIC LABOR

TECHNOLOGIES OF THE VISIBLE AND OF THE INVISIBLE IN ANCIENT ROMAN ARCHITECTURE

Text: Maria Shéhérazade Giudici

Fig. 1

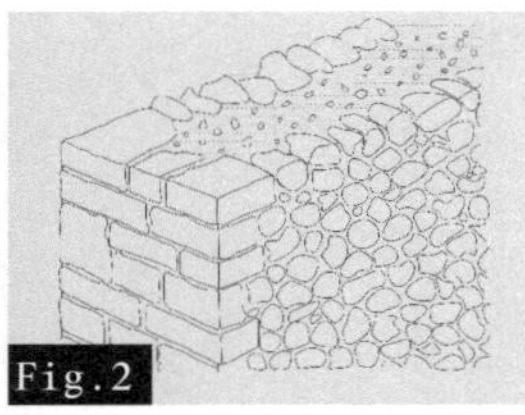
Fig. 2

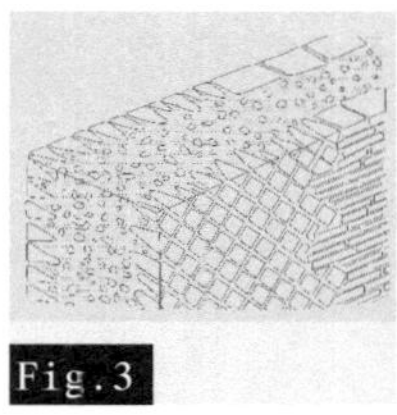
Fig. 3

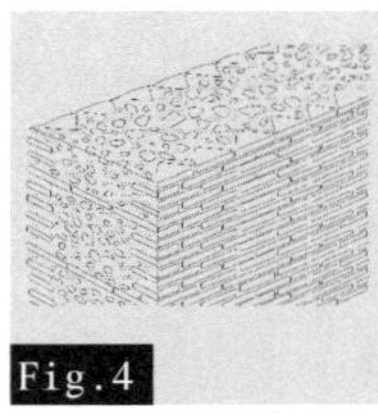
Fig. 4

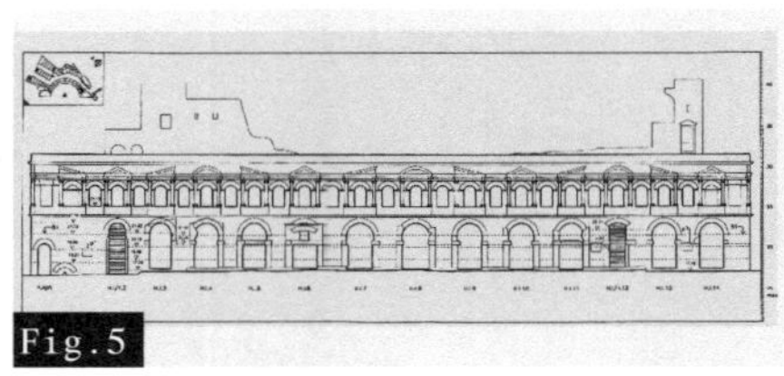
Fig. 5

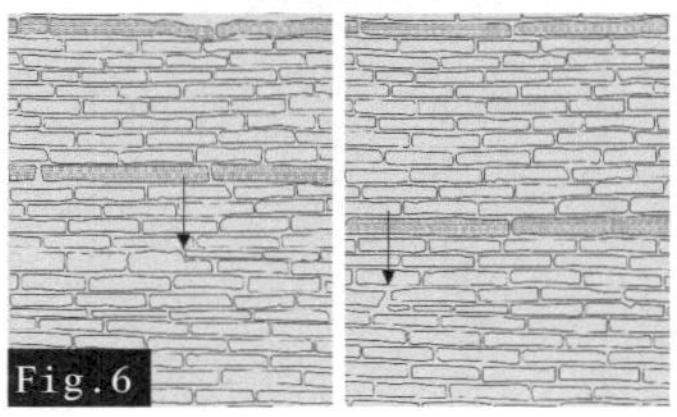
Fig. 6

Fig. 7

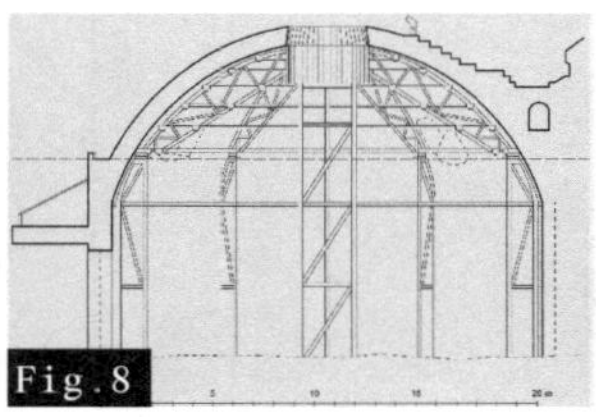
Fig. 8

Fig. 9

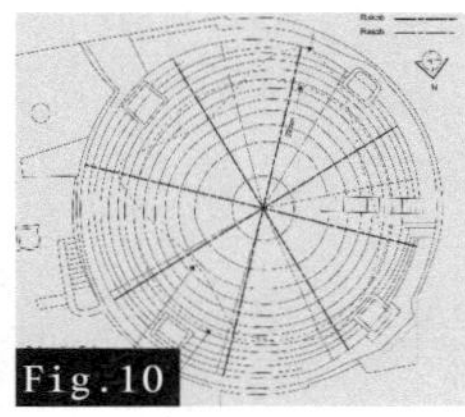
Fig. 10

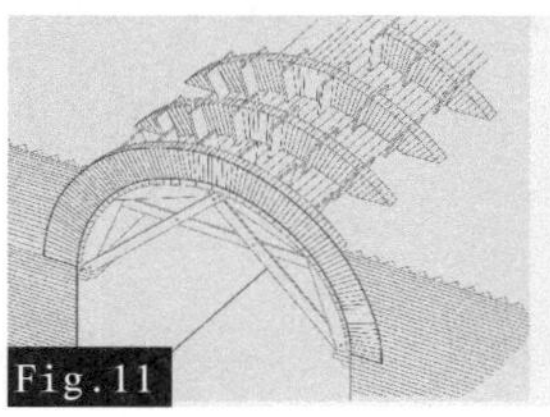
Fig. 11

Fig. 12

Fig. 13

Fig. 14

Fig. 15

European architecture firms generate 50% of their revenue from planning new buildings. The figures vary widely by country: (resp. rank; figures in %) → 1. Romania ● New construction 72 ● Heritage preservation 7 ● Refurbishment / adaptive reuse 21 → Poland ● New construction 70 ● Heritage preservation 8 ● Refurbishment / adaptive reuse 21 → 3. Croatia ● New construction 66 ● Heritage preservation 19 ● Refurbishment / adaptive reuse 15 → 22. UK ● New construction 43 ● Heritage preservation 17 ● Refurbishment / adaptive reuse 40 → 23. Denmark ● New construction 35 ● Heritage preservation 40 ● Refurbishment / adaptive reuse 24 → 24. Italy ● New construction 16 ● Heritage preservation 33 ● Refurbishment / adaptive reuse 50 → In Germany, refurbishment and adaptive reuse projects (53%) now outnumber new construction in Germany.

Fig. 1 Giovanni Battista Piranesi, *Ponte Ferrato, Called the Bridge of Cestius*, 1756, copperplate etching, 40 × 60 cm

"Hoc opus, hic labor," says the Cumaean Sibyl to Aeneas in Virgil's eponymous epic poem.[1] This much-cited verse translates to: "Here's the task, here's the hard work." Four words summarizing what, two millennia later, Hannah Arendt would describe in her *The Human Condition* (1958) as the difference between the *animal laborans* and the *homo faber*: the distinction between the capital-w Work—the emancipatory, productive, creative *Opus*—and *labor*—mere toil, that is to say—while still putting them on the same level.[2] Indeed, the ever-pragmatic Romans knew very well that there is no *opus* without *labor*. How much the first is contingent on the conditions of the latter is nowhere more evident, perhaps, than in Roman production of large-scale architecture.

Opus, in Latin, refers not only to the oeuvre or the final product, but also to the technique by which concrete and stones are shaped into walls: masonry. With the invention and rapid spread of the use of concrete, Roman building technique underwent a dramatic evolution in the first century CE. The new composite material not only accelerated the erection of vertical walls, but also made it possible to build daring vaulting systems.[3]

The Romans had all the ingredients to produce a precursor to modern concrete—though different in the sense that it was never handled in a liquid state. Rather, it was an aggregation of rubble called *caementa*, kept together with *pozzolana* mortar. But the techniques to give shape to this *Opus caementitium* evolved over time and were essentially shaped by labor conditions. This evolution remains poorly understood to this day, as most literature focuses on the material itself rather than the process of construction and the organization of labor.[4] However, history—and the remains of building projects from antiquity—remain an object lesson on how architectural expression and the built environment as a whole are linked to material conditions, social structures, political power relations, and processes of raw material extraction.

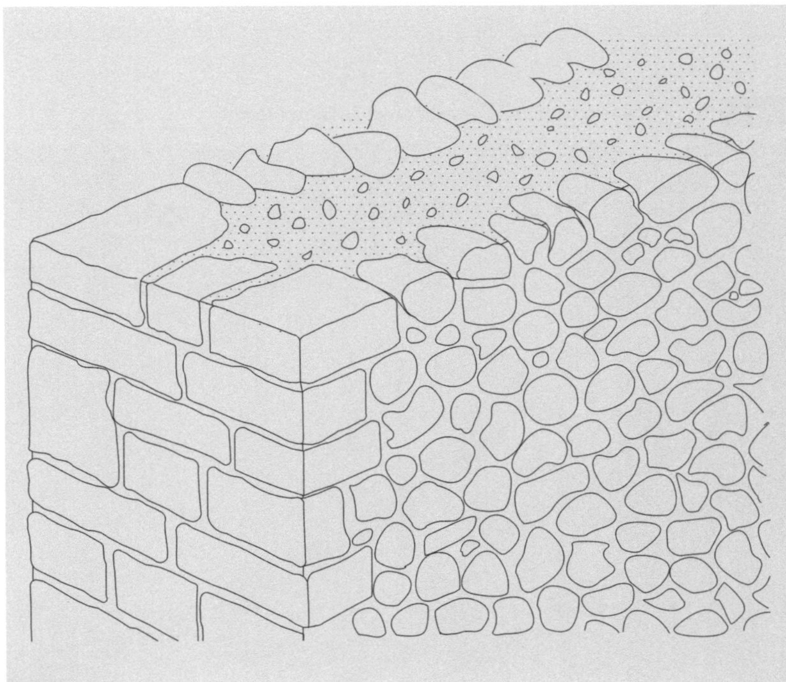

Fig. 2 *Opus incertum*

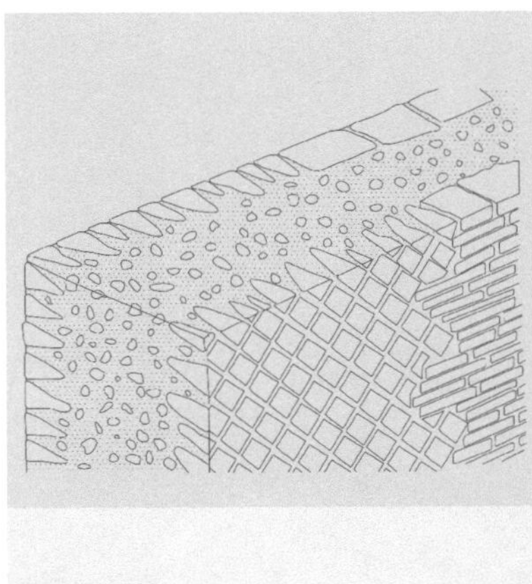

Fig. 3 *Opus reticulatum*

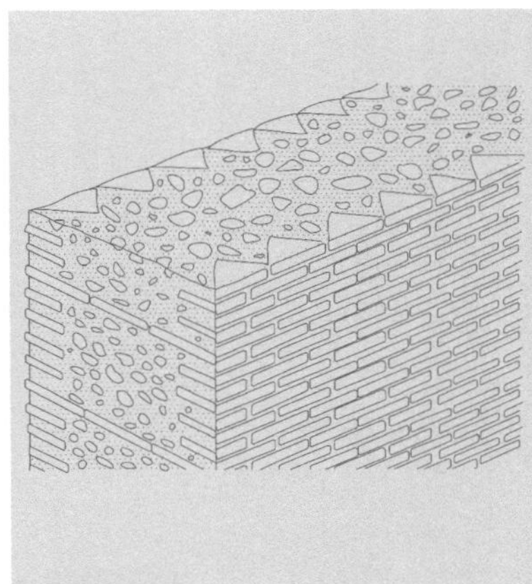

Fig. 4 *Opus testaceum*

Building as a Form of Welfare

During the transition from Republic to Empire in the last century BCE, waged construction workers became increasingly important subjects in Roman society.[5] Rome had recently established itself as a power in the Mediterranean, and with this flourishing hegemonic role came a period of large-scale infrastructure construction including roads, aqueducts, monuments, and places of worship. Late-Republican monuments were usually built using a technique called *opus incertum*, a type of wall lined with unhewed stone, called *caementa* (fig. 2). This masonry type required great care and craftsmanship, as the irregularly shaped stones had to be chosen one by one to fit together. Most of the workers on the construction site were free men, paid a relatively stable wage for their expertise—slaves represented a minority.[6] Wage workers could be paid just for the days they were needed; as building was seasonal work, it was economically inefficient to force slaves, who needed to be provided for year-round, to perform this kind of work.[7]

In the first century BCE a different technique arose, which significantly decreased labor costs. Called *opus reticulatum*, it was made using stones of even size and with a square section as lining (fig. 3).[8] These stones could be produced off-site and year-round—also by slaves—compensating the increase in preparatory labor by reducing wages on-site, where radically deskilled workers could easily and rapidly place the standardized stones.[9]

This rationalization of construction work allowed the state and powerful landlords to retain the services of a vast number of free, waged workers, some without any specific skill. The construction industry therefore became a massive source of employment and income, essentially pacifying the lower urban classes. It is on the era's monumental construction sites that the political consensus for the Empire itself was built.

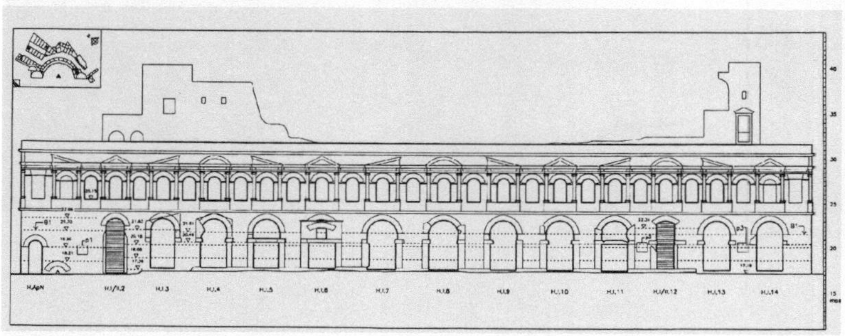

Fig. 5 Two-dimensional facade projection of Trajan's Market

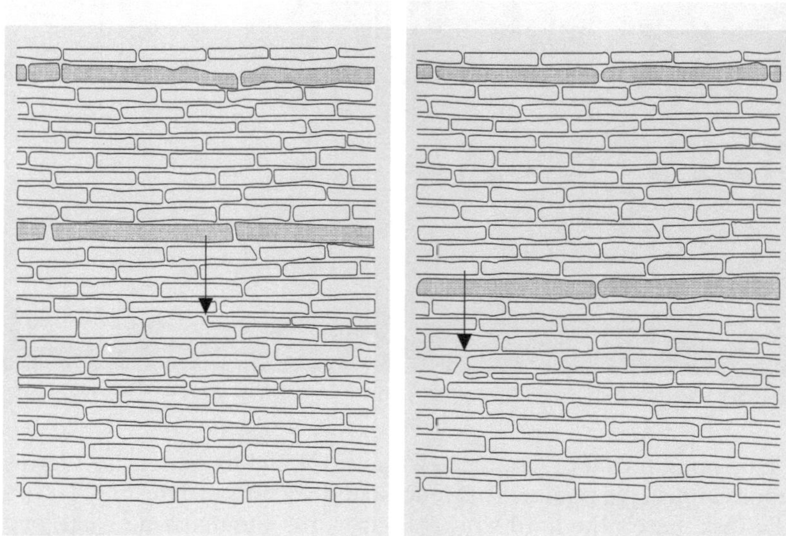

Fig. 6 Transition between two masonry segments

Fig. 7 Giovanni Battista Piranesi, *View of Part of the Upper Hemicycle of Trajan's Forum*, 1756, copperplate etching, 14 × 21 cm

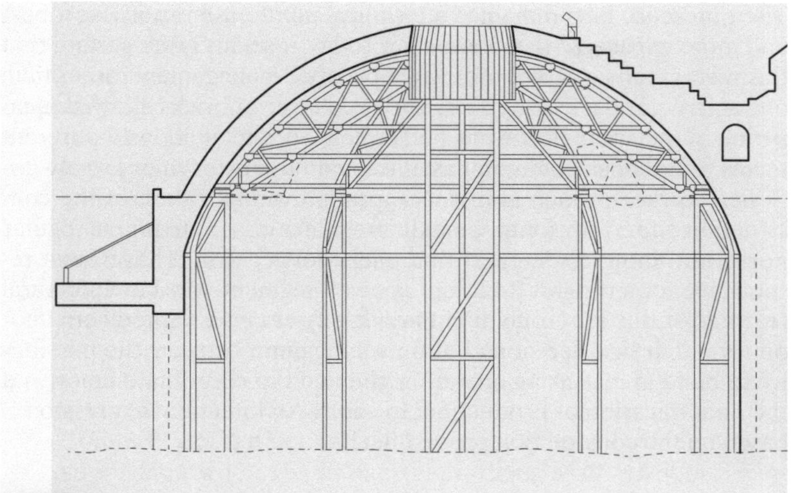

Fig. 8 Schematic section of the Pantheon showing the falsework

Fig. 9 Francesco Piranesi, *Section of the Length of the Pantheon That Illustrates the Pronaos, or Portico, and the Interior of the Temple*, 1786, copperplate etching, 48 × 68 cm

Form Follows Process

Rome was ravaged by a fire in 64 CE, during Emperor Nero's reign. While annals have left dire pictures of this disaster, the lower classes in reality applauded the reconstruction and rejoiced in the sudden rise in employment offers, which resulted in their economic situation improving quickly.[10] However, the large volume of rapidly built architecture that Nero and his successors left behind was only possible thanks to a long supply chain which initially had little to do with the construction industry, and yet developed innovative techniques that provoked deep changes in terms of form, scale, and site management.

After the fire, Nero appropriated a large area close to the Forum to build a phantasmagorical compound, the Domus Aurea, considered the earliest documented trace of formal experimentation with vaulting.[11] Less well known is the fact that this experimentation could only happen because of groundbreaking innovation in the making of formwork. This development was enabled by a significant progress in the craft of carpentry, which archaeologists have equally found evidence of in the ships built during this period.[12] Only with this increased sophistication in formwork production could complex shapes such as those in the Domus Aurea be realized, creating a class of skilled and commercially successful carpenters.

In turn, such advancements in carpentry would have been unthinkable without the development of metallurgy. Only in the first century CE did Rome gain control over Noricum, an Alpine region in present-day Austria with important iron ore deposits.[13] Metallurgy made huge advancements around the mid-first century, including the production of iron saws to produce long and precisely cut wooden planks used in centerings.[14] This allowed builders to produce vast vaulted spaces like the Colosseum.[15] Early Imperial architecture was therefore made possible not only thanks to architects or masons, but also thanks to ironmongers, toolmakers, and carpenters who sometimes worked hundreds of miles away from Rome. The monuments still visible in Rome today are merely the result of a process starting with steel extraction in colonies located in contemporary Austria.

Material Cycles

At the same time, a simplification in the construction of walls was achieved through the introduction of *opus testaceum* (fig. 4). This technique initially repurposed roof tiles as wall facings for an *opus caementitium* wall core,[16] but the mid-first century saw brickyards start producing purpose-made bricks in several dimensions.[17] This development made the task of construction workers even simpler and more standardized than with *opus incertum* or even *opus reticulatum*.

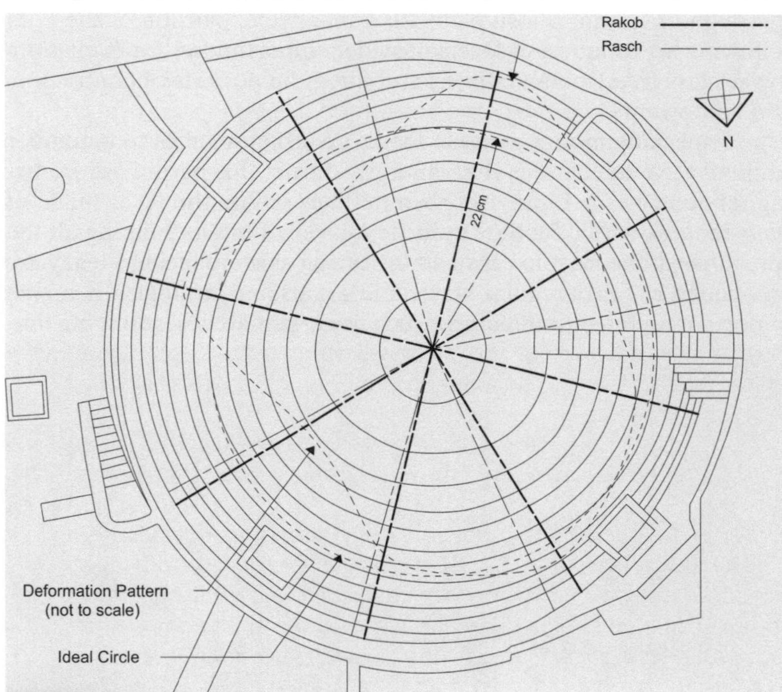

Fig. 10 Schematic floor plan of the Pantheon

From an economic point of view, the construction industry was a well-oiled machine: The state paid building contractors, who obtained their building materials from landowners, who in turn sold the resources abounding on their estates.[18] It is precisely this supply chain that warrants closer inspection to shed light on the reasons for the formal evolution of Roman architecture. On any big construction site, several contractors would work in parallel and virtually independently from each other.[19] Each small-scale entrepreneur probably employed a few dozen workers and bore responsibility only for a section of the site. A few state employees were in charge of centralized control, monitoring the collaboration between different groups.

The contractors usually supplied their own construction materials, buying it from estates scattered around Rome.[20] This area was almost entirely owned by powerful—often aristocratic—Roman families. Surprisingly, this situation has changed little in the twenty centuries since, a staggering percentage of land still being owned by only a handful of family clans. The trickle-down system's remarkable efficiency stemmed from the fact that the elites profited just as much from the construction boom as well-off and small-scale entrepreneurs—among them freedmen or subcontractors of the estates charged with bringing their materials to market. This procurement process flourished during

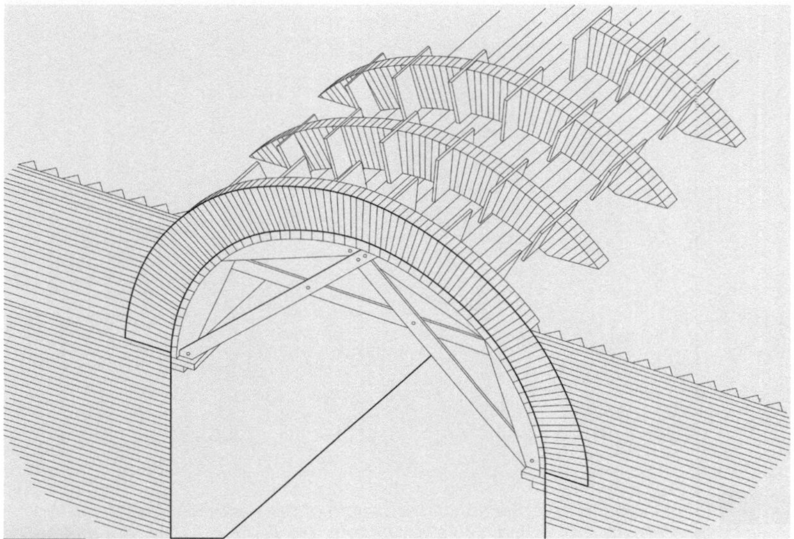

Fig. 11 Schematic axonometric view of the formwork used in building a vault

the reign of Trajan, whose plans for a massive expansion of the Fora following his conquest of Dacia provided opportunities for even more lower-class free Roman citizens and filled the pockets of contractors and landowners.

Especially his eponymous Trajan's Market testifies to a number of innovative techniques that emerged during this period before being refined (fig. 7). Lighter horizontal lines striate the walls made of *opus testaceum* (fig. 5); they indicate a layer of bricks running all the way through the masonry instead of serving as mere facing.[21] They are positioned at fairly regular vertical intervals and strategically match important architectural features such as certain arches' springing line. Their presence long remained a technical puzzle, as brick is less robust and more expensive than *caementa*. Today, it seems quite certain that this was actually a choice motivated by labor management rather than out of structural necessity. First, the even layer of bricks allowed measuring of the amount of work performed. Second, it allowed different teams to establish common baselines and targets for their largely unskilled workers, which points to a granular organization of the construction site. Additionally, small irregularities occurring at regular horizontal intervals suggest that each worker would have been responsible for a roughly 2-meter-long wall segment. Most architectural features of this era—one might argue: any era—were predicated not on formal design decisions, but on what cannot be seen: the possibility to build arches using centering, the need to coordinate labor, and the quantification of production. In short: Architectural expression is based on the construction process itself.

Projecting the Void

A very specific class of entrepreneurs saw its clout rise during this period. Engaging with architecture at the time meant designing the negative space—i.e., the formwork—and organizing labor far before the actual building process. After all, the centering represented a large part of the problem of vault construction. Many features of Roman construction indeed cannot be understood without taking the centering into account. In Giovanni Battista Piranesi's famous plates depicting the Ponte Cestio, protruding elements appear right underneath the arch (fig. 1). These elements have no purpose in the bridge's functioning and only served as strategically placed supports for the wooden centering over which the bridge was subsequently built. Similar features can be seen in a number of buildings of this period: Many seemingly decorative elements of classical architecture, especially

Fig. 12 Giovanni Battista Piranesi, *A View of Part of the Intended Bridge at Blackfriars, London*, 1764, copperplate etching, 42 × 62 cm

cornices, are nothing but support ledges for formwork and centering that allowed carpenters to use the expensive imported timber more efficiently.

The specific intricacy of a centering, moreover, lies not in its erection as much as in its removal. Often, carpenters would include custom stabilizing elements that would be cut out once the vault had settled, thereby letting the centering detach and fall. The weight and size of the centering made this operation rather difficult, so builders sought to achieve cheaper, slenderer centerings which would detach more easily while simultaneously being stable enough so that the vault would not suffer from deformation. The study of deformations in extant vaults has revealed a radial pattern—proof that attempts were made to lighten and simplify the centering by using ribbed formworks on which the boards would rest.[22]

By the early second century builders had refined a range of techniques that would counteract deformation in the *caementa* and reduce the risk of damage from the (premature) removal of the formwork. Perhaps the most prominent of these methods involved the use of brick ribs. While bricks have a lower structural performance compared to concrete, the curing of the latter could take time in larger buildings, and the result could be ruined by uneven curing. This so-called "concrete creep," in which parts of the mass shrink more than others, was prevented by segmenting the vaults with brick ribs. The Pantheon[23] is a key example of this technique, which was rather expensive, since bricks were by no means a cheap material (figs. 8–10). This kind of structural innovation would have been impossible without the Empire's strength through colonial expansion under the Nerva-Antonine destiny in power during the second century CE. A total of 30 percent of extant bricks were produced under one of its Emperors, Hadrian, a clear sign of the city's wealth at that time. The brick industry was a source of steady income and a way of laundering the spoils of colonial violence.[24]

Central Planning

It is worth considering once again the previously analyzed web of relationships in the building industry as it pertains to Roman bricks. The relationship between client—the state, Emperor, or large donor—and contractor essentially did not change in the first centuries CE, nor did the composition of the labor force. A new set of actors emerged, however. The raw materials for bricks did not go directly from landowner to contractor, but were transformed into a usable product in a brickyard. The latter were mostly run by small entrepreneurs who rented their brickyard from the estate owners, who also provided them with the primary materials.[25] Not less than 30 percent of landowners were actually wealthy women; even more surprisingly, 6 percent of brickyards were also managed by women. Two of them, Domitia Lucilla and Arria Fadilla, were in fact the two main suppliers of bricks for the massive building site of Hadrian's Villa in the third decade of the second century CE.[26]

The story of these women also reads as a cautionary tale: Both had sons who went on to become Emperors, respectively as Marcus Aurelius and Antoninus Pius. The subsequent absorption of their brickyards into the property of the Empire was symptomatic of a broader process of wealth concentration and redistribution which slowly strangled what, anachronistically, we might call the era's "middle class" in favor of a class of increasingly skilled managers—architects, or controllers—able to cut costs, steer material flows, and organize large-scale building enterprises. One of the first structures to suffer from this centralization of means of production was the interclass alliance clearly identifiable in the previously described supply chain for bricks.

Economic turmoil and a state apparatus struggling to hold together an unbearably vast Empire led to a remarkable drop in brick production during the third century CE, mirrored by the evolution of brick ribs: A calculated attempt to use as little brick as possible can be seen in barrel vaults of that period, spurring the transition from full-brick ribs such as those still visible in the Pantheon, to vaults using many fewer bricks by arranging them in lattices (fig. 12). While saving material, this technique required a much more sophisticated design ahead of construction. The use of this increasingly expensive material with structural advantages of little significance in the case of small vaults can look puzzling, especially since these ribs were used in virtually all vaults at the time. The answer lies, again, in the advantages of a clear division of tasks on the construction site. Once the ribs were set, less skilled workers or slaves could come in and fill the lattice with *opus caementitium*. A lot of planning, design, and expertise went into such attempts to simplify the construction process. This substantial advancement in design competence made the construction of very large public works possible even in an age of turmoil and economic uncertainty. The massive Baths of Caracalla, for instance, represented a big effort by the state to offer recreational spaces to a disenfranchised population, while also offering it an opportunity for employment (fig. 13).

Architecture as Physical Manifestation of Policy

Rome slipped into a political and economic crisis in the mid-third century. A protracted process of parallel skilling (of planners) and deskilling (of workers) reached its apex when Emperor Diocletian introduced *corvee* labor—i.e., forced labor that every subject had to perform for the state without compensation—which portended the end of the free construction industry. Diocletian also introduced

Fig. 13 Auguste Choisy, "Thermes de Caracalla," in *L'art de bâtir chez les Romains*, Paris, 1873, plate 5

a blanket land tax that applied throughout the Empire starting in about 287 CE. Roman landowners often offered payments in kind, which in most cases meant construction materials: timber, lime, stone, brick. Moreover, the *collegia*—the Roman equivalent of guilds—were forced to offer their services to the Emperor.[27] Effectively, the state took control of the building industry. There was, however, no incentive to provide good-quality materials or to work efficiently. It comes as no surprise then that the architecture of the time serves as an indicator of rapid economic decline.

An example of the architecture produced under these conditions is the partially preserved Nymphaeum of Minerva Medica (figs. 14–15). The design of the octagonal dome is extremely sophisticated: The less money and skilled labor the Emperors had at their disposal, the more their planners got creative to compensate. The result is intriguing in that it is made out of poor-quality material, but still spatially innovative. As many other buildings of the same era show, architects were not above recycling. In this case, they incorporated single-use amphorae, used in the transport of oil, which not only lessened the load of the wall, but also replaced more valuable material since they came at no cost.[28] This is another clear sign of the extreme centralization of the system: The byproduct of colonial imports was reused for the construction of state-led architectural projects. The state had become a gigantic enterprise seeking to recycle its own waste—but for a crumbling political system, it was too little, too late. The collapse of the social alliances that had fueled the building frenzy of the second century engendered the collapse of the Roman building industry, and once colonial resources began to run dry, there was no way to revitalize an ecologically and socially unsustainable practice.

Two millennia later two observations hold true: First, the formal qualities observed in the often-sentimentalized architecture of Roman antiquity were not ends in themselves. Instead, they were always a function of the dominant material conditions of production. Innovation was dependent on—and sometimes a by-product of—the strategic use of financial means, labor, and natural resources, the rallying of political support, and the tapping of available supply chains. Centralized powers have often used the construction industry as an artificial economic engine to employ their subjects when in need of consensus.

Second, the steadily refined division of labor led to a progressive deskilling of construction workers. This development had its countereffect in the parallel rise of a class of managers and designers, whom we would today call "architects," increasingly estranged from the social and material conditions they (re)produced. Their increasingly complex designs sought to offset the scarcity of (skilled) labor. Design became an accomplice of power. When the state sought to centralize the control of construction, architecture became the literal manifestation of policy. The walls and vaults of their palaces and monuments crystalize these class asymmetries to this day.

Faced with the ecological and social crises of our own time, we have to ask ourselves whether most of these points might not, after all, still hold true, as scarcity and constructed scarcity, social and colonial violence, and a demonstrable inadequacy of the nation-state as political subject risk leading the construction industry to a standstill. It is incumbent upon today's architects to reflect on how the structural violence playing out on construction sites every day directly flows from the surrounding political context. Architects who accept—or even enable—such violence may fortuitously create something of sublime beauty in the process, but they also expose themselves to blame. For a clear-eyed look at the past begs the question: If the walls we build today could talk, what story about us and our society would they tell in two millennia?

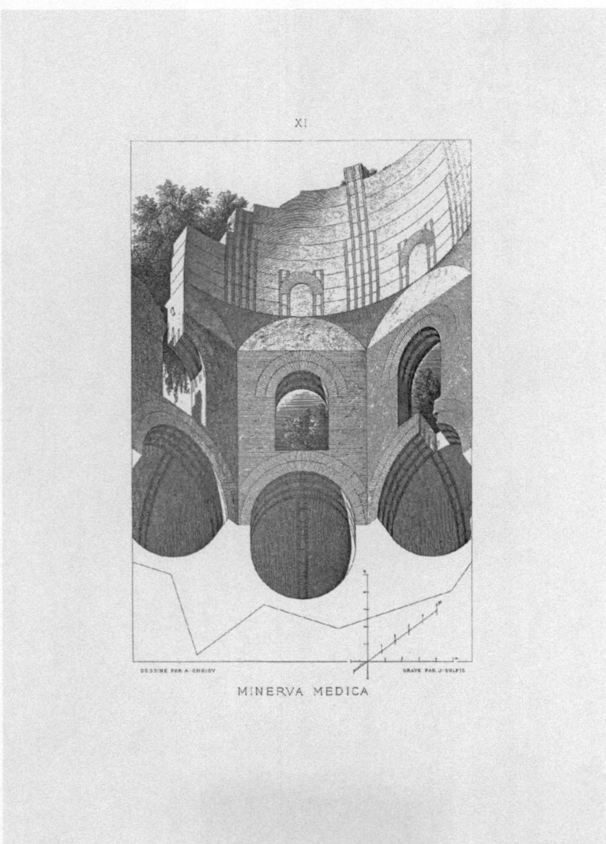

Fig. 14 Auguste Choisy, "Minerva Medica," in *L'art de bâtir chez les Romains*, Paris, 1873, plate 11

Fig. 15 Giovanni Battista Piranesi, *Remains of the Temple of Minerva Medica*, 1756, copperplate etching, 13 × 20 cm

1 Virgil, *Aeneid*, book VI, 129.
2 Cf. Hannah Arendt, *The Human Condition* (1958), 2nd ed. (Chicago: University of Chicago Press, 1998).
3 This shift is also commonly known as an "architectural revolution." See John Bryan Ward-Perkins, "Materials and Methods: The Roman Architectural Revolution," in *Roman Imperial Architecture* (New Haven: Yale University Press, 1981), 97–120.
4 Cf. Giuseppe Lugli, *La tecnica edilizia romana con particolare riguardo a Roma e Lazio* (1957; Rome: Giovanni Bardi, 2016).
5 See Peter Astbury Brunt, "Free Labour and Public Works at Rome," *The Journal of Roman Studies* 70 (1980), 81–100.
6 See Lynne C. Lancaster, *Concrete Vaulted Construction in Imperial Rome: Innovations in Context* (Cambridge: Cambridge University Press, 2005), 18–19.
7 See Jean Andreau and Raymond Descat, *The Slave in Greece and Rome*, trans. Marion Leopold (Madison: The University of Wisconsin Press, 2006).
8 Frank Sear, *Roman Architecture* (1982; London: Routledge, 2021), 76–78.
9 See Jean-Pierre Adam, *Roman Building: Materials and Techniques* (1984), trans. Anthony Mathews (London: Routledge, 2005), 20; ibid., 259.
10 See Anthony A. Barrett et al., eds., *The Emperor Nero: A Guide to the Ancient Sources* (Princeton: Princeton University Press, 2016), 149–70.
11 Cf. William MacDonald, *The Architecture of the Roman Empire*, vol. I (New Haven: Yale University Press, 1965, 1982), 122–27; Larry F. Ball, *The Domus Aurea and the Roman Architectural Revolution* (Cambridge: Cambridge University Press, 2003).
12 Cf. Roger B. Ulrich, *Roman Woodworking* (New Haven: Yale University Press, 2007); Guido Ucelli, *Le navi di Nemi* (Rome: Istituto d'Archeologia e Storia dell'Arte, 1950).
13 See John Francis Healy, *Mining and Metallurgy in the Greek and Roman World* (London: Thames and Hudson, 1978), 233.
14 Ulrich, *Roman Woodworking* (see note 12), 45–50.
15 See Ward-Perkins, *Roman Imperial Architecture* (see note 3), 70.
16 See Vitruvius, "Methods of Building Walls," in *The Ten Books on Architecture* (1st c. BCE), trans. Morris Hicky Morgan (Cambridge: Harvard University Press, 1914), 51–53.
17 See Sear, *Roman Architecture* (see note 8), 131.
18 See Margareta Steinby, "I senatori e l'industria laterizia urbana," *Epigrafia e ordine senatorio* 1 (1982), 227–37.
19 See James C. Anderson, *Roman Architecture and Society* (Baltimore: Johns Hopkins University Press, 1997).
20 See Herbert Bloch, "The Roman Brick Industry and Its Relationship to Roman Architecture," *Journal of the American Society of Architectural Historians*, vol. 1, no. 1 (January 1941), 1; ibid., 3–8.
21 See Lynne Lancaster, "Building Trajan's Markets," *American Journal of Archaeology*, vol. 102, no. 2, (April 1998), 283–308.
22 The work of Friedrich Rakob and Jürgen J. Rasch is particularly significant, as highlighted in George R. H. Wright, *Ancient Building Technology*, vol. 3, "Construction" (Leiden: Brill, 2009), 273–74.
23 See Robert Mark, "Reinterpreting Ancient Roman Structure," *American Scientist*, vol. 75, no. 2 (March–April 1987), 142–50.
24 Margareta Steinby, "L'industria laterizia di Roma nel Tardo Impero," in Andrea Giardina, ed., *Società romana e impero tardoantico*, vol. 2. (Bari: Laterza, 1986), 99–164.
25 See Paul Weaver, "Imperial Slaves and Freedmen in the Brick Industry," *Zeitschrift für Papyrologie und Epigraphik*, vol. 122 (1998), 238–46.
26 See Tapio Helen, *Organization of Roman Brick Production in the First and Second Century A. D.: An Interpretation of Roman Brick Stamps* (Helsinki: Annales Academiae Scientiarium Fennicae, 1975), 22–23.
27 See Jean-Michel Carrié, "Les associations professionnelles à l'époque tardive: Entre *Munus* et convivialité," in Jean-Michel Carrié and Rita Lizzi Testa, eds., *"Humana Sapit": Études d'Antiquité Tardive offertes à Lellia Cracco Ruggini* (Turnhout: Brepols Publishers, 2002), 311–15.
28 See Arturo Zaragozá and Fernando Vegas, "Wider, Lighter, Faster: Building Vaults in the Medieval Mediterranean," in Paula Fuentes and Anke Wunderwald, eds., *The Art of Vaulting: Design and Construction in the Mediterranean Gothic* (Basel: Birkhäuser, 2019), 11–28.

THE PYRAMID AND THE LABYRINTH

Text: Will Orr and Ricardo Ruivo

Fig.1

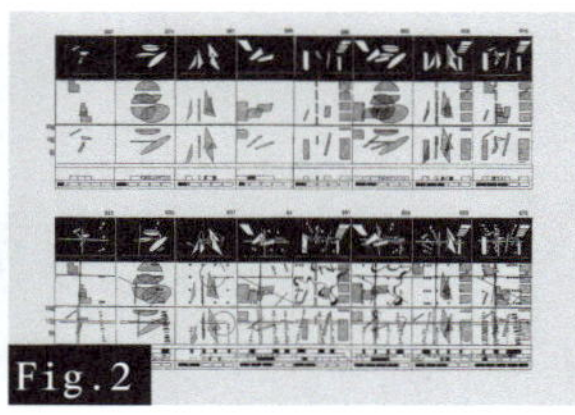

Fig.2

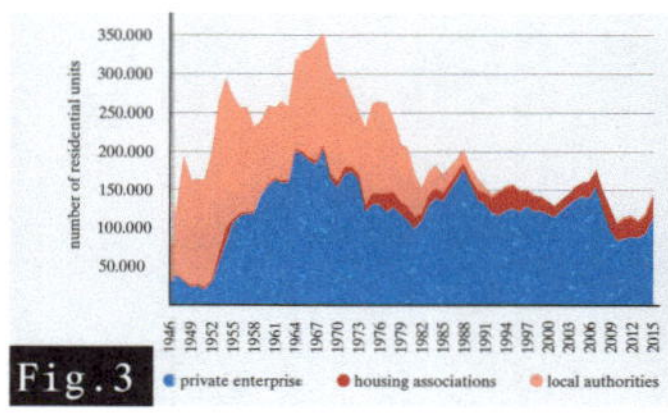

Fig.3

Fig.4

Fig.5

With a current workforce of 620,000, the number of architects in Europe has grown by 100,000 in the past decade. This translates to an average of one architect for every 1,000 EU citizens. However, the figures vary widely across countries. Italy and Cyprus have the highest concentration of architects, while Luxembourg and the Baltic states have the fewest architects per capita. 81% of all freelance architects in Germany would choose to study architecture again, while only around 70% of salaried architects would do so.

Fig. 1 The architecture of the event: “The greatest architecture of all is the fireworks: It perfectly shows the gratuitous consumption of pleasure,” mused architect Bernard Tschumi in 1974. His theoretical observations, in which he dissolved the interdependence of form and function, culminated twelve years later in a half-hour fireworks display at Parc de la Villette in Paris.

Architectural academia has long had a complicated relationship with architectural practice. This relationship is most harmonious in periods of economic growth, when education expands in step with employment, as it did in the public sector–led heyday of the welfare state or during the neoliberal private-sector boom years. When the number of jobs is in decline, the relationship becomes more fraught. In such moments of crisis, academia develops notions of autonomy; these notions are the ideological expressions of a need to find new clients. As Will Orr and Ricardo Ruivo show using the UK as an example, in the long crisis stretching from 2008 to the present, this academic autonomism has grown to absurd proportions, as if it were trying to become its own client.

Introduction

In his 1980 *The Sphere and the Labyrinth: Avant-Gardes and Architecture from Piranesi to the 1970s*, Manfredo Tafuri distanced himself from the critique of architectural ideology he had developed in the preceding years.[1] Giving up on the explanatory and critical power of political economy—perhaps even giving up on the progressive power of architecture in general—he entered a labyrinth of historical and discursive fragments from which he would never return.

In fact, this move is indicative of the radicalization of a weakness present in Tafuri's earlier critiques of operativity—i.e., critiques concerning the conception of an "immediate agency" of architecture—in which he focused on creating space for historical research independent of the practical demands of architectural design.[2] However, Tafuri never fully considered that this critique might itself be operative: Even if it were not directly instrumental to architectural design, it still held ideological power within the academic discourse.

There is an exception to this blind spot. In a 1976 interview with Françoise Very, Tafuri appeared to be concerned by the uselessness of architectural education, which he described as cut off from the economics and social utility of building production.[3] Saying that beyond the production of literal buildings, architects' publications catered to other "culture markets," Tafuri acknowledged the material pressures exerted on academia—while still maintaining that these markets were autonomous from one another, rather than part of a larger dynamic. Looking back from the vantage point of today's economic hellscape—when the construction industry, the academic market, and especially the relationship between the two have been cast into serious doubt—we might ask ourselves: Has anything changed? How does the architectural discipline position itself in a world in which—as the sales pitch goes—"architecture has never been more needed," if the discipline itself is more stratified, split, and cut off from building production than ever before? Is the academy still trapped in Tafuri's labyrinth, or would another metaphorical structure be more appropriate?

A Great Disciplinary Reset?

The outbreak of the Covid-19 pandemic exacerbated the profession's latent crisis. This development has been a source of concern for academia, as a lack of jobs threatens to reduce students' consumer confidence in the material returns on the investment made in their education. This anxiety is reflected by a series of recent publications, seemingly aimed at restoring this confidence by promising alternative career paths: Keller Easterling's 2020 book *Medium Design* and that same year's September issue of *Architectural Review*, titled *Letters to a Young Architect*, are paradigmatic.[4]

Published the following year, the collection of essays *Architects After Architecture: Alternative Pathways for Practice*, cuts to the point.[5] The texts, representing the examples of a wide range of architecture graduates now "practicing" at some distance from the customarily

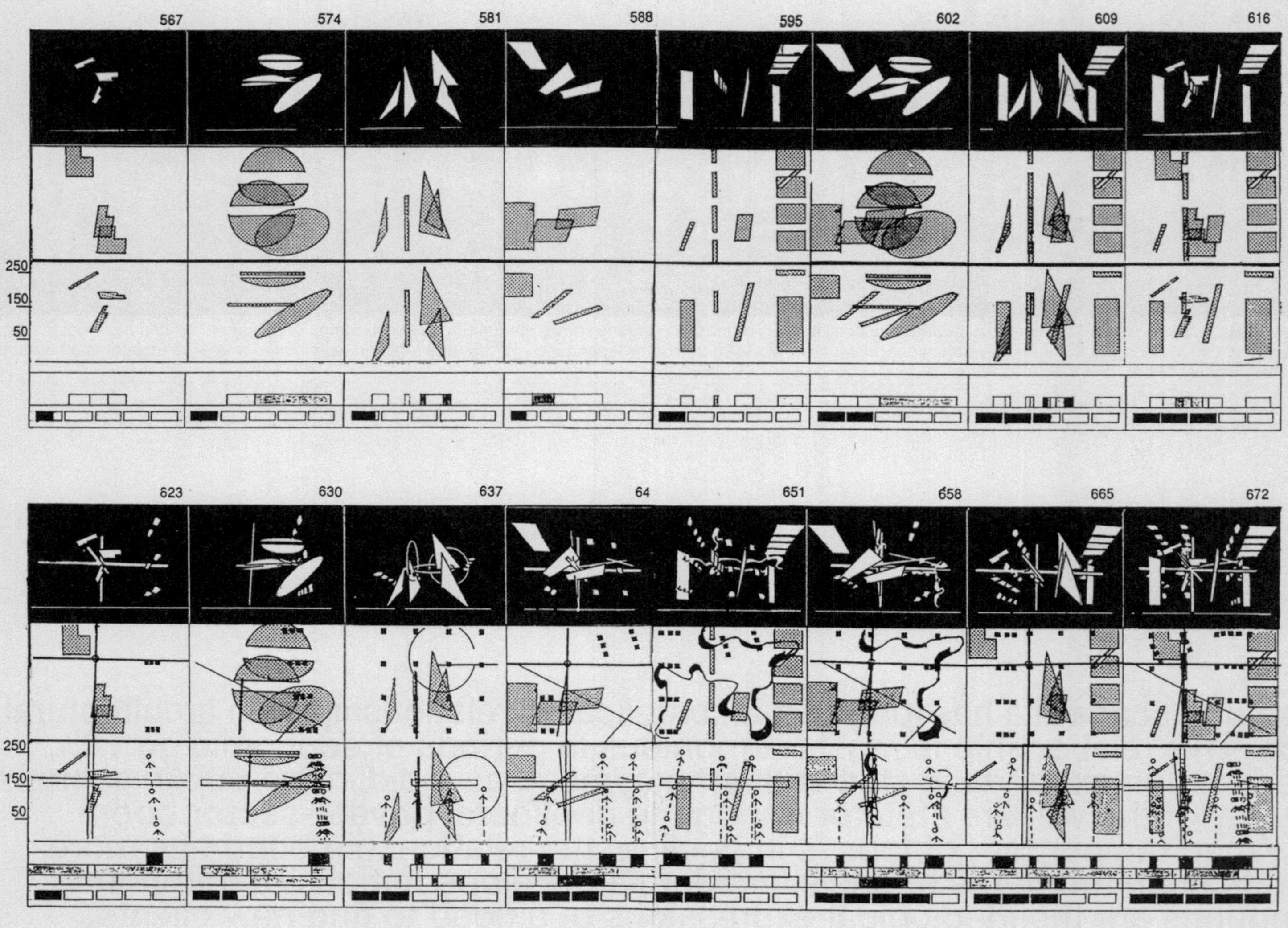

Fig. 2 In the 1992 fireworks display, the organizational principles of Parc de la Villette, designed by Bernard Tschumi, were repeated with the superimposition of points, lines, and surfaces. He developed a special notation system for this purpose.

defined design or planning profession, are offered as guidance and consolation: "Many of the people and practices presented in this book also forged their paths in times of crisis. Faced with great challenges, they were forced to re-evaluate their priorities, and to reinvent the way they work in order to move forward."[6]

However, the collection is not offered solely as a list of emergency measures; it is also offered as a critique. The introduction begins with a rejection of the solitary architect as "singular hero,"[7] just as one *Letter to a Young Architect* repudiates the "Renaissance man" or "orchestra conductor."[8] Against this quasi-mythical figure, they suggest the architect as mediator.

Key to the attraction of the notion of an architect-as-mediator is its appeal to collaboration, to architectural practice as a collective and open endeavor. One might think this is aimed at suggesting an alternative to the private market; instead, it offers a model of the architect as an entrepreneur, located somewhere else entirely in the chain of production to consumption (not necessarily even of buildings): in the position of a middleperson[9]—a post-construction industry disciplinary reset not unlike the post-productive economy, finance sector-led "Great Reset" proposed at the 2020 edition of the Davos World Economic Forum.[10]

Architects After Architecture points to myriad other markets in which the architect can sell their cultural panache: as developer (of real estate or video games), cartoonist, fashion designer, journalist, curator, celebrity chef. This inevitably begs the question: What, then, is the point of maintaining the disciplinary title of "architecture"? Ultimately, the question is mainly of an academic nature: Faced with the fact that a large number of architecture graduates do not go on to practice as architects, the universities face the task of preserving the value and brand familiarity of an architectural education once the latter loses its connection with architectural work as it is normally understood.[11]

As the professional crisis has become more acute following the 2008 financial one, these publications' editors' gambit is to transform what would normally be considered a liability into a selling point, claiming the achievements of architecture graduates outside the profession are a function of their education: "But rather than sweeping this cohort under the carpet, pretending they don't exist, and letting them find their own way, what if we were instead to acknowledge their diverse roles and pathways as a sign of success? … What if architecture were promoted as a generalist degree, a way of thinking about the world, rather than a step toward professional accreditation?"[12]

This promotion of architectural training as cultural polymathy is testament to a growing split between the discipline's academic and professional institutions. The notion of "architects after architecture" may appeal to the academy—after all, they produce architects, not architecture—but what does it mean for those still concerned with producing architecture? Even students who insist on producing literal architecture need to find alternative modes of funding it—following committed projects like + POOL, Assemble's Granby Four Streets, Real Estates' The Ingot, or Alejandro Aravena's Quinta Monroy, all embedded in—respectively—Kickstarter schemes, art grants, fictitious financial instruments, or new mechanisms of debt accumulation. What about the many unemployed architectural workers in the UK's building sector? Will they, too, have to resort to Kickstarter or even retrain for their own discipline? Has "learn to mediate" become the new "learn to code?"

We can read these recent publications like the *Architectural Review* issue and *Architects After Architecture* as gestures aimed toward boosting morale, particularly that of current and prospective architecture students. Whether that is true or not, their efforts are remarkably similar to those meant to reassure investors during times of crisis and uncertainty in the financial markets. The irony here is that such efforts have previously failed precisely for those markets, whose crash was so catastrophic for architectural employment in the first place. In any case—so far, at least—financial markets other than the construction economy have bailouts and quantitative easing to make good on such calls for optimism. This casino economy is now backed by public money. But on what grounds does confidence in the architectural discipline rest? Whose money is it backed by? Has the discipline become a bubble unto itself?

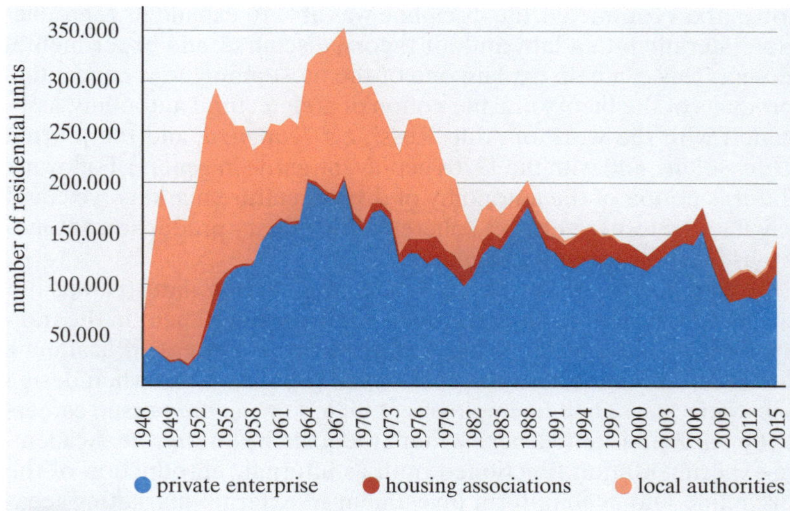

Fig. 3 Evolution of the housing market in the UK

Boom

In the four decades before 2008, the financial markets themselves, particularly the increasingly central real estate sector, were backing the architectural market. As labor productivity rose faster than wages, consumption capacity in the neoliberal economy was increasingly maintained by credit: Consumers bought goods in the present with future wages. In such a framework, the expansion of the economy could only be sustained by an ever-growing debt bubble with the housing market at its core. As described by Grace Blakeley in *Stolen* (2019), commercial and housing markets were vital to the entire financial system: "By 2007, mortgages were no longer just mortgages. The debt that had been created by the banks in the boom between the 1980s and 2007 had been transformed into the plumbing of the entire global financial system."[13]

The only way to maintain market confidence in the real estate credit bubble was to bring in more consumers, an expansionist drive often referred to as a macro-economic form of the Ponzi—or pyramid—scheme. This bubble would continue to absorb the real economy, where real wages were in decline and investment in productive sectors was increasingly unprofitable in comparison to the multiple financial products of the casino economy. This process is commonly referred to as financialization.[14]

Into the Labyrinth

This expansion was neither the first of its kind, nor the most important structurally. The architectural field had been under continuous expansion since the vast public-sector investments in the construction of the postwar European welfare state. This simultaneously expanded higher education and provided public jobs building public infrastructure, increasing the number of professionals in the field. Universal access to housing, education, and healthcare were virtually achieved. Unemployment was all but eliminated, both in the broader economy and in the architectural field itself, even as there were more architects than ever before. When this expanded field faced the consequences of the welfare state's degradation beginning in the 1970s, including cuts in public jobs and building programs, it required a new main client. This client was emerging at the same time: A large capitalist real estate sector, which ultimately became the central pillar of the financialized economy as a whole.[15]

When after 2008 opportunities in architectural academia provided a possible pressure release for the legion of graduates facing unemployment, the situation was reminiscent of an entire era, from the 1970s to the 1990s, where something similar was accomplished at a larger and more historical scale. This era saw the development of an academic production partially independent from traditional job training. As the job market contracted, the discipline was able to expand its reproduction laterally into a labyrinth of theory, discourse, and experimental design. This can help explain one of the most ambiguous conceptual products of the theory era: the notion of architectural autonomy, associated with the work of Aldo Rossi, *La Tendenza*, and the journal *Oppositions*, and with the 1970s neo-avant-garde in general. Following Tafuri's notion of the autonomy of diverse culture markets, we could say that the term refers to a sphere of disciplinary production autonomous from the activity of building.

The decline of the welfare-state construction industry was not mirrored by a reduction in the mass academic enrollment in the transition to neoliberalism. What shifted was the content of academic work and its connection to professional training. Even when design jobs were scarce and unemployment high, some could pursue careers within academia as teachers, writers, theorists, historians, etc. Academic experimentation functioned both as internal reproduction of the discipline and as long-term investment in external marketing techniques.

When the real estate market took off, this investment earned massive returns for the so-called starchitects, whose offices also produced (generally less lucrative) opportunities for the still-growing cohorts of architecture graduates. Emerging from their discursive chrysalis, architects could drop the critical pretense of autonomy and move on from deconstructing the welfare state toward constructing the neoliberal one. As the title of Michael Speaks's 2003 essay bluntly put it, "Theory Was Interesting ... But Now We Have Work."[16] In the emergence of an expanded real estate sector, the autonomous culture markets for architecture found their shared premise in one market in particular; Rossi's theoretical search for the urban artifact found its *raison d'être* in the gentrifying dynamics of the Bilbao effect.

The new role of the architect was to provide aesthetic value added for real estate developments to be sold to an affluent sector of the population whose housing needs had already been met. For each job that disappeared designing mass-fabricated social housing and free schools, another emerged, producing either the prestige urban objects that post-industrial cities used to compete in the global market of tourism and real estate speculation or the veritable fortresses of upscale developments surrounding them.

Architecture was a prestige profession in the late 1990s and early 2000s, and academia continued to expand, providing a veneer of innovation and artistic expression over the mounting inequalities, social tensions, and profound economic instabilities of the neoliberal economy.

Bust

While the capitalist economy is subject to an endless cycle of boom and bust, the 2008 financial crash was not just an encore of the 2000 or even of the 1987 Black Monday ones. It was a crash specifically triggered by the bursting of the real estate bubble, as the financial markets came to realize the unpayability of its housing debt pyramid. The normal mechanisms of neoliberal management were completely insufficient to overcome this crisis. Instead, the most sacred tenets of neoliberal policy—free markets as well as deficit and inflation control—were abandoned in favor of state takeovers and direct public funding (though not of the banks themselves, but of their private debt and its repayment).[17]

The normal order of business was interrupted and would never really recover. Private financial capital, the absolute ruler of a wholly financialized economy, was comatose, but kept on life support through constant injections of public funds. Vast amounts of public spending—unseen since the welfare state's prime—were back in vogue with the neoliberal pseudo-Keynesianism of quantitative easing. Public deficits skyrocketed, only modestly curbed by systematic upward wealth transfers enforced through corporate tax cuts and austerity programs responsible for drastically exacerbated social inequalities.[18]

This had an obvious effect on the status of the real estate market, the central client of architecture since the 1980s. Until 2008 the financial pyramid had rested on the ever-expanding bedrock of property speculation. In 2008, that bedrock dissolved into quicksand, and states began injecting banks, insurance companies, and the stock market with public capital. The profitability of the financial markets was again assured, but now mostly detached from real estate.

Inside the Pyramid

As real estate shrank, so did the number of architectural jobs.[19] A massive downturn in job openings without a matching contraction in architectural education created a material split between academia and the job market it was accustomed to serving. [20] Public or private, normal architecture jobs were increasingly unattainable. Cut off from Ponzi finance, the expanded neoliberal academic field itself became a pyramid scheme.

If the academy functions as a straightforward vendor of degrees, it relies upon external job markets for the value of its product. As those markets ebb away, and public investment in education is cut by austerity policies, architecture schools must attempt to construct alternative job markets for their students. The growth of research funding in the first decade of the millennium, the holy grail of academia's financial survival, was mostly an illusion, lagging far behind the needs.[21] In order to sustain themselves, schools would have to offer jobs to their own students, and morph architectural education into the production of the marketing materials to entice even more students. The academic job market would need to become an increasingly wider slice of the total job market for the discipline.

The meaning of the discipline cannot remain the same in this context as when it worked for industry. Architectural education already shifted from privileging planning and technical competency to the production of aesthetic value added in the 1970s and 1980s. But now, that value added has become detached from construction altogether. The fundamental skill of an architect trained for this market is now the capacity to sell architecture itself as a brand.

The Architecture of the Deal

At once artist, activist, philosopher, and entrepreneur, the architect as synthetic mediator can apparently lay claim to any line of work, so long as architecture still carries brand recognition and the promise of value added. The polymath strategy therefore transforms the architecture degree into a culturalist MBA, helping the graduate leap over the increasingly defunct construction market and directly into pure financial deal-making (or NGO philanthropy, neoliberalism's good cop). Architects abandoning all in the discipline that is useful to society are left with making a business out of selling the cool factor.

But even this cynical professional path is only a ploy, nothing more than marketing for a product to be sold *within* the academy. This is the point where the operative criticism Tafuri attacked—discursive production serving the external market—collapses in on the operative criticism Tafuri failed to notice—discursive production serving academia itself as a market. Publications like *Letters to a Young Architect*, *Medium Design*, or *Architects After Architecture* do little to address this disciplinary crisis other than to reassure the most important remaining consumer base: students. While student enrollment remains relatively high, it hides the underlying crisis, namely that the material prospects of an increasing number of graduates depend not on the

Fig.4 More than 100,000 spectators witnessed the event at Parc de la Villette in Paris in 1992.

reproduction of the profession, but on the reproduction of student enrollment. In fact, the above publications demonstrate to these prospective consumers the correct path to follow: Students must eventually take their turn as the avant-garde of disciplinary hype. They are trained to become the teachers of—and marketers to—future students, moving up the pyramid in a process which only functions to the degree it can draw in an increasing number of newcomers.

Conclusion

Tafuri, along with an entire generation, entered the academic labyrinth in the 1970s. It is clear today that the discipline never left. Architecture's commitment to its autonomous split from reality has finally led it to its historical cul-de-sac. Reading its political-economic genealogy, it becomes clear that the labyrinth is *also* a pyramid—a formal ambiguity that Tafuri would have undoubtedly appreciated. The irony is tragic in the present historical moment when nothing is more urgent than a vast new public construction program—to address at once the enormous and still compounding housing crisis, a necessary social reconstruction (be it of a welfare-state or a socialist society), and the vast range of infrastructure reform and development needed to address the climate crisis. For that, it needs to link arms with a new client yet to emerge. It needs to politicize itself, not in the performative guise of a political architecture of ethics and mores, but through involvement in real politics, and with real political struggles and agents.

Architecture—and architectural education—need a structural course correction, as does society at large. More than that, the discipline needs to become part of a course correction *in* society at large. Without a new progressive social client, a new public building sector—indeed, without a structural transformation of the overall political economy—all that architecture can be is a vain sideshow to a much greater catastrophe. With that new client, it could leave behind the morbid structures it has preserved itself in, and again build something useful.

1 Manfredo Tafuri, *The Sphere and the Labyrinth: Avant-Gardes and Architecture from Piranesi to the 1970s*, trans. Pellegrino d'Aciero and Robert Connolly (Cambridge: MIT Press, 1990).
2 Cf. Manfredo Tafuri, *Theories and History of Architecture*, trans. Giorgio Verrecchia (London: Granada, 1980).
3 Cf. Françoise Very, "The Culture Markets," interview with Manfredo Tafuri, *Casabella* 619–20 (1995), 36–45.
4 Keller Easterling, *Medium Design: Knowing How to Work on the World* (London: Verso, 2021); *Architectural Review* 1474 (September 2020).
5 Harriet Harriss et al., eds., *Architects After Architecture: Alternative Pathways for Practice* (New York: Routledge, 2021).
6 Ibid., 7.
7 Ibid., 8.
8 Klaus, "Letter to a Young Architect," *Architectural Review* 1474 (September 2020), 32–33.
9 This line of disciplinary strategy is most evident in Keller Easterling, "The Activist Entrepreneur," in Dana Cuff and John Wriedt, eds., *Architecture from the Outside In: Selected Essays by Robert Gutman* (New York: Princeton University Press, 2010), 318–23
10 John Rennie Short and Michael Orlando, "No, Covid 19 Won't Kill Our Cities. Here's Why," *World Economic Forum*, February 4, 2021, accessed June 6, 2024, www.weforum.org/agenda/2021/02/covid19-cities-urbanisation-migration.
11 According to a RIBA Survey, in 2017, only 70% of architecture graduates were working in the architectural field a year after graduation, including freelance and part-time work, as well as a substantial number of people with a second job outside of architecture. Only 5% of respondents stated they did not work in architecture by choice. Cf. Royal Institute of British Architects, ed., *RIBA Student Destination Survey 2017*, accessed June 6, 2024, 4, riba-prd-assets.azureedge.net/-/media/GatherContent/RIBA-Student-Destinations-Survey/Additional-Documents/REPORTRIBAStudentDestinationsSurvey2017pdf.pdf.
12 Harriss et al., *Architects After Architecture* (see note 5), 14.
13 Grace Blakeley, *Stolen: How to Save the World from Financialisation* (London: Repeater, 2019), 147.
14 Blakeley notes how the amount of debt in advanced economies rose from 68% of GDP in 1980 to 438% in 2007, and how in 2007 in the UK, funds invested in mortgages alone were equivalent to 67% of GDP. Cf. ibid., 155. Citing Robert Fitch's *The Assassination of New York*, Samuel Stein gives an American example of the preponderance of real estate speculation over the productive economy: "From the 1950s to the 1990s, [New York City] lost 750,000 manufacturing jobs while its land values soared from USD 20 billion to USD 400 billion." Cf. Robert Fitch, cit. Samuel Stein, *Capital City* (London: Verso, 2019), 45.
15 Public housing construction has continuously declined since 1968 and had all but disappeared by the mid 1980s; see Ministry of Housing, Communities and Local Government, ed., *House building: New Build Dwellings, England. December Quarter*

Fig. 5 In 2009, Tschumi's fireworks were restaged for the exhibition *First Works: Emerging Architectural Experimentation of the 1960s and 1970s* at the Architectural Association in London.

2019, Statistical Release, March 26, 2020, accessed June 6, 2024, 9, assets.publishing.service.gov.uk/government/uploads/system/uploads/attachment_data/file/875361/House_Building_Release_December_2019.pdf. The real estate boom would take off in the 1980s but was already on the rise in the 1960s; see Malcolm MacEwen, *Crisis in Architecture* (London: RIBA Publishing, 1974).

16 Michael Speaks, "Theory Was Interesting … But Now We Have Work," *Architectural Research Quarterly*, vol. 6, no. 3 (2002), 209–12.

17 "The panic selling that had started in 2008 had eroded the value of banks' assets to such an extent that many were now effectively insolvent … The problem was capital, not liquidity. In effect, the banks had to be forced to take money from the state in exchange for shares—they had to be nationalised.' Blakeley, *Stolen* (see note 13), 172.

18 In the year 2018 alone, the income of the bottom 20% of earners in the UK dropped by 1.6%, while that of the top 20% of earners rose by 4.7%. 4 million children now live in poverty. Between 2010 and 2016, the number of people sleeping in the streets doubled, and the number of homeless children rose 65%, to a staggering 123,000. The number of unhoused people rose 16% in 2016, with the life expectancy of an unhoused person now at 43 years for men and 47 years for women. At the same time, currency was printed in incredible amounts, breaking all neoliberal rules on inflation control. In 2008, UK banks were given GBP 500 billion, and between 2009 to 2019, USD 10 trillion were distributed as part of quantitative easing schemes between the US Federal Reserve, the Bank of England, the European Central Bank, and the Bank of Japan; see ibid., 172–74.

19 In 2009 unemployment claims by architects instantly skyrocketed in the wake of the crash by 760% in a single year. These numbers might be an underestimation by 30%, and estimates by the construction union UCATT were 100% higher; see Jenny Percival, "Architect Job Losses Soar as Crunch Hits Construction," *The Guardian*, March 20, 2009, accessed June 5, 2024, www.theguardian.com/business/2009/mar/20/architecture-job-losses-construction-unemployment.

20 While the number of undergraduate students in architecture in the Greater London area remained relatively stable at just above 3000 between 2009 and 2015, the number of jobs in the architecture sector fell dramatically from 22,500 in 2010 to 12,200 in 2015 (and from 62,500 to 49,200 in the UK as a whole); see: Mark Wingham, *Working Paper 86: London Architectural Sector* (London: Greater London Authority, March 2017), accessed June 6, 2024, 24, 34, www.london.gov.uk/sites/default/files/architecture_paper_wp86.pdf.

21 Research funding never really constituted a new extra-academic market, but merely a neoliberal "results-driven" twist to leftover public funding for academia. In the 2012–13 fiscal year, between the UK Government, the EU, and mostly public UK Research Councils, at least 77.3% of architecture-related research funding for UK universities was public money; see ibid., 43.

PUBLIC PRACTICE

Finn Williams in conversation with Jakob Walter and Paul Barth

Fig.1

Fig.2

In the wake of the 1980s neoliberal turn, the UK's public sector lost its capacity to plan proactively. The country's authorities have since become increasingly reliant on external consultants, especially as concerns the built environment. To once again invest them with agency and provide architects with alternative pathways to working in conventional offices, Finn Williams and Pooja Agrawal founded the nonprofit Public Practice, which places architects in public-service jobs.

In a 2021 survey of its members, the Federal Chamber of German Architects found that salaried architects working in the public sector earned an average gross annual salary of €67,943, with a median salary of €68,000. For architects with less than ten years of professional experience, the average annual gross salary was €56,400. Approximately 47% of architects over the age of 61 in Germany work in the public sector as employees or as civil servants. For architects under 40, the figure is 15%.

Fig. 1 With around 1,500 employees, the London County Council Architects' Department was one of the world's largest architecture firms in the 1950s.

Jakob Walter: I have recently come across an increasing number of architecture students interested in working in the public sector. Is there any evidence that this is part of a larger trend?

Finn Williams: I think so. It's definitely a trend I have seen throughout my own career: When I graduated in 2007 the possibility of working in the public sector as an architect wasn't even on the radar for many of my peers. Only four decades earlier, in 1976, almost half of architects in the UK were employed in the public sector. But when Margaret Thatcher became prime minister in 1979 and started implementing a host of neoliberal policies, there was a significant shift in who plans and builds cities from public to private sector. That shift continued through successive governments right up to the time I graduated. Then, in the wake of the 2008 global financial crisis, it only got worse. Public-sector planning departments had their budgets cut by 43 percent over a period of ten years. Specialists such as architects were often among the first to be let go as a result of austerity policies. By 2016, the share of architects working in the public sector had shrunk to less than one percent.

At the same time, something else was happening: In the early 2000s, the building industry, particularly in London, was starting to reach new heights. Architecture found itself increasingly at the service of more and more exclusive private interests, operating at ever higher budget levels. When the 2008 crash came and some of that work disappeared, I think it made a lot of people question: "Who am I doing this for? Why did I want to become an architect in the first place?" It's no coincidence that a lot of new offices or collectives challenging established commercial models of practice began to emerge in this period. For me and my peers, this was the point where we started to look around and think about alternatives to working in a commercial practice and making some rich developer even richer. There had to be ways that we could make our skills useful to a broader public. I joined Croydon Council, a local government on the outskirts of London, in 2009, which was a relatively unusual move at the time. Back then, most architecture students' ambition was to work for one of the more established big-name architects in London like Zaha Hadid, Norman Foster, or Richard Rogers. By the time we started Public Practice nearly ten years later, you could sense a real shift in students' interest and willingness to go into the public sector. There's been a real flip in perceptions of what is considered a meaningful career in the meantime.

JW Ricardo Ruivo and Will Orr reflect in this issue on the fact that a growing number of trained architects turn their backs on the profession's primary role. Isn't working in the public sector just another strategy to avoid building things?

FW If you see the role of the public sector as being limited to enacting regulations, you could see joining its ranks as a retreat from designing. But from my perspective, the public sector actually offers architects far more agency as designers than working in a private practice ever could. The typical architect's role today is too often flattened to choosing an aesthetic wrapping for a set of preconditions that will have been decided further upstream, such as location, size, or program. All of those decisions tend to be made before an architect ever gets hold of the brief. If you're serious about making meaningful architecture, you need to reclaim agency over those questions. Now, there's lots of different ways of going about that. There are some architects who are attracted by money and become developers. I chose to follow how political decisions influence the built environment and see how architectural thinking might bring more creativity or spatial understanding to those decisions. For me that's still design and architecture, even if it doesn't involve drawing many lines and it's sometimes as simple as the structure of a compelling brief, the form of a genuinely inclusive participation process with local residents, or a plan for how to guide a particularly important decision through the political process. Why would any of those be things architects shouldn't use their expertise and energy on?

I don't see a fixed line where you suddenly stop being an architect. In fact, I'd say proper architectural work depends on its agency in influencing upstream planning decisions.

JW Briefs should be seen as design problems, too?

FW Yes. And you can design more than briefs. If you look at the best new housing schemes being built in the UK—from Mikhail Riches's Goldsmith Street to Peter Barber's work in London—most of it is being driven by local authorities. In fact, a number of authorities in the UK are building their own in-house design teams as well, consisting of people who aren't just writing briefs and bringing in external consultants, but actually designing the buildings themselves. I think it's counterproductive to try to draw a distinction between an architect who sits in a practice and does lovely drawings and an architect who works in a strategic capacity. Both can be creative and wield a big influence.

JW What led to you cofounding Public Practice? How good is the UK already at public planning?

FW What I saw firsthand working at Croydon Council, and then for the Mayor of London, was that over more than four decades local authorities had systemically lost their ability to plan proactively and be propositional. When faced with budget cuts, their capacities shrank to reacting to proposals from the private sector. After a while, it became clear that the private sector alone wasn't going to meet the real need for affordable housing or tackle social imbalances. So, on the one hand, progressive local authorities had a desire to build back their expertise on the built environment. On the other, the exact kind of people who could help them had a prejudice against the public sector: They saw it as slow, bureaucratic, and unable to provide roles for experts like them. They weren't even thinking of looking for a job in a local authority.

Over the decades, the public sector and architecture had drifted apart, and authorities didn't know what to look for in a candidate. Vice versa, a public-sector job ad didn't make sense to architects. As a result, the public sector had become increasingly reliant on HR agencies who would provide them with staff for short periods of time at unbelievable costs. The agency staff would often move somewhere else after a few months without developing the same commitment to the place or the job as an employee. That was an immense waste of resources.

JW So, you had authorities with the need and the resources to employ people on one side; on the other, you had architects and other built environment professionals who wanted more meaningful work but didn't know how to find it. All they needed was a matchmaker to bring them together?

FW Exactly. After my experience in Croydon, I moved to the Greater London Authority, where I worked together with Pooja Agrawal. We received support from colleagues and the Mayor of London to develop a model for how this could work. We had lots of conversations with authorities about their needs, and with practitioners about the kind of roles they would be interested in. Once the idea for Public Practice emerged, we secured enough seed funding to set it up as an independent social enterprise. It has now matched over 260 people to roles in over 70 authorities, but I think the critical thing it does is creating new forms of practice within the public sector. This isn't just about just filling existing positions; the vast majority of the jobs offered through the program are new kinds of roles. Public Practice also helps to design these job descriptions.

JW How does Public Practice exactly work, and how is your organization structured?

FW Usually, it starts with an authority realizing it needs to do something it hasn't done before or doesn't have the capacity for. The first step is for the authority to apply to Public Practice and prove that task is something they can't already do with their existing staff's expertise. Public Practice isn't a way of displacing existing staff or replacing standard models of recruitment. It's about asking what kind of additional built environment expertise can be brought in. That application is then shaped into an outline job description, and an idea of the kind of candidate they need. Placements are a minimum of twelve months, as that's the minimum time we found you need to make a meaningful difference in the public sector, but there is no maximum. Positions can even be permanent. On the other side of the equation, Public Practice works hard to generate applications from a wide range of built environment practitioners with diverse backgrounds, experiences, and expertise. Those applicants go through an extremely thorough assessment and matching process, which is carefully designed to include aspects of diversity, equality, and inclusion. If the right candidate can be found for a role, they are proposed as a match. And if both the authority and the candidate are happy with the match after meeting each other, the whole placement process gets underway. Successful candidates join a cohort of around three dozen so-called associates, and take part in a twelve-month-long program including a learning and development course which helps them transition into their new role.

JW In a way, you could understand Public Practice as an exchange program from the private sector to the public sector.

FW In a way—but it's for a wide range of professionals including people toward the end of their career. The salaries range from 30,000 to 70,000 British pounds a year, which compares quite well to the private sector. If you think of it as an exchange program, you have to admit it's pretty much a one-way exchange. In the three years I ran Public Practice, over 90 percent of the applicants came from the private sector. And over 90 percent of them stayed on in the public sector after the end of their placements.

Paul Barth: I wonder if Public Practice could be useful in other European countries as well. After all, the UK is not exceptional in the way governance and government expertise have been privatized. Planning authorities are now desperately seeking new employees across the continent. But in Germany, at least, working conditions seem better in the private sector than in government agencies.

FW I believe it could work elsewhere. But it would be worth first testing that presumption about working conditions being better in the private sector. When we started Public Practice, a lot of people assumed it wouldn't work because people coming from the private sector wouldn't accept being paid less. In reality, a lot of people actually got paid more by authorities, while at the same time enjoying better working hours and more holidays. The real issue was less about pay and more about the perception of the kind of work you do if you go into the public sector.

PB How do you convince a local authority to hire someone instead of bringing in an external consultant?

FW When the public sector commissions architects or other built environment consultants, it not only pays the wages of the individuals, it also pays for the profit and overhead of the companies they're associated with, as well as for the whole procurement process. Public Practice would often create new jobs by saying, "Suppose you have a budget of 100,000 British pounds to spend on a consultant to do six months' work. Instead, you could use half of that budget to employ the same person for twice as long directly inside your organization. The public sector needs a shift in perspective. Insourcing is simply better value for money than outsourcing. Of course, it's riskier because it's less flexible, but there's a real value added to having that kind of expertise embedded within an organization over time and having it related to

Fig. 2 Group photo of the architects and planners placed in public-sector jobs by Public Practice in 2022

a place. In-house staff can really get to understand the communities they work for, can collaborate more easily with other disciplines and departments, and at the end of a project, their knowledge is retained.

JW Every year, thousands of people apply for your placement program. You seem to have set off a trend.

FW Well it's not just Public Practice. We're one of a number of organizations out there who are helping to dispel outdated myths about public service—including, for example, the Institute of Innovation and Public Purpose at University College London. There is no doubt that the three dozen people placed by Public Practice every six months are a drop in the ocean of the structural change that needs to happen in the UK's public sector, but our work definitely has an impact beyond that number. There are a lot of people who apply to the program but end up working their way into the public sector through other routes. Conversely, quite a few authorities have thought of creating new roles just because they see that they exist through Public Practice. We never set out for Public Practice to be the only way that authorities recruit. In fact, the sooner the public sector doesn't need Public Practice to recruit staff the better. But there's a long way to go before you get there at a national scale. In its early years the program was focused on London and its surrounding region, but since Pooja Agrawal took over as Chief Executive, it's been scaled nationally. There's a huge need across the UK.

JW Will this bring back the city-run architecture office?

FW At one time in the 1950s, the London County Council Architects' Department was the largest architecture office in the world. Part of me loves the idea, but we live in totally different times. Even if the public sector is now taking more responsibility for the built environment—not just homes, but other kinds of social infrastructure as well—we are far from the political conditions of the postwar-era welfare state. Today's conditions call for a less centralized power. That's why Public Practice is a dispersed network embedded in many different organizations. The first cohorts from 2018 have already worked their way into influential positions in different kinds of public authorities. I suppose if you compared that network of over two hundred people to private-sector consulting agencies, it would be among the biggest multidisciplinary built environment practices in the UK. The difference is that they're not all in one place, but working in places that really need them. And finally, they're working in the public interest, and therefore have more impact collectively than any single big office.

PB The role of the state would then be less in building and more in management?

FW I think this idea of management, maintenance, or care is a really important point. The public sector needs to recover its role as steward of place over time, which is increasingly important as the profession becomes more aware of how much damage every new building is doing to the environment. We need to ask ourselves: How can we make the most of architecture's capacity to create spatial identity and quality through design so that we actually take care of our built environment without resorting to the assumption that change can only happen through demolition and development? I think there's no better place for an architect to practice than the public sector if you want to take on that responsibility.

ASSEMBLE

Assemble in conversation with Olaf Grawert

Fig. 1

Fig. 2

Fig. 3

Fig. 4

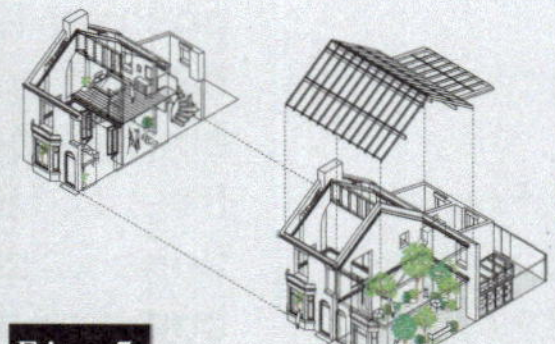
Fig. 5

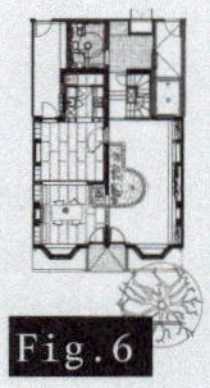
Fig. 6

Fig. 7

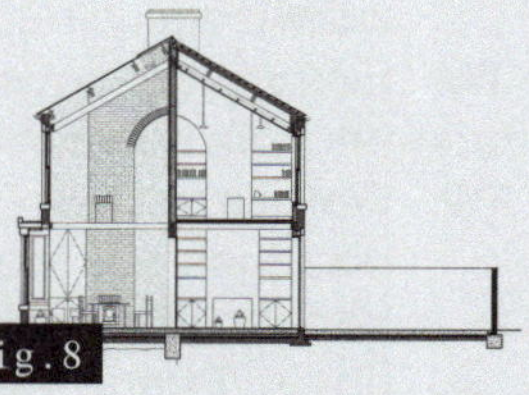
Fig. 8

ORGANIZATION

● OFFICE

Name	ASSEMBLE INDUSTRIES LLP, ASSEMBLE DESIGN LTD., SUGARHOUSE STUDIOS LTD.
Founded in	2010, RESP. IN 2018 IN THE CURRENT LEGAL FORM
Registered in	LONDON
Legal form	LIMITED LIABILITY PARTNERSHIP OWNING SEPARATE LIMITED COMPANIES

● PROJECTS

Total	404
completed	137
public	73
private	64
Current	38

● TEAM

Total	23
by gender	42% M, 54% F, 4% X
average age	30
nationalities	GBR, MNG, DOM, IRL, UKR, RUS, POL, CHE, NZL, CHN
Partners	9
Managing Directors	4
Employees	20
Freelancers	3
Working students	0
Interns	0

FINANCES

● INCOME PER MONTH / YEAR IN EUROS

Total	122,238 / 1,466,854
Construction projects	94,038 / 1,128,450
Teaching	11,284 / 135,403
Other external activities including lectures	6,583 / 78,995

● EXPENSES PER MONTH IN EUROS

Total	68,650
Staff costs	46,682
Average salary (employees / freelancers)	3,009
Average salary (interns)	
Rent and operating costs	10,298
Office supplies	4,805
Insurance, consulting, and legal fees	5,492
Travel expenses	1,373

Olaf Grawert: You are known for your collective approach to self-initiated projects. Tell us about the evolution of what ultimately became Assemble and about its current structure.

Assemble: Assemble is a multidisciplinary architecture and design practice in London. We are structured as a partnership across different disciplines, with each partner owning a series of separate limited companies to undertake the different types of work we do. We started as a collective, and while we maintain a lot of that collectivity, there is now a hierarchy in that there are employees. It's important to us that there's a route for any employee to become a partner. This way, we maintain a democratic approach, albeit with more structure. The aim is for a model that gives stability and viability while reducing hierarchy to a minimum.

OG Do the founders have a special role in the office?

A No. With the partnership model, all partners have an equal stake, and we expect the practice as well as its values to evolve as the partners change. Instead of an equity model, we have a system where you accrue points over time. So, if an asset like the company or one of its buildings were to be sold, the profit from the sale would be distributed to all the people who have contributed to the practice over its lifespan. Those points are kept even after you leave, though they are being diluted continuously because points accrue over time. This applies to the founders, too. The system doesn't deny that the original founders have invested in the practice, even if they move on, but also doesn't privilege control of the company for founders after they've left. If a single shareholder could control 20 percent of the company after they'd left, that would tell new partners coming in that they can never have an equal stake.

OG You describe Assemble as a multidisciplinary practice rooted in paths considered alternatives to architecture as a profession. Is this a function of your different professional backgrounds?

A In the beginning, we started doing a series of projects as volunteers and as a result, the original mix was much more by accident. It was predominantly as a group of friends that we got to work first on the Cineroleum and then on the Folly for a Flyover, two projects from which the practice evolved. This was not planned, but came about through self-organizing. Over time there's been an ongoing conversation about who we employ and how we create the team's mix of skills, which today includes law, sociology, and social anthropology. However, the majority of us studied architecture, and a few worked in crafts. We're always in conversation about how to steer the practice, but for now we're most focused on architecture, design, the built environment, and our workspace. It's a delicate balance between our own aspirations, what work is available, and the pragmatics of what clients find interesting.

OG Was the success of working as a team a stroke of luck or do you have tools to make the collaboration work?

A Both. At first it was luck. We started this as a hobby since there was no sure route to financial stability. This labor of love included loving the dynamic of working with many people and having many conversations. That can be tortuous, byzantine, and glacial. In the end, it's a self-selecting process: Either you like this amorphous and anonymous structure or you don't. It isn't necessarily the best model for working; I wouldn't recommend it to everyone in any situation, but it's how we want to work.

Tools like Action Learning have been quite helpful. It's a way of structuring meetings, constructing group conversations, and tempering embedded hierarchies. We talk about having no hierarchy, but this doesn't account for the differences between newer team members and longer-term members who have more clout. We want to avoid this, and let new voices share interesting ideas. We've also done personal and general reviews as well as workshops on unconscious biases and on how to work with each other in productive ways.

Working as a big group is likely easier than, say, as a group of three, where you can gang up on someone. For instance, with members split five against five on an issue, you have to work out a solution because neither group is radically wrong. If, instead, it's eight against two, it's unambiguous where the weight of opinions lies. Bigger groups mean decisions are clearer. Groups require work, consciousness, and constantly thinking about how you engage others around you.

OG The Cineroleum was your first project, which you also initiated yourselves. How did this dynamism take off and how did your practice evolve over time, especially regarding your projects' importance and profitability?

A It emerged from a general dissatisfaction with the kind of work we were doing as recent Bachelor's graduates going into the recession, and also from a desire to maintain some of the ambition and collective work we had started exploring at university. This led to us directly contacting the landowner of an empty gas station and asking if they'd be willing to let us use it. They gladly

Fig. 2 Two dilapidated row houses were joined together to create the winter garden used by the neighbors. The crumbling intermediate floors were removed and the roof was fitted with a skylight, creating an impressive triple-height interior.

Fig. 1 Granby Winter Garden is part of a larger revitalization project carried out by the Granby 4 Streets Community Land Trust on its own initiative in Liverpool. In addition to organizing community activities in public spaces and street greening, the residents also renovated vacant buildings with the help of Assemble.

Project	GRANBY WINTER GARDEN
Category	CONVERSION
Use	COMMUNITY WINTER GARDEN
Size	150 M²
Architecture	ASSEMBLE
Client	GRANBY 4 STREETS COMMUNITY LAND TRUST
Location	CAIRNS STREET, GRANBY, LIVERPOOL
Year	2016-19

Fig. 3 The interior of the building under construction

Fig. 4 The Granby Winter Garden is where the neighborhood meets informally, tends the plants together and organizes events and gatherings.

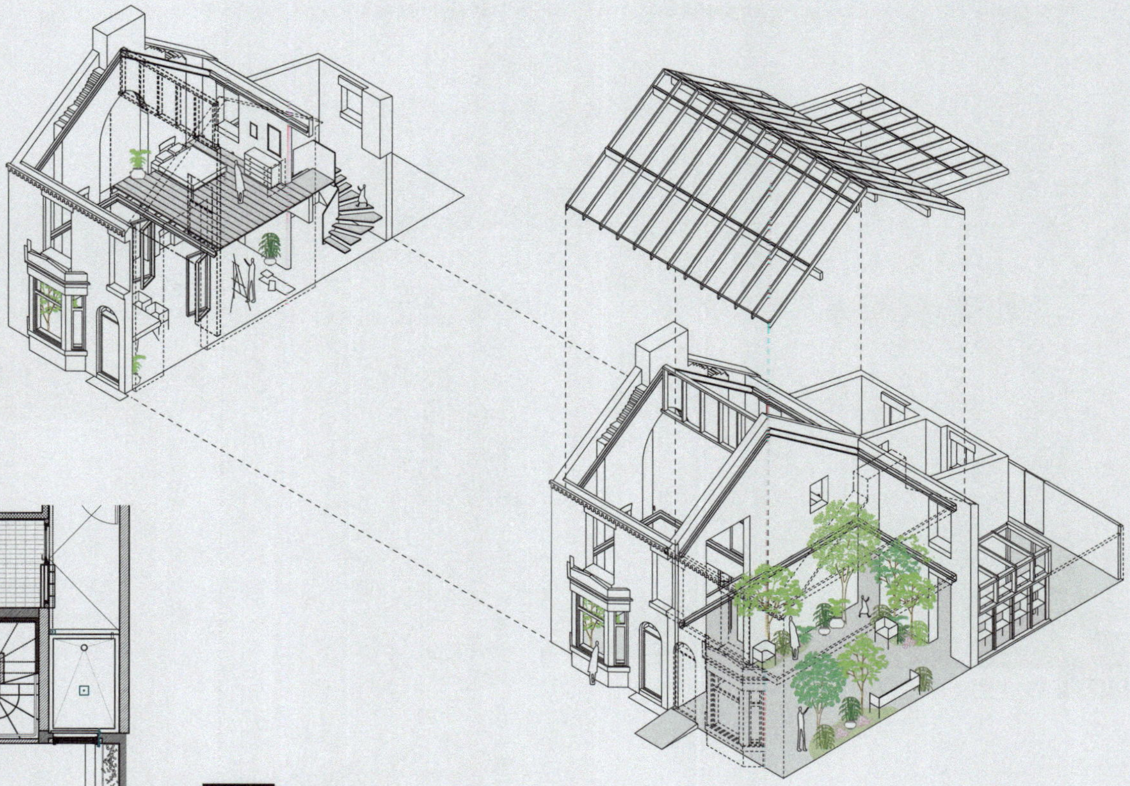

Fig. 5 Isometric view

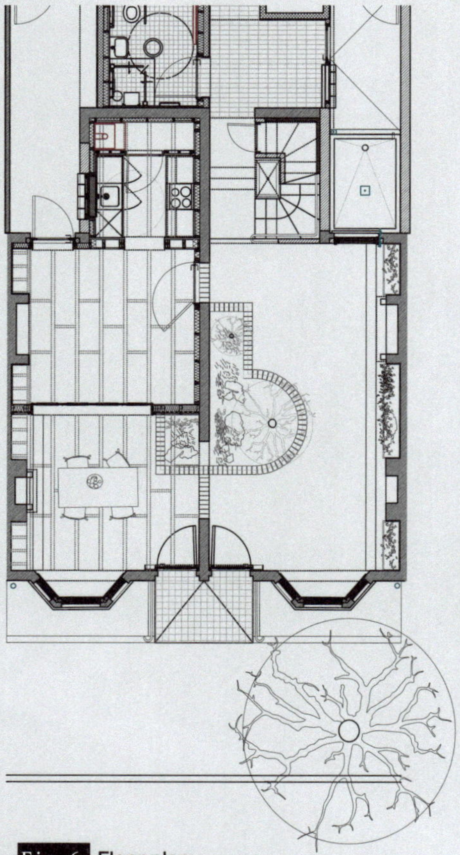

Fig. 6 Floor plan

Fig. 7 Elevation

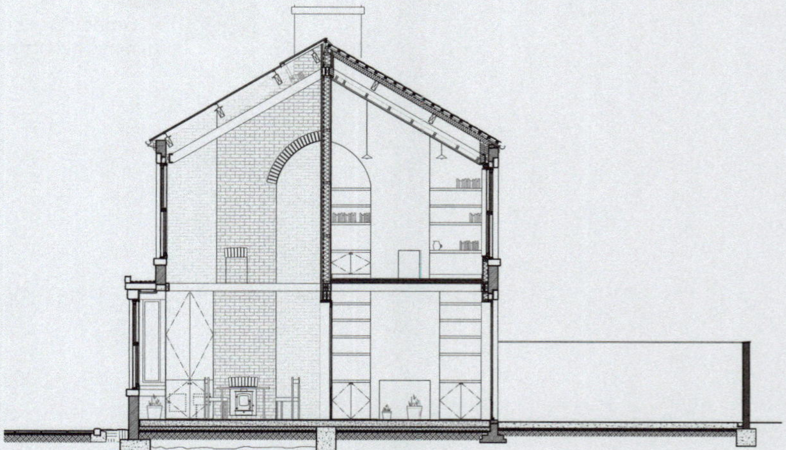

Fig. 8 Cross-section

did, since it had been the site of a housing scheme put on hold because of the recession. We started a fundraising campaign, with everyone paying about 50 to 100 pounds, and got a small grant, which enabled us to make the project happen.

The first proper—i.e., paid—project of scale was a public tender for a series of public spaces in the London suburb of Croydon. It was the first competition in which we were up against more established architects. The planners responsible for this project at Croydon Council, Finn Williams and Vincent Lacovara, trusted us even though we had no prior experience. It's often these kinds of individuals who make a difference; if local authorities stick to a tick-box exercise, things won't change, especially here in the UK. In Switzerland, public competitions have reserved spaces for emerging practices while in Flanders, the *Bouwmeester* system tries to make things more equitable. Here, the system is ruthlessly capitalist and caters to established practices. There's a reason why many internationally reputable UK-based practices build very little public work of scale in the UK itself.

The most important project is our long-term work since 2013 on Granby Four Streets in Liverpool. It gets published the most, was one of the projects cited for the Turner Prize, and was shortlisted for the Mies van der Rohe award. We've evolved a lot in terms of our work through that experience. It is architectural work that is more considerate of context and communal arrangements. But Sugar House Studios, the workspace we inhabit and manage, is just as important. Here, we create affordable workspace for craft production, which we have spun off into a separate company.

OG How do you finance your practice?

A As of now it's almost entirely through projects. Five years ago, one-third of the money came from teaching. That made the difference between surviving on very little and having some level of comfort. As the practice became more stable and robust, it increasingly proved to be the center of gravity. We teach less, keeping only our lecture programs at Cambridge and UCL, as well as our permanent position at EPFL in Lausanne. They're now quite small in terms of income share.

Our earlier model for the practice was much more like a collective of freelancers; teaching was personal. In 2016 we made the big decision to pool all our income, finally making us a practice where everyone was pulling in the same direction. As freelancers, the work was structured in a more libertarian fashion, despite its social aims, until we decided to make our decisions explicitly as a collective.

OG Looking back on your experience over the years, which subject should be taught more at universities?

A Insight into other ways of thinking. Teaching is still incredibly centered on the Global North. This comes with big weaknesses because it prejudices certain ways of thinking and ethical standpoints. The practice could benefit from a socioeconomic education addressing the structures by which decisions and development happen. Rather than learning about these things from an architect-practitioner who only has an understanding of them through their own experience, it would be interesting to have a proper economist give a lecture series. Architects shouldn't try to be economists or politicians, but that doesn't mean that they don't have to understand those dynamics. The same holds true for ecological aspects. Architects pretend to be experts in areas that they're not, and as a result, they don't respect the real expertise in these very important fields.

OG Which advice would give a new generation?

A Don't underestimate your agency. Grit and risk do pay off, especially when you're young and can take risks. It's worth taking them when the consequences of failure are smaller.

Additional copy editing by Sam Ghantous

ARGE.CO

The members of the cooperative Milena Buchwalder, Lorenz Bachmann, Laszlo Blaser, Theresa Behling, and Lukas Fink in conversation with Olaf Grawert

Fig.1

Fig.2

Fig.3
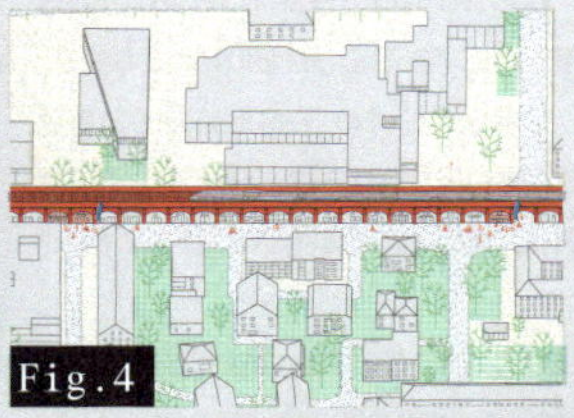
Fig.4
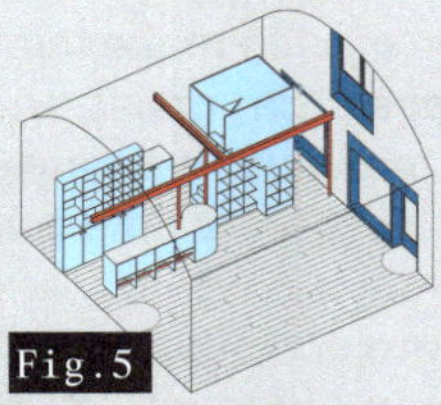
Fig.5
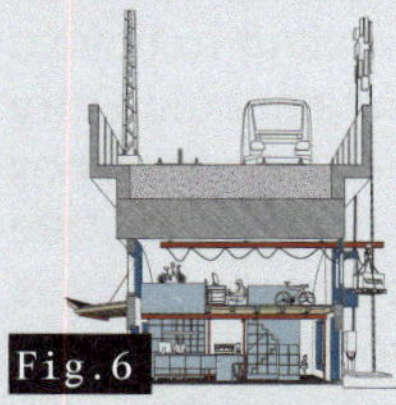
Fig.6
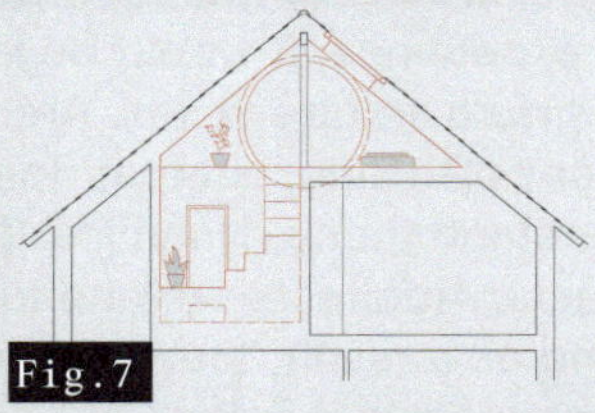
Fig.7
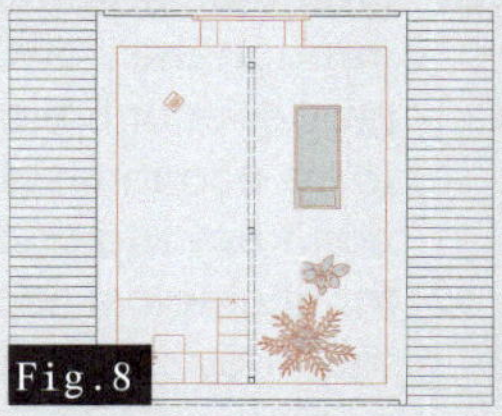
Fig.8

Fig.9

Fig.10

Fig.11

Fig.12

Fig.13

Fig.14
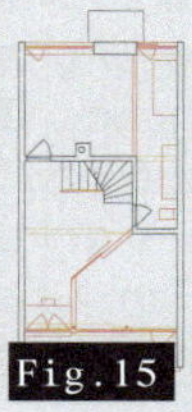
Fig.15

Fig.16

ORGANIZATION

OFFICE

Name	ARCHITEKTURGENOSSENSCHAFT C/O
Founded in	2021
Registered in	ZURICH
Legal form	COOPERATIVE

PROJECTS

Total	55
completed	17
public	17
private	38
Current	23

TEAM

Total	14
by gender	71% M, 29% F
average age	32
nationalities	CHE, DEU, ITA, FRA, NLD
Partners	14, 7,1% EACH
Managing Directors	14
Employees	14
Freelancers	0
Working students	0
Interns	0

FINANCES

INCOME PER MONTH / YEAR IN EUROS

Total	45,517 / 546,198
Construction projects	40,965 / 491,578
Teaching	4,097 / 49,158
Other external activities including lectures	455 / 5,462

EXPENSES PER MONTH IN EUROS

Total	39,781
Staff costs	33,018
Average salary (employees / freelancers)*	2,984
Average salary (interns)	
Rent and operating costs	2,785
Office supplies	995
Insurance, consulting, and legal fees	995
Travel expenses	1,990

* GROSS

Olaf Grawert: On your website, you describe yourselves as a collaborative platform of independent architects; this is followed by a list of fourteen names. Should ARGE.CO be understood as a conglomerate of fourteen independent practices? How does this system function, and how did you come up with it?

Milena Buchwalder: Our collective, Architekturgenossenschaft C/O, i.e., ARGE.CO, emerged from a group of friends, most of whom met while studying architecture at ETH Zurich. A few years after graduating, many of us slowly became self-employed and wanted to start their own practice. So, we asked ourselves how we could collectively establish an appropriate structure without necessarily always having to work together.

Lorenz Bachmann: Most of us finished our studies somewhere around 2017. Afterward, we all gathered experience in the field, and around five years later most of us were working on our own projects. At this point a sort of vacuum emerged, because we all were resisting becoming employees, but also reluctant to create our own limited liability companies. This situation led to the idea of ARGE.CO.

Laszlo Blaser: When we founded ARGE.CO, we weren't primarily interested in economic growth. Instead, we were searching for a lean structure that would enable us to carry out specific individual projects of varying scales. In this sense, the co-op, or *Genossenschaft* in German, is just a legal form for carrying out these projects, not a company in its own right. From the beginning, we agreed that everyone should be able to work on individual projects and preserve their own responsibility. Everyone has their own sub-account, into which fees are deposited and from which wages are paid. A certain share of the wages, however, goes to the collective. This allows us to pay insurance, administration, and bookkeeping fees. Anyone who receives wages thus pays for the cooperative's operations and, indirectly, becomes one of its shareholders. This approach, however, ensures that there is no cross-subsidizing between individual projects, as is typical at architecture firms. In the event a member has no project of their own, they can join someone else's project.

Theresa Behling: At the outset, the idea was entirely pragmatic, but since then we've discovered the structure's inherent programmatic potential. It has encouraged more intensive exchange among us, increasing the desire for collaboration. But this also poses new challenges for our decision-making structure and financing system.

Lukas Fink: Some of our goals and values will likely change again. As we mentioned, at the beginning our focus was on sharing costs. To find the right structure for this, we sometimes sought advice from a trustee. Today we are trying to figure out how we can continue developing the existing structure into a solidarity-based one.

OG You are a cooperative rather than a limited liability company, which is the conventional organizational form for architecture firms in Europe. Among other things, the laws regulating the German equivalent, called GmbH, protect individual shareholders from personal liability by requiring a minimum founding capital of 25,000 euros. Why did you decide to start a co-op instead?

LaB One major difference between a cooperative and a limited liability company is that the former is a voluntary collective of a flexible number of members, whereas the latter has a fixed number of shareholders. Thereby a co-op has the advantage of distributing responsibility across many more shoulders.

LF We are a cooperative of fourteen members, who are ultimately liable collectively for any individual member's actions. This influences the question of personnel growth, which is something we wrestle with a lot.

OG Does that mean you are all individually authorized to function as signatories of ARGE.CO?

LaB Yes and no. The cooperative is liable as a legal entity, with its collective capital. This, however, can be set as low as desired. If everyone puts only one Swiss franc into the collective capital, the company is liable only for the amount in the company account. In principle, we are not privately liable. Ultimately, however, it's similar to a GmbH, where there is a board of directors with authority to act as public signatories.

LoB Only in contracts with clients do we still have individual authority to act as signatories. To ensure mutual trust, we have signed a Memorandum of Understanding. This agreement articulates our ideological principles.

TB A GmbH is quite strict when it comes to incorporating new members. Registering a new member involves administrative overhead and costs. Whereas for admission to a co-op, all that's needed is a share certificate—which is much easier to manage.

OG Do any of you have employees of your own? If so, how would they fit into your system?

MB Not at the moment. But if one of us were to hire an employee, they would become part of the co-op after a certain amount of

Fig. 1 The Veloflott bicycle shop, designed by ANA, is located in one of the arches of a train viaduct from the 1850s that runs from Innsbruck Central Station toward the Saggen neighborhood on the banks of the river Inn. Previously, the premises housed a darts club.

Project	BOGEN 131
Category	RENOVATION, INTERIOR FITTINGS
Use	COMMERCIAL
Size	80 M^2
Architecture	ANA - MEMBER OF ARGE.CO + DAVID FINK
Client	VELOFLOTT GMBH
Location	INNSBRUCK, AUSTRIA
Team	DAVID FINK, LUKAS FINK, TOBIAS FINK
Structural engineering	TRAGWERKSPARTNER ZT GMBH
Year	2020-21

Fig.2

Fig.3 The ground-floor sales area is partitioned by sculptural built-ins. The floor above contains a workshop, storage areas, and an office.

Fig.4 Site plan

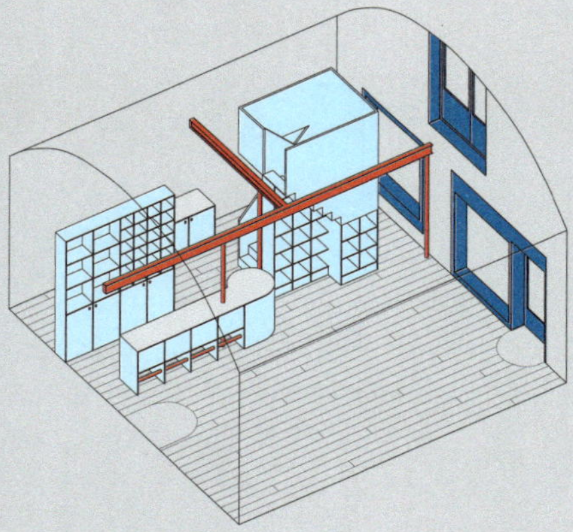

Fig.5 Isometric view

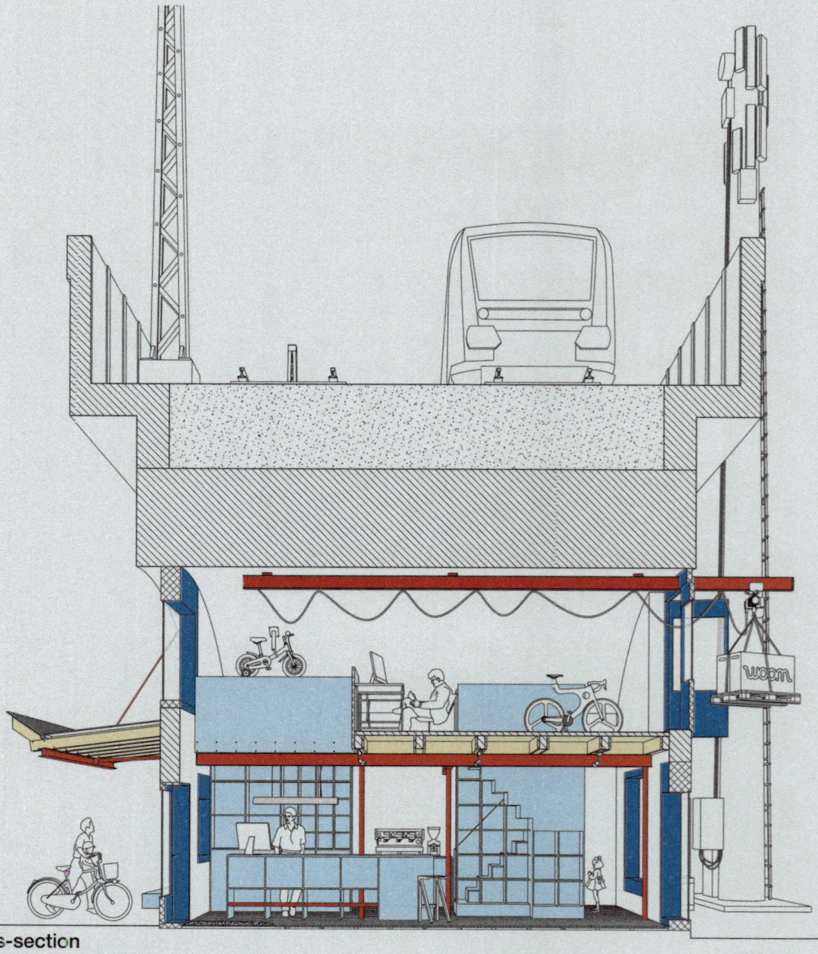

Fig.6 Cross-section
Goods can be delivered directly to the 2nd floor using an overhead crane.

time. We decided on this in advance. What this means is that, the way we work now, there is no hierarchy. There are no employees, only collaborators—or rather: We're all employees.

OG How does this mentality define your concept of solidarity?

LaB I think solidarity was a fundamental starting point. In our case, this means having collective security that enough money is being generated for the administrative tasks while we are able to tackle projects independently. With the cooperative having fourteen members, administrative overhead and individual risk is lowered. And the structure is not dependent on just one person, or a few people. This means that if I don't have a project and end up working for another office, it is very easy to dissolve my working relationship with the co-op without changing its legal structure. And if a new project arises, I can join the cooperative again just as easily.

MB This kind of security comes into play on many different levels. On the one hand, investment costs are much lower if we share them. On the other, we profit from our status as employees, because we don't need to worry about covering social security contributions on our own.

I'd also like to mention that one-quarter of the collective currently consists of inactive members. We differentiate between two contribution models. One is an obligatory annual contribution, the other is determined by the costs incurred by being a practitioner. These include professional liability insurance and bookkeeping, which are pooled and then distributed according to your individual income determined by a quarterly statement. The additional contribution for active practitioners is approximately one percent of this income.

OG It seems that the cooperative brings financial and organizational advantages, but do you need to be on the same page conceptually? Do you have differences in values—both in terms of the type and size of projects, but also the self-image of ARGE.CO itself?

LaB We have always shied away from formulating a concrete approach for the collective. We are more interested in letting the sum of our projects define our approach.

LF As we have already discussed, we are trying to build a solidarity-based structure. This is already a set of values we share. But we also try to separate this from our actual architectural production. In this sense, we are not a conventional firm, presenting itself to the outside world with a particular style. Authorship and responsibility for the output ultimately belong to the respective individuals.

OG During your studies, did the issues you address through your collective already play a role? How does your knowledge acquired back then relate to your current reality?

LF Our knowledge stems more from experiences after graduation, as well as from our frustrations with the existing office structures in which we worked. The question of corporate structure wasn't discussed much during our studies, mostly because it wasn't part of the curriculum. But I've noticed some changes on this front.

MB I can confirm that. I am a few years younger than the average member of ARGE.CO, and I went through different training. My education concentrated more on how to work, less on where or in what position. Sometimes even the product itself became marginal to some extent, leaving room for the adaption of production processes. At the same time, it strikes me that many of us are simply not ready for the conventional reality of the profession. Many of our individual futures remain uncertain, much as they did before. This was another reason for us to team up.

OG What entrepreneurial advice would you give to younger people entering the profession?

MB Join a sociocracy workshop! Making decisions within a group is a complex business. It has worked well for us over the past year. Last week we all attended a workshop where we learned how to work and reach decisions sociocratically. Everyone formulates their individual proposals, and one of the central rules is that consent—i.e., acceptance, as opposed to consensus as complete accordance—is required within the group. To reach consensus, discussions continue until everyone is persuaded and agrees on a proposal. With consent, on the other hand, you ask whether a proposal contradicts the common goal, and whether someone therefore wants to veto it.

LoB For us as well, decisions initially are only binding for half a year. After that, they are reviewed again.

LaB On a more abstract level, I recommend taking responsibility. There's a difference between being an employee, simply punching the clock, and doing work you actually identify with. With our model, you can be both employee and employer, and that has a value in itself.

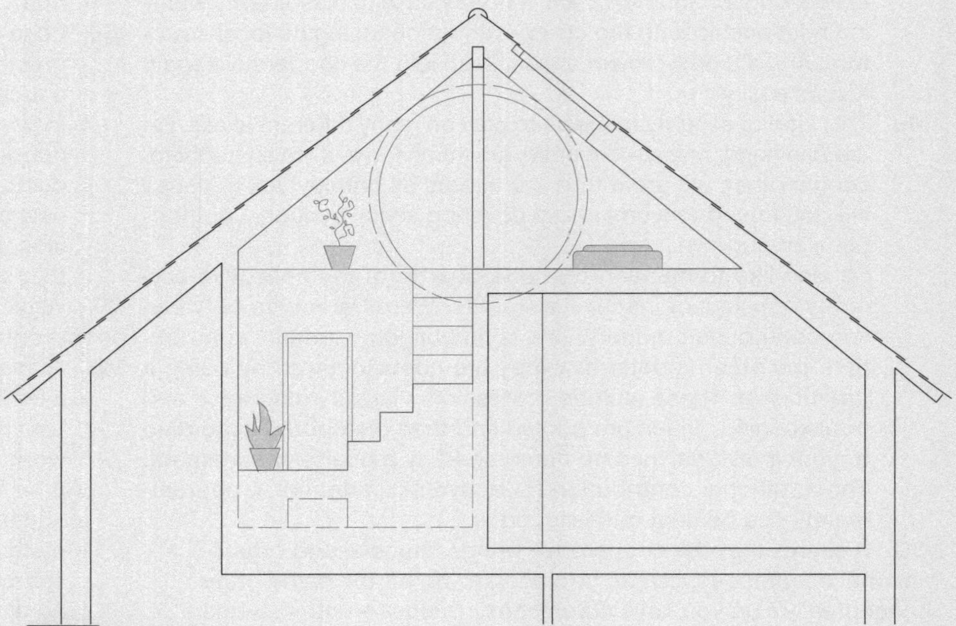

Fig.7 Cross-section

Fig.8 Attic floor plan

Project	ROOF WITH OCULUS
Category	ATTIC EXPANSION
Use	RESIDENTIAL
Size	38 M²
Architecture	LORENZ BACHMANN – MEMBER OF ARGE.CO, ANDREAS REIMANN, RÜDIGER KREISELMEYER
Client	PRIVATE
Location	MEILEN, SWITZERLAND
Year	2018–19

Fig. 9 A storage room lies behind a mirrored door, accessible from the staircase's landing.

Fig. 10 In the attic area, the client wanted a place to retreat.

Fig. 11 The attic expansion was realized in one of a series of single-family homes built at the end of the Second World War as part of a job-creation scheme on a former vineyard in the village of Meilen.

Fig. 12 Haus Barthweg is part of a 1970s row-house estate in Innsbruck that has been renovated multiple times across the years. A new sense of spaciousness was created inside the house through minimal structural interventions.

Fig. 13 Floor-to-ceiling windows connect the upper floor with the recessed balcony

Fig. 14 Interior fittings are kept simple, bare, and open to the possibility of expansion and conversion.

Project	HAUS BARTHWEG
Category	CONVERSION
Use	RESIDENTIAL
Size	150 M²
Architecture	ANA - MEMBER OF ARGE.CO
Client	PRIVATE
Location	INNSBRUCK, AUSTRIA
Team	LUKAS FINK, TOBIAS FINK
Year	2022-23

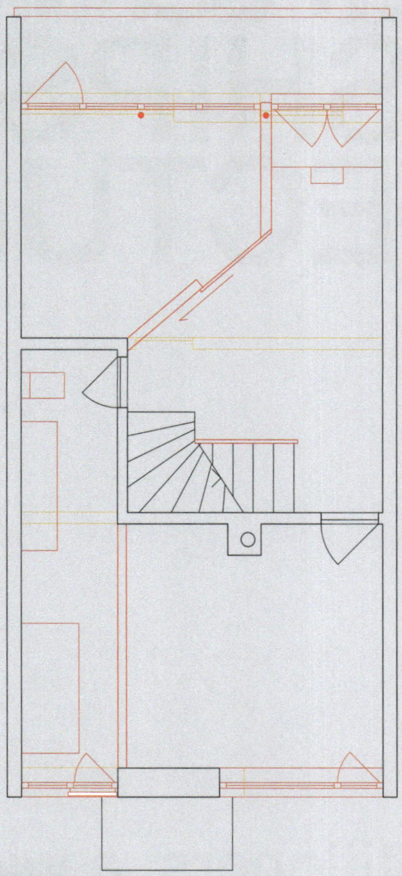

Fig.15 Attic floor plan
The bathroom is drawn out to reach the facade, connecting it to natural light and ventilation in the process. The hallway is transformed into a light-filled multipurpose space.

Fig.16 Section

FORMALIZING WORK RELATIONSHIPS IN ARCHITECTURE FIRMS

Text: Jakob Walter

Among architecture practitioners, a widespread sentiment about workplace dynamics being "unique" —i.e., incomparable—hides the fact that almost every architecture firm contains the same fundamental work relationship between two types of actors as any other workplace: the employer and the employee. The belief that work relationships in the architecture world are somehow different from other fields stems from the fact that both the employer and the employee seem to pursue the same goals. Everyone simply calls themselves an architect. But that may not be the whole truth. While a principal's name on the door ties their personal identity to their practice, that calculation does not apply to those working for them.

In a 2021 survey of its members, the Federal Chamber of German Architects found that salaried architects working in the public sector earned an average gross annual salary of €67,943, with a median salary of €68,000. For architects with less than 10 years of professional experience, the average annual gross salary was €56,400. Approximately 47 % of architects over the age of 61 in Germany work in the public sector as employees or as civil servants. For architects under 40, the figure is 15 %.

The employers, whose names often come up first when discussing the firm, hold significant power. They can distribute the firm's earnings, decide team compositions, and make pivotal, risky decisions in the pursuit of fame or tenure. On the other hand, the employees might not aspire to entrepreneurship, a position in academia, or notoriety; many just want a stable, well-paying job, but often lack transparency about earnings, staffing decisions, job security, and career advancement.

Instruments to negotiate the details of this relationship—and the discrete goals of principals and employees—have been created around the world, some of which could be applicable to architecture offices. Recently, calls for unionization have gained prominence in global architectural discourse. However, a closer look at different models of representation reveals that there's no one-size-fits-all model for improving working conditions for salaried architects.

Unions

Architecture offices, like other businesses, operate within a functional legal framework. This framework includes employment contracts defining the employer-employee relationship and have been supplemented by workplace protection legislation. For example, mandatory injury insurance for workers in Germany dates back to 1884. However, labor legislation varies significantly across countries, making it difficult to apply one country's solutions directly to another. In recent years, calls for unionization have gained prominence across North America. Employees in the architectural sector and other industries have sought—with varying degrees of success—to unionize their workplaces. The most visible such attempt was the ultimately unsuccessful January 2022 campaign to unionize over one hundred employees at SHoP Architects in New York, which garnered significant online and media attention.

Labor unions play a crucial role in defining employer-employee relationships around the world, albeit with significant differences across countries. In some, like the United States, unions bargain directly with the employer to formalize workplace relationships. The Architectural Workers United (AWU) platform exemplifies this by guiding architects to join the International Association of Machinists and Aerospace Workers (IAMAW) and establish company branches to legally represent employees. A few months after the failed unionization attempt at SHoP, a significantly smaller New York-based office, Bernheimer Architecture, was the first to unionize in over eighty years, joining the IAMAW in September 2022.

In contrast, unions in Europe often organize on an industry-wide basis. They negotiate collective agreements (*Tarifverträge*) that apply to all employees in an industry, ensuring consistent working conditions across the market and prohibiting companies from competing by undercutting each other's labor costs. However, architecture lacks specific organizations representing either side, making such agreements unrealistic in the short term. Notable exceptions include the union GPA in Austria and the Union of Architects and Designers (FAOD) in Denmark, both of which have managed to negotiate industry-wide collective agreements with employers.

Professional Associations

Professional associations also play a role in representing architects. But despite various institutions representing architects' concerns before legislators and other actors in the building industry, they usually favor employers, by which they are often led. This is true for organizations such as the Association of German Architects (BDA) and the Federal Chamber of German Architects (BAK), the BNA in the Netherlands, the Syndicat d'Architecture (SA) in France, and the American Institute of Architects (AIA) in the United States.

Muyiwa Oki's election as President of the Royal Institute of British Architects (RIBA) in 2023 therefore represents an anomaly: An employed architect, Oki was elected with the support of the so-called "transition lobby," which operated a successful social media campaign that garnered support among student RIBA members. After winning, he declared banning unpaid overtime for architectural workers as his primary objective. While such attempts at modernizing traditionally management-led institutions such as the RIBA deserve praise, they will not resolve these associations' fundamentally conflicted nature given that they have to represent both employers and employees. They can therefore hardly be seen as the path to better working conditions for architects.

Alternatives

Although professional associations are often inadequate tools to represent employment rights in architecture firms and unions do not hold the same negotiating power in every country, the rediscovery of unions in the US architectural discourse is a reminder for architects everywhere to explore the unique labor protection laws their country has developed and verify if they can be applied to the context of architecture employment.

Another example is the German works council *(Betriebsrat)*. Works councils have a strong tradition in Germany, where they can be formed in any company with more than five employees as guaranteed by the German constitution. These works councils are legally empowered to represent their colleagues and negotiate with employers on workplace issues, have strong rights to be informed about and question employer decisions, and their establishment does not require employer approval. However, their presence in German architecture firms is rare. Despite 38 percent of the overall workforce being represented by works councils in Germany, where they wield significant power in employer-employee relationships, they have notably been overlooked in the architectural sector. As elsewhere, employee well-being in German architecture offices still depends on the employer's good will. In a country where employed architects have recently looked enviously at US efforts to unionize, the chance for their rights to be enforced by a works council goes unused. The fact that the works council represents workers anonymously means that individual employees are taken out of the firing line in disputes with their superiors and at the same time their concerns are given more emphasis. This is particularly beneficial for those groups that suffer from structural discrimination, such as women or young employees. A works council in Germany is helpful in enforcing the reduction and redistribution of workload or better pay for overtime as well as employee-friendly work-from-home and holiday arrangements or training measures. But just as with unions, works councils are not a one-size-fits-all solution: Outside Germany and Austria, they are much less powerful.

Conclusion

Worldwide calls for unionization in the architectural sector fanned an online frenzy at the onset of the decade. However, their lackluster report card should not deter employees in architecture firms from seeking better working conditions through formalized relations with their employers, especially in times of economic uncertainty. Unions may seem like the only viable path in North America, but might not be the most promising avenue in other parts of the world. While unions have been at the center of a mostly online discourse, every country presents its own options.

Looking into your country's unique labor laws is worthwhile. Maybe works councils are the preferable option to negotiate your rights as an employee, maybe unions are. But there might also be another pathway altogether yet to be discovered and put to use for architects: a tool for constructive working conditions in architecture firms that makes sure the goals everyone in the office is working toward are not just a single person's aspirations. As the example of the German works councils shows, it might not require much to gain a negotiating position. Maybe that position has been there all along. It just hasn't yet been discovered by our profession.

TRUSTING IN ALTERNATIVES

Gabu Heindl in conversation with
Jakob Walter and Sascha Kellermann

Fig. 1

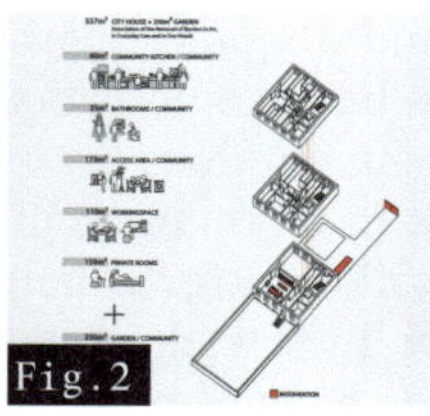
Fig. 2

Fig. 3

Fig. 4

Fig. 5

Institutions of the welfare state have been experiencing the impact of funding cuts for a number of years now all across the Global North. This trend has had its effects on architecture practices as well. Is there a way out of the neoliberal utility paradigm that takes economic profit as its sole objective? Is it possible to counter it with new economic and architectural models? A conversation with Vienna-based architect, urban planner, and author Gabu Heindl.

Greece (60%), Italy (56%), Finland (54%), Croatia (54%), Romania (54%), and Sweden (53%) have the highest share of women in the architectural workforce. → The proportion of women is lowest in Slovakia (25%), Austria (24%), and the UK (27%). → In Germany, women make up 42% of the workforce in the sector. 47% of European architects are partners, directors, or sole practitioners.

Fig. 1 The performative intervention titled *Fitting* was based on an idea by Gabu Heindl and brought to life in 2011–13 in Vienna, Paris, Graz, and other cities to raise the subject of the appropriation of public space. The concept and choreography are by Willi Dorner.

Jakob Walter: Your practice rests on various pillars: You are head of the Architecture Cities Economies department at the University of Kassel, where you focus on alternative economic models; at the same time you're a practicing architect and founded your own company, GABU Heindl Architektur, in 2007. What impact does your work in the academic context have on your architectural practice?

Gabu Heindl: I try wherever possible to translate my political aspirations into my practice's output. From early on, back when we were young architects, we decided for instance not to work on any suburbanizing single-family homes, nor on any senselessly (self-)exploiting projects.

To the contrary: In 2016, we supported the Viennese nonprofit Verein für die Barrierefreiheit in der Kunst, im Alltag, im Denken (Association for Accessibility in Art, in Everyday Life, and in Thinking) in converting a three-story, turn-of-the-century building into a single-kitchen house for a large flat-share based on solidarity; we called it the *Intersektionales Stadthaus* (Intersectional Townhouse). Like its members, this nonprofit association has hardly any money, so most of the users had to move in to what was still a building site as they could not afford to rent two places, their old apartment and their share of the new house, in addition to funding the construction work. As for fees, we decided that everyone on the construction site would earn exactly the same hourly wage, independent of whether they were working primarily on the construction or on the computer. In that constellation it was beautiful to see how consciously everyone treated other people's hours.

The nonprofit also put into practice an alternative rental model based on solidarity. Instead of a fixed rent per square meter, everyone pays only as much as they can afford and gets as much space as they need. Hence, a wheelchair user who needs space to be able to move around lives next to someone who can fit her office and bedroom on a much smaller footprint. The former can pay 200 euros a month, the latter 600. Even if, at first sight, this doesn't necessarily have much to do with the economy of our office as a company, it is absolutely crucial for us to decide whom we work for and how the client looks at the value of that work.

JW This way of practicing architecture is not something every company can afford to do. What are working conditions like in your office?

GH In Austria, there's a collective bargaining agreement for architects that sets minimum wages across the industry; of course, we pay that. Some commercial offices can undoubtedly pay more. What an architecture practice such as mine can offer, with a certain ethical claim, is work that, hopefully, is actually meaningful. Whether or not you are able to afford a certain type of practice is a matter of social policy. Even in a comparably affordable city like Vienna, an office like mine faces the dilemma that the cost of living is steadily rising for the members of my team, and many newcomers to the city have no other option but to take the expensive rentals they are offered on the private market. Your career chances essentially depend on the respective social security systems. If these aren't in place, you can call on people to be critical, radical, and self-confident as much as you want and tell them not to accept every project out there—at the end of the month, rent is due for all of us. Only when you don't have any existential fears can you actually be free in your own professional choices. Only then can we all start to focus more on what issues we want to work on. Do they seem meaningful and are they in line with our own political convictions? And can we, as architects, do work for which there is no lobby? With this in mind, I very much hope that the community of smaller offices continues to exist.

JW Where does your political awareness stem from?

GH My basic trust is definitely due to the fact that I grew up in the Austrian welfare state at a time when there was a consensus that no child which needed help and assistance would be left behind. I was always able to co-finance my education through stipends and scholarships—from school, to high school, to university—and I would still want every child to get that kind of financial support today. It provided access to education independent of your social class, and that sort of thing produces a sense of security, even if many people look at it today—after the dismantling and devaluation of the social security system—and think that security is guaranteed above all by solid financial backup from your family. At any rate, my generation gained self-confidence through what was essentially unconditional support from the state. But we shouldn't look back at that period with too much nostalgia, either, particularly as regards the discrimination of marginalized groups.

Sascha Kellermann: It is precisely with your activist mindset that you seem to find clients who want to build projects like the Intersectional Townhouse. Such alternative architectural concepts first need to be developed, and the overtime invested in that development has to be financed somehow. What does an acquisition strategy that enables you to work outside the contradictions you describe look like?

GH It's not as if I simply give activist groups my business card and say: "Hi there. I'm a political architect." It's more about slow processes of building confidence. In my early days of self-employment, I took part in conventional competitions, partly because we wanted to gain a foothold in the public discourse as an office—knowing full well that we could realistically expect to win one in ten of them. That said, the other nine proposals can be turned into a study or a project that also garners recognition. It has always been important to me to attend and organize lectures and debates, something I have frequently done since I first started teaching at TU Graz. That's where I found out that it is interesting to help shape the discourse in addition to designing buildings. I was a member of panel discussions on multiple occasions. At some point, after I had won a competition for a school I then built, the Austrian National Real Estate Company

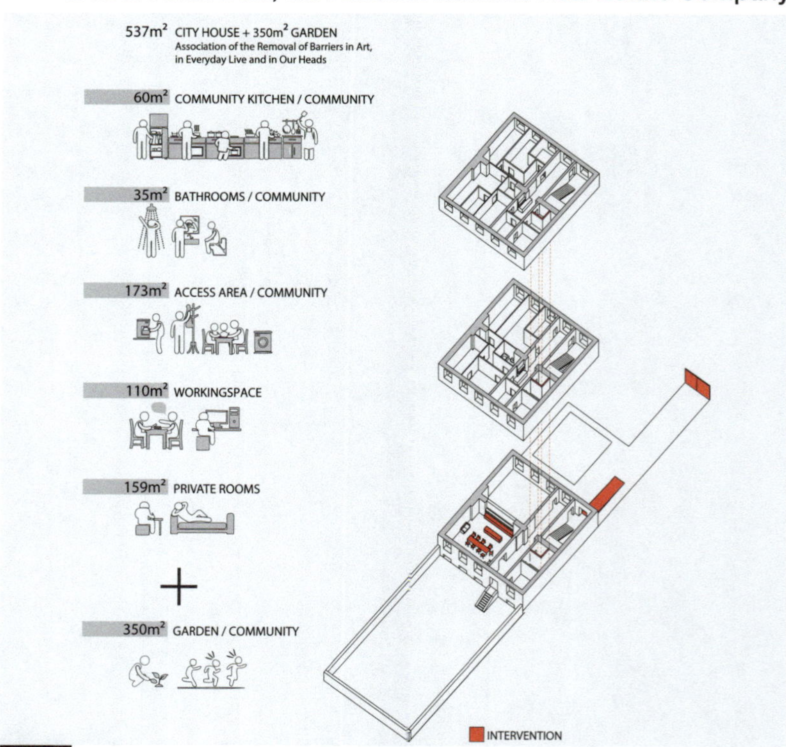

Fig. 2 GABU Heindl Architektur, Intersectional Townhouse, Vienna, 2016
Spatial subdivisions for living together collectively

asked me to become a member of its advisory council. That was at a time when there were fewer and fewer public competitions. This position allowed me to advocate for keeping those doors open. I believe it is important for us to play an active role in public committees and in urban planning.

Many of the NGOs and self-organized groups with whom I work today have not always had the best of experiences with state-run, top-down organizations and urban planning and are often very skeptical in this regard. It required time and effort to create a feeling of trust and make it clear that not all urban planners work on behalf of private interests in the pursuit of profit. Only when such trust exists will people contact you in search of support in making their project a reality—and sometimes without actually having much of a budget. Often, our support in the beginning of any project is to explain how to realize it economically: Where can the clients apply for funding? What are the real costs? We explain that architects cannot work for free, but that architects' wages are not the lion's share of building costs. On the contrary: If we make smart choices during the planning phase, the building itself will often be cheaper. It is precisely when budgets are tight that a dedicated architect can save you a lot of money.

JW The sums people inherit from their parents are growing with each generation, and just as you set ethical standards for your work, some heirs set ethical standards for their wealth. Surely there's an opportunity here to divert this money into alternative architectural projects.

GH That was exactly the case with the Intersectional Townhouse. The owners had inherited some cash from their Nazi grandparents and initially felt they didn't want to touch money from such a source. But in the long term, the question was no longer *whether* to use the money but rather *what for*. They eventually decided to use it toward a meaningful, non-speculative solidarity project. This touches on the fundamental question of the historical distribution of money and thus also the question of how to set a redistribution project in motion—on a small scale, at least. To my mind, it is crucial to make it clear to people that they can invest their money in a feminist, progressive project while also safely investing it, since it is nonetheless parked in real estate. Nonprofit projects like these are also capital investments. Yet, the additional parameters make the difference: Whether people have expectations of a higher return—and the focus is on value added in line with market principles—or whether the value added of a project is actually of a more social or ecological nature instead. As architects, we have the chance to support alternative or collective forms of ownership and possession.

SK Would an ideal working environment for architects not be one where the staff do not have to constantly think about how to realize their political ideals on the side? Shouldn't the tasks be socially meaningful *per se*, so that it would be unimportant what personal mindset I bring to work?

GH Sure, it would be great if that were the reality in both society and the architectural profession. But the need to position yourself will remain. We tried to respond to calls for a better working environment by introducing a four-day workweek, among other things. It's something we have been doing in my practice for some time now, as I think it's important to have three full days for other things—days when everyone can decide for themselves what they want to do, whether you want to lie on the couch for three days or work on other projects during that time. For me personally, it's important to teach and to write in addition to my work as an architect. Teaching and writing interact productively with work on a construction site.

Fig. 3 GABU Heindl Architektur, Intersectional Townhouse, Vienna, 2016
In collaboration with Verein für die Barrierefreiheit in der Kunst, im Alltag, im Denken, this three-story house in a courtyard in Vienna's Ottakring district was transformed into a single-kitchen house in a cooperative planning and a collective conversion process. It houses a large flat-share organized around the principles of social solidarity.

JW On the one hand, you advocate for a culture in which small practices rival for competitions in what is essentially a free market. On the other, you emphasize the safety function played by the welfare state; you're against public–private partnerships; you teach alternative economic models. How do you square free competition with restriction imposed by the state?

GH Architecture competitions—as a cultural praxis which repeatedly proves that there are many alternative routes for developing any particular site—are something I continue to find persuasive precisely for that reason: In an age when people constantly say there is no alternative to the way things are going, architects are producing alternatives. The major dilemma of competitions is that the labor invested is seldom paid for, and that the contributions—as contributions to a discussion—simply get lost in the ether. It would, for example, make sense to hold public jury meetings and create processes that can trigger a democratic discussion if we as planners have already laid the foundations for that. My take on competitions is therefore somewhat ambivalent. Of course, there's a vast amount of unpaid work and ideas that get lost, but we need constructive debate around proposals on how we want the future of our cities to look like. If every place could develop in so many different directions, why are so many projects still developed in the same way? We need to find a way of expanding the public discussion as it relates to a collection of ideas while reducing the economic competition.

JW Can you imagine a large-scale solution as opposed to this individualistic approach? One of these was the London County Council Architecs' Department, a large structure established by the welfare state, the likes of which could perhaps be more effective than competitions or nonprofit work.

GH It is difficult today to really believe in this kind of centralized, government- or municipality-run structure. But smaller practices like mine often already work in shared structures. We share space and the office infrastructure—that's already everyday practice. And in the Vienna office world, at least, there is an increasing number of projects where practices collaborate with one another, structured around loose networks. More formal networks generate a kind of collective knowledge that can, for example, be tapped via a mailing list, just as can information on potential partners, specialist planners, and tradespeople with whom one could collaborate. Now that can't really be equated with a truly collective work process, but it is nevertheless a collective organizational tool. It was in the wider context of one of these networks, the IG Architektur (interest group of architecture practitioners), that the organization of something like a small architects' strike happened: The City of Vienna held a competition for a large school campus to be developed as a public–private partnership. Ironically, they wanted me to join the jury, but I didn't want to give them a leg up and declined. Subsequently, many participants, instead of submitting competition entries, handed in beautifully designed protest posters bearing the slogan "We won't design your PPP school!" In the end, some practice nevertheless won the competition, but we did manage to draw the City of Vienna's attention to the fact that we architects are organized in a quasi-trade union and collectively refuse to plan such a neoliberal project. It was thanks to this existing network that architects were able to organize the refusal so swiftly.

Fig. 4 A competition held by the City of Vienna in 2015 for a school campus sparked a great deal of criticism from planners, as it was supposed to be developed as a public–private partnership. Many architecture practices responded by submitting protest posters instead of designs.

JW The opinion that the professional practice of architects as a whole needs to be fundamentally questioned has grown louder recently. Why are so many young people still studying architecture? Given the plethora of current crises, should we even still be building things? Where should we be directing our efforts instead?

GH I would by no means contend that there are too many young people studying architecture. Actually, there are too few. After all, we're talking about our built environment, and that, to paraphrase a quote by Margarete Schütte-Lihotzky on architecture, is something that affects everyone's lives! In this light it would make sense for a large number of people to understand the issues at play. The misunderstanding here tends to stem from the fact that people think studying architecture must invariably have something to do with building new buildings. As a professor of urban planning and now for ARCHITECTURE CITIES ECONOMIES, I have always been speaking of urban *conversion*. To a large extent, going forward everything will be about converting, expanding, improving, and renewing the existing. Of course, there will also be new buildings, but we will focus much more carefully on what really needs to be built anew and what can be converted, and how we can protect resources in the process. We'll need a lot of creativity to tackle the repairs to the legacy of modernist urban spaces, for example. The problem, though, is that there still are entire generations of students who graduate from university having only focused on building anew. Now that has to change, meaning we should also instill in students the self-confidence to go down these new paths. Which brings us back to the question of how to make a living. All those students who are asking today how they will be able to sustain themselves and their practice in five years' time, given rising rents, should find out that their training offers an invaluable tool. After all, they are the ones who can create alternative living spaces, who can plan the adaptive reuse of vacant spaces, even if they may need to initiate the projects themselves.

JW For their own use, too?

GH Yes, why not? We will need to be active on many different levels if we are to set in motion a paradigm shift. That is why I want my students not only to know how they can design affordable and ecological housing, but also how they can fight for the opportunity and the right to access project developments—not just for themselves but also for everyone else. If we want to counter the despair among students, we need to highlight the agency they already have. To understand their own power, they need to have a sense of how the built environment relates to its underlying economic, ecological, and social conditions, as only then will they themselves later be able to explain this system to others. And we have to make clear to them that, during their studies, they can try out creating the visual representations of what they want to champion politically. We can all use our visualizing and Photoshop skills toward a particular goal; it is, however, a matter of choosing that goal. We can, for instance, produce drawings that present the potential embedded for society in buildings which have been earmarked for demolition. But if we are not able to make that alternative visible, if we cannot convey that alternative to others, then there will be nothing to talk about, and the demolition of too many buildings will probably continue.

Fig. 5 GABU Heindl Architektur, *Draußen im Gefängnis* (Outside in Prison), Krems, 2009–11
In this art-in-architecture project, the men's prison yard at a correctional facility in Krems was redesigned to feature leisure and sports zones.

SK In other words, your aim is to give your students the tools to realize their own political ideas in the built environment?

GH I feel that the world is lacking in reified ideas and alternative scenarios, and that's something we must try and change politically. Now, we don't all have to go into politics, of course, but as architects we have to become more insistent—and more radical. We need to be able to convey, in both visual and economic terms, what we want to change in the world. That way, we can highlight credible alternatives to the structures of the current real estate market. As chair for architectural design and critical economy, I ask the students for a good design proposal, but also for the development of the corresponding economic models to finance their alternative for a certain place. And we likewise highlight how we can benefit from the existing creativity of potential clients and how, together with the latter, we can work to create a city that is more equitable. Architects who call themselves "not political" actually take a very political stance, if you ask me, albeit one that is fatal because they give up on the possibility that anything might change and therefore contribute to maintaining the status quo of the relations of production in architecture.

SK I would contend that the vast majority of architects would claim to be unpolitical.

GH It is impossible to avoid being political. If we believe that we can't intervene in anything, then we just abet the way things are. The fact that the younger generation is, once again, increasingly politicized shows that many people do not subscribe to that claim. If I were a student today, given the massive crises I, too, would fundamentally question the validity of the current curricula. As faculty, we face a didactic challenge, namely to teach students how they can understand, design, and create socioecologically sensitive spaces in a system in need of more radical critique, especially since there is no guarantee that they will actually be able to put these skills to work toward a more ecologically, socially, and economically just way. Yet, our task is to give them the confidence that the architectural profession continues to be meaningful. And while we're at it, I'd like to take the opportunity to reject the romanticization of everyday office work. I, too, spend a lot of time gazing at Excel spreadsheets. But if that's part of what has to be done for a project to succeed—to experience how, for example, the users of the Intersectional Townhouse create a beautiful space for marginalized people to have the space they want while paying what they can afford—then that's definitely worth the effort.

NATURE OF HOPE

INTERNATIONAL ARCHITECTURE BIENNALE ROTTERDAM 2024

Text: Saskia van Stein, Janna Bystrykh, Hani Salih, Noortje Weenink, Alina Paias, Catherine Koekoek

Fig.1

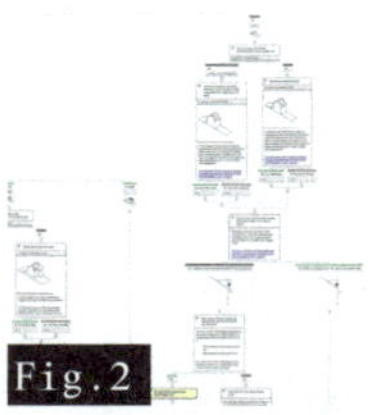
Fig.2

Fig.3

Fig.4

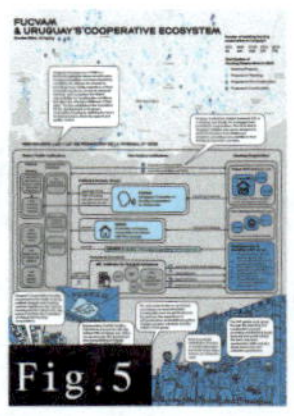
Fig.5

Fig.6

Fig.7

Fig.8

Fig.9

Fig.10

Fig.11

16% of European architecture practices participated in a competition in 2022. → Belgian firms work an average of 1,903 hours each year on competitions, while Danish firms invest just 95 hours. → Austrian firms invest an average of €214,261 (incl. staff costs) in competitions per year; Italian firms invest just €4,154 (incl. staff costs). → The average prize money is €120,960 in Norway and €1,756 in the Czech Republic.

Liaison-Building as a Cultural Strategy

Saskia van Stein

The disciplines of architecture, landscape design, and urban planning play a substantial role both in the genesis of the present accumulation of socio-ecological crises and in the radical changes necessary to address this planetary condition. Despite the fact that architecture as a discipline is a meaningful proponent and fabricator of alternative environments, the leeway architects as a profession actually possess to create better conditions of coexistence is currently highly limited. Rather than committing resources to economically, socially, environmentally, and materially sustainable practices by championing regulations and standards that could drive beneficial change, the political-economic framework at the national and supranational levels across the Global North continues to uphold a construction industry responsible for 40 percent of greenhouse gas emissions and one-third of all waste produced globally.

Since its first edition in 2003, the International Architecture Biennale Rotterdam (IABR) has drawn attention to architectural culture in a broad sense, and in particular to the value of analysis, research-based design, and the importance of producing alternative models. While historically, architecture has been narrated in triumphant terms, lionizing so-called starchitects and revering spectacular objects, this eleventh edition of IABR is a discipline's reflection on its complicity in processes of material extraction, real estate speculation, labor exploitation, toxic waste production, and CO_2 emission. As such, IABR functions as a platform to participate, host, make, learn, and engage with the disciplinary self-interrogation of architecture.

As the title *Nature of Hope* suggests, the 2024 IABR's stance is, however, not one of resignation. Rather, the Biennale takes up Immanuel Kant's conceptual question "What may I hope?" through an architectural and territorial, practice- and materials-based lens. Within this research frame, the curatorial team, consisting of Janna Bystrykh, Catherine Koekoek, Alina Paias, Hani Salih, Noortje Weenink, and myself, has built and initiated multiple liaisons, culminating in the main exhibition, an assembly space called "Practice Place," twenty-six "Botanical Monuments" spread throughout Rotterdam, in addition to an extensive public program. As an ensemble, *Nature of Hope* works with an understanding of the inseparability of "nature-culture," generating public awareness of the real risks of the current polycrisis, while showcasing design-based perspectives that move beyond quick-fix solutions and toward substantial socio-ecological transformations.

Nature of Hope highlights architectural propositions that critically reevaluate traditional methods, operate beyond disciplinary confines, and minimize environmental impact while maximizing material efficiency and resilience. However, this transitional moment for architecture calls not only for reducing the carbon footprint of built objects by transitioning to new, bio-based materials, but rather for the mainstreaming of a systemic and circular understanding of a broader construction economy.

The Dutch landscape, for one, has been the negotiating table for many fundamental changes linking space to the forces that define it. This situation is best captured by the term *polderen*. At once a noun designating the large swaths of land in the country protected from the sea by a system of dikes and a verb denoting the activity of discourse and consensus-seeking, the term reflects the technocratic, rationalized origin of the Netherlands—i.e., its territory—on the one hand, and its consensus-oriented democracy—i.e., its map—on the other hand. A series of farmer-led protests in the Netherlands, which started as a way to air grievances over a national directive seeking to halve the country's livestock, and which grew into large-scale protest movement against top-down planning, came to a head in 2022. These protests can be understood as a particular instance of a more pervasive schism between territory and map, as stakeholders experience pressure under transitional reforms. It was against this backdrop that the mission of IABR 2024 started to emerge: The obfuscation of complex, systemic issues and false reactionary promises of nostalgia as implicit admissions of a futureless vision draws attention to the urgency for cultural initiatives to elaborate alternative desirable futures for the way we share space. Simultaneously, the demands for fundamental shifts in design practice must also be reflected in an altered role for cultural institutions. No blueprints are readily available for either of those tasks. We begin, therefore, from the bottom up, step by step, practice by practice, learning how to forge paths in entangled conditions, without the naïvely hubristic certainty of a masterplan.

Against a climate of schism, IABR approaches its mandate through liaison-building at various scales of what one might consider locality. In a rapidly changing, risky world, exhibitions are vital platforms for education, cultural exchange, and innovation. Beyond the event every two years, the institution can ensure enduring support of burgeoning practices, agents, architects and designers, ideas, and experimentation that follow very different temporalities. The work of liaison-building is not only a step toward dissolving the dichotomy between proximity (here) and distance (there), it also constitutes tangible efforts at a material and intellectual strengthening by trying to distribute the "load" of our times more equitably. From policy-making, to brick composition, to self-repairing concrete, these different prototypes—whether material, conceptual, activist, or legislative—play an essential role as structural supports in the renovation of our field. For *Nature of Hope*, we drew inspiration from German philosopher Ernst Bloch, who wrote: "The work of [hope] requires people who throw themselves actively into what is becoming, to which they themselves belong." We took this call literally by actively throwing ourselves into the future of the architectural practice, by creating a space of collective, sometimes complicit, belonging. Climate justice can only germinate when materials and ideas across geographies, histories, and disciplines such as our own, can invent ways of interfacing beyond their locales. If any desirable, viable, and joyful future is collaborative in structure, its medium is the liaison.

Fig. 1 Installation view

Learning from Land-Based Practices
Janna Bystrykh

The term "regenerative" first became associated with spatial practices in the 1980s in the United States. In the context of organic farming, it captured attempts at improving soil health and biodiversity and has since grown into a holistic approach seeking to restore soils, rebuild local communities, and repair systems of food production. Regenerative farming connects different scales, from small vegetable producers to large-scale precision agriculture, organic farms, ranches, and many more. Although no certificate codifies adherence yet, regenerative agriculture is both a movement and a practice based on five shared principles focused on improving and maintaining soil health, including the maintenance of soil coverage, limits on chemical or mechanical soil disturbances, a focus on the biodiversity of crops, keeping living roots in the soil, and the integration of livestock grazing into crop-farming cycles. A growing number of farmer-led organizations focused on building and sharing practice-based, ecological, and indigenous knowledge has emerged across the United States and internationally, offering important primary input for academic research on soil health and food systems and for governmental agencies responsible for regulating agriculture, food safety, and conservation.

A similar knowledge exchange does not yet seem to exist between architects and built- and natural-environment regulators. In 1996 landscape architect John T. Lyle applied the spatial concept of regeneration to the realm of design, linking buildings and the built environment to their potential impacts on ecosystems and human well-being.[1] Trying to approach architecture as a regenerative practice—as the combined situated, architect-defined, and profitable best practices for designing, constructing, and managing the built environment and contributing to the restoration of ecosystems—could help accelerate a comprehensive shift toward a just and ecological practice of architecture. This can only be achieved by integrating collective, practice-based professional knowledge, and fostering its exchange with other fields of expertise.

Our relationship with nature should be informed by more than its capacity to store carbon. A 2021 United Nations report found that while many actions currently aimed at mitigating climate change have fewer positive outcomes for biodiversity than expected, those aimed at preserving and restoring biodiversity generally have a net-positive effect in terms of achieving climate goals.[2] Climate action today often solely focuses on reducing carbon emissions through technical solutions and shifting to renewable energy, preserving and expanding carbon sinks, and emission trading schemes, which, while certainly having a positive impact, frequently reveal themselves to be detrimental to biodiversity. Similarly, shifting the focus away from simply reducing emissions to strengthening the bonds undergirding the built environment might bring about necessary transformations in the construction industry. A regenerative architecture practice could help connect the needed restoration of biodiversity to community well-being, material circularity, just labor practices, and the realization of a built environment based on coexistence. In transitioning to renewed, renewable, or circular materials, architects should seize the opportunity to reconsider these materials' entire chain of production—from their source to their next use, including working conditions, transportation systems, and more.

Afforestation projects have become established climate actions to increase carbon sinks and source bio-based materials but may cause a loss of biodiversity as they often follow a monoculture approach. So-called trait-based forestry, on the other hand, is an example of regenerative, biodiversity-focused action that links ecological forest management and harvesting specific tree species for timber while potentially enhancing the biodiversity of a forest area, and simultaneously achieving climate goals.[3]

Limited research has been conducted on the economic viability of a transition to a regenerative architectural practice. The economic profitability of regenerative agriculture in comparison to conventional farming practice is evident in the reduced input (of fuel, fertilizer, chemicals, and labor) and the buildup of topsoil.[4] Such a type of tangible financial incentive is also necessary for a collective shift away from today's building practice, and will likely have to emerge initially through external financial mechanisms and legislation as we gain more knowledge about its potential financial advantages, which could lie, for example, in reduced costs for materials and their transport. The 2024 IABR offers an array of insights into how the relationship with nature and communities is becoming a stronger part of the profession and its economy. Emerging is a shared narrative and practice-based movement offering a beginning of a regenerative model for architecture, possibly also based on a set of shared principles aimed at improving social and natural ecosystems, similar to soil health principles in regenerative agriculture.

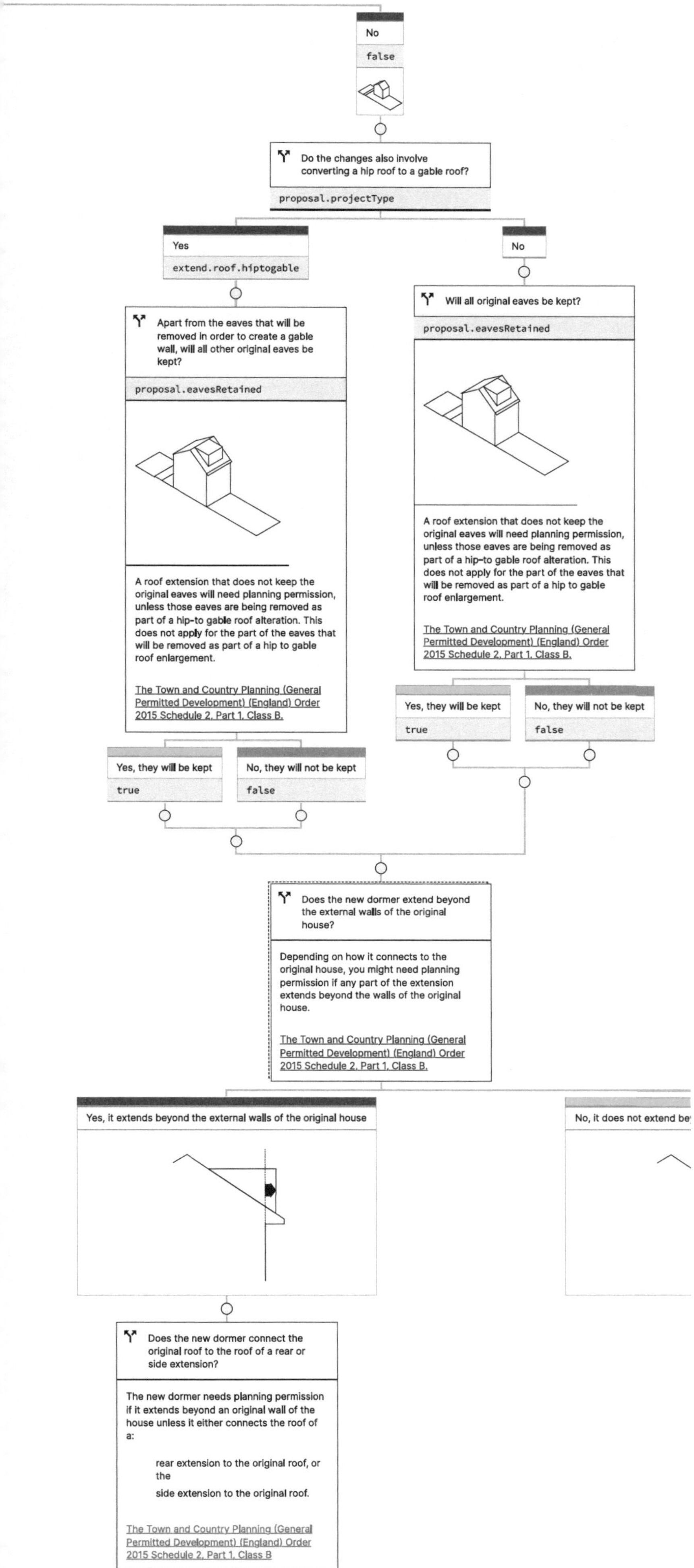

Fig. 2 Detail of the flowchart of the Plan× interface developed by Open Systems Lab, which simplifies English planning law into an easy-to-use platform intended to help homeowners, planners, and authorities alike navigate the complicated system

Infrastructure and Systems

Hani Salih

Whether through intentional decisions or unplanned externalities, most of the things around us are designed, as direct or indirect results of policy and investment. Our everyday lives are supported by layers of infrastructure, from systems of delivery, such as the logistics machine that waits for us to tap “buy now” on our phones, to the value systems that dictate what is prioritized when making planning or political decisions.

In architecture, this notion of predictability depends on a network of actors to facilitate the flow of means of production, labor, and raw materials on any building site. But beyond the material aspects, various incentives and disincentives prop up patterns of consumption and depletion, path dependencies, or extractive economies far from the actual construction site. Political allegiances, by-products of decisions made centuries ago, ossified into notions of what and, perhaps more importantly, who goes where; the inertia of what has come before still bending the waters of this river to its will, tainting its waters with its own muddied history.

Systemic thinking is at the heart of the way in which we’ve approached this edition of the biennale. Scanning the horizon for those who are working at the juncture of architectural practices and other disciplines—planning policy, community empowerment, or ecological preservation, to name a few—*Nature of Hope* showcases different ways in which these practices have articulated themselves within a network of relations.

Architects and designers have an ability to analyze systems, holding them in respect to their other parts and reinterpreting their outcomes. The challenge of what can be done in the face of the current polycrisis can be addressed by deploying architectural thinking and critical spatial analysis as a means to draw together different political-economic layers. Occupying the spaces between these systems to test new configurations of design, production, and knowledge is, therefore, an important first step, as is thinking more deeply about how we can form connections across various systems—be they operational systems or systems of value.

At the far end of Gallery 0 in the Nieuwe Instituut, for example, draped from the ceiling, a thirty-meter-long white curtain is inscribed with the graphical representation of the logic framework that makes up (part of) the English land-use and planning policy. This work, “Rules as Code: Plan×,” began as a collaborative effort between Open Systems Lab and the local authorities of Southwark, Lambeth, and Buckinghamshire in the Greater London Area. Its aim was to provide assistance on the necessity of a planning permission to make alterations to a house or property in England.

The project sought to simplify and reinterpret the thousands of pages of policy palimpsest, a result of decades, if not centuries, of legislation, into easily navigable code. Using digital tools to address the challenges of the past, its impacts are manifold, allowing the public to engage more directly with the system democratically, but also helping to reduce the burden placed on often under-resourced local planning authorities. The result is design thinking used as a tool beyond the built form, turned inward at the discipline’s own infrastructure, carving out time for architects to think about alternative ways of practicing in an increasingly complex landscape.

Fig. 3 *The Beacon* is held in place by the principle of tensegrity (a portmanteau for tensional integrity): The bamboo elements are compressed inside a network of tensioned cables. The removal or cutting of any piece of the structure leads to its collapse, making it hard to remove quickly. These structures have become useful architectural elements of protests around the world since their first use by Extinction Rebellion UK in 2019. *The Beacon* shown in the *Nature of Hope* exhibition space was assembled collectively with Extinction Rebellion Rotterdam and several activists from northern and central Europe.

Fig. 4 The Uruguayan Federation of Mutual Aid Housing Cooperatives (FUCVAM) promotes bottom-up housing development based on the self-organization of local communities. The mutual aid model has played a crucial role in Uruguay's sociopolitical history and in the democratization of urban development. With the project COVIVEMA 5, the mutual aid housing model was brought to the center of Montevideo, the Uruguayan capital. Rising land values forced the cooperative to increase the density of its development and pioneer the country's first ten-story self-construction project. The massing is organized around a public square, which was co-designed by future residents and neighboring communities.

Resistance as (Architectural) Practice
Noortje Weenink

Resistance requires a fundamentally positive outlook: a belief in the potential to improve current circumstances and in other people's ability and desire to partake in this imagined future. Resistance of any kind embodies an active form of hope: one of choice, determination, and persistence. To resist is to fight, withstand, refuse, and counter*act*. Every gesture of resistance implies the desire to replace what is countered with something else—however hopeful or bleak that something may be.[5] Spatial designers can encourage social and political change by designing the built environment to facilitate such activist events. However, architecture also has the potential to overcome its passive role as an environment in which these actions take place and, instead, to become an *actor*.

Architect Morgan Trowland and artist Julian Maynard Smith's *The Beacon*, centrally located in the exhibition space, is another example illustrating how architecture can empower both design professionals and activists in the collective fight for systemic change. Designed as part of Extinction Rebellion's 2019 protests in the United Kingdom, *The Beacon* draws on historical architectural experiments with a structural principle called tensegrity, developed in the 1960s and 1970s by figures like Buckminster Fuller and Cedric Price. The structure is composed of a network of bamboo poles held in compression and steel cables held in tension and is easily reproducible. Employed in climate protests around Europe, bamboo beacons are used to quickly occupy public spaces, and can be climbed by activists to gain an overview of the situation. Climbing the beacon also delays its removal by the police: Cutting the interconnected elements would cause the structure to collapse and the height of the structure requires police to use special equipment, which complicates eviction. Thus, the architecture itself effectively becomes part of the action.

Even after people and physical structures have been removed from the protest site, the networks and social bonds that are formed persist.[6] In Uruguay, the mutual aid system illustrates how relations between governments and citizens can be reshaped to resist the commodification of housing development through collective spatial production. The IABR shows the history of mutual aid construction in the country through four exemplary buildings, including COVIVEMA 5, a residential complex located in the center of the Uruguayan capital, Montevideo. In the mutual aid system, which has been well established in the country following a series of protests in the late 1960s, future residents—often from a poor, working-class background—form a cooperative. They purchase construction land to build, own, and maintain housing as collective property. Nonprofit, independent Institutes for Technical Assistance advocate and coordinate collective land acquisition, assisting the cooperatives by giving legal advice and supporting financial negotiations, design, and construction work, as well as democratic decision-making throughout the process. The Uruguayan Federation of Mutual Aid Housing Cooperatives (FUCVAM) is the country's oldest, largest, and most active social movement on housing and urban development: Today, more than 730 cooperatives with over 35,000 members are federated under FUCVAM.[7]

By employing their familiar tools, skills, and knowledge for nonviolent activism, both architects as individuals and the architecture they produce can join the resistance for a hopeful and livable future.

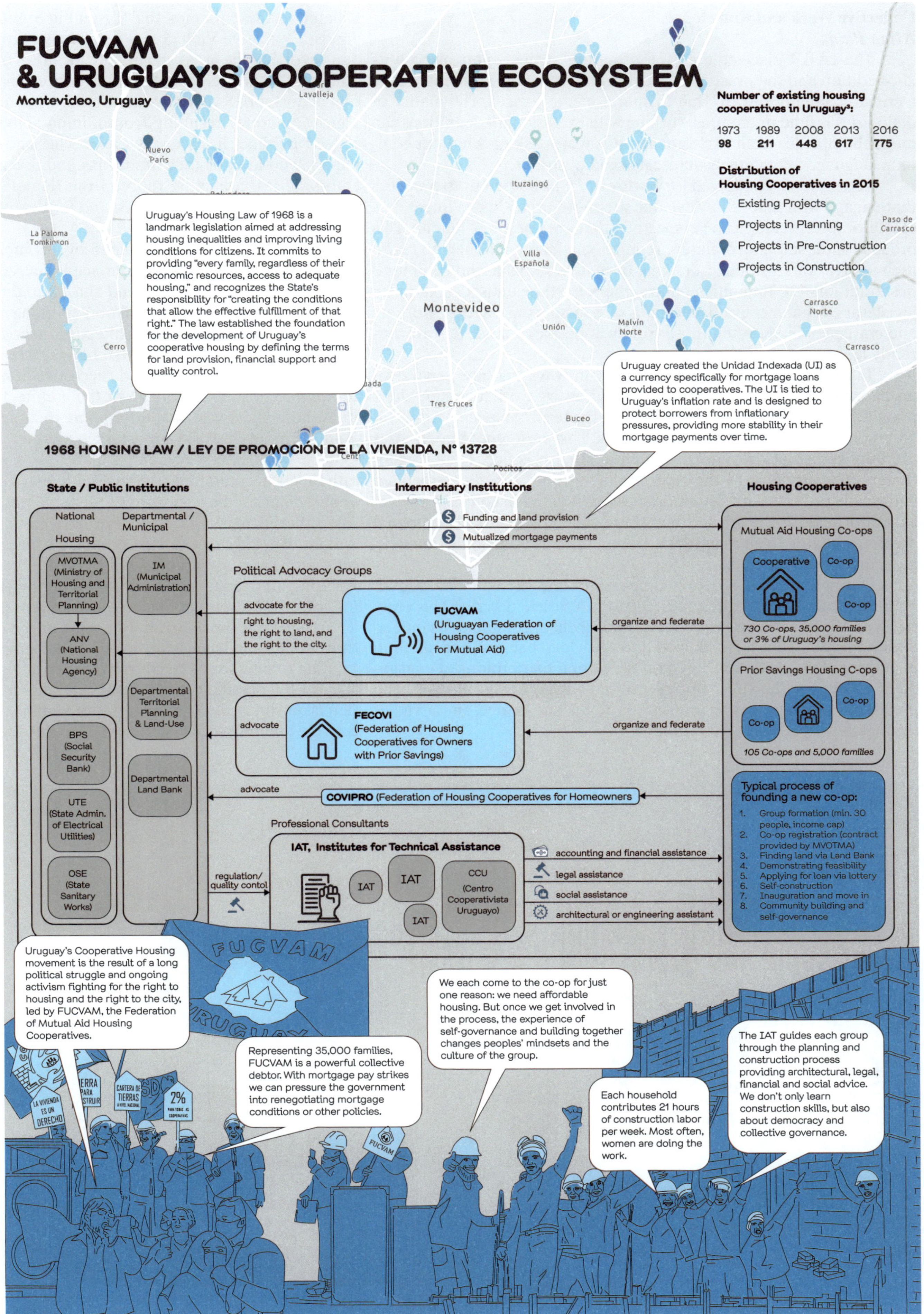

Fig. 5 "FUCVAM & Uruguay's Cooperative Ecosystem," part of the research project "Commoning the City" by the Remaking Cities Institute at Carnegie Mellon University led by Prof. Stefan Gruber in collaboration with Master of Urban Design students. The drawing is by Yi Zhou.

Collective Work and Knowledge
Alina Paias

The IABR places the notion of nature at the center of both its 2024 edition and the practice of architecture. By doing so, it engages in a critical contention with what this term means exactly. The matter of definitions is fundamental, as working with exclusionary definitions can make the practice itself exclusionary. It is worth asking what our common language as architects obfuscates and obstructs.

The research conducted for *Nature of Hope* has led us to practices that engage with nature in ways that are more urban, more queer, less scenic, or interpreted from perspectives that are not solely human. This broader understanding of nature requires spatial practitioners to revise their sources of knowledge, drawing from diverse fields and communities. Traditional communities, philosophers, Earth scientists, economists, legislators, organizers, activists, and, of course, construction workers and craftspeople are often those from whom spatial designers are currently learning the most.

Tapping into sources of knowledge in ways that are generative instead of exploitative involves looking at how we work together. Many practitioners we spoke with prefer to use the term "alliance" over "collaboration" for collectively authored work. This preference underscores the importance of definitions in architectural practice. These practitioners are wary of how the term "collaboration" is often associated with single projects with fixed start and finish dates. In contrast, alliances are formed for the advancement of a collective political and social project, implying longer lasting and deeper bonds beyond the immediate scope of work.

During the 2024 IABR opening symposium, architect and founder of the Bogotá-based office APLO Pedro Aparicio described his practice with Black, Indigenous, and traditional fishing communities on Colombia's Pacific Coast. He likened it to the "deep hanging out" method in anthropological studies, based on the notion that prolonged engagement allows for the site's embedded knowledge to reveal itself. The practitioner then acts as an interpreter of this knowledge, amplifying it through new spatial configurations.

Related to these themes, the "Listening Station on Practices of Hope amidst Extractive Violence" is a collective project from Sápmi in Sweden, involving the areas around the localities of Malmberget, Koskullskulle, and Gällivare. Malmberget, in particular, epitomizes the colonization of northern Sweden, with the mining town now being consumed by a growing crater resulting from mining activities. Karin Reisinger, a trained architect, has acted as a researcher and ally to the women of the region, who archive their traditions and document their loss through embroideries, collecting rubble from demolished houses, organizing farewell festivals for buildings slated for demolition, writing, and walking ancestral paths.

These practices are sustained by a combination of intelligent resource use and redirection from academic, cultural, and public institutions in Western Europe and the United States, along with non-commercial exchanges and relations. Among allies, housing, food, and transport can be traded for architectural services.

These non-commercial exchanges are also present at the R-Urban Poplar, a self-described "eco-civic hub" in Poplar, London. In addition to hosting the offices of the architecture studio public works and other collectives, the hub is home to anaerobic digesters, a mushroom farm, in-vessel composters, a kitchen, a dining space, a classroom, a workshop space, and a materials store. These are all shared with the local community in the Poplar district. In a substantial shift of what it means to be a steward of the built environment and its inhabitants, public works is an active and co-equal participant in this community-building effort sustained by microeconomies, gift economies, and swap economies, where skills for building, making, and repairing are traded as part of learning programs, enabling collective and informed interventions on the shared premises and beyond.

These examples highlight a shift in the definitions and types of knowledge that have historically constituted architectural practice, pointing to new forms of collective work and skill exchange. This shift suggests the possibility of an architectural practice liberated from commercial exchanges and strict terms of viability, focusing instead on collectively building space and knowledge through deep bonds.

Fig. 6 Bird's eye view of the R-Urban Poplar in London

Fig. 7 The installation *Give and Gain* by the London-based architecture office public works showcases the evolution of the R-Urban Poplar and maps out all the complex relations that make the project possible. The books, zines, and objects on the table were produced at the self-described "eco-social hub" in East London's Poplar district.

Fig. 8 Event held in the exhibition's "Practice Place" in summer 2024

"Practice Place": Conditions for Hope
Catherine Koekoek

If the design disciplines are to contribute to building hopeful futures (as *Nature of Hope* proposes they can), we need to transform both our practice and the concrete materials with which we build. This feminist insight—that, "it matters … what thoughts think thoughts," as Donna Haraway writes, or Audre Lorde's observation that "the master's tools will never dismantle the master's house"—implies that process and product are inseparable.[8]

Prompted by the widespread feeling that, in times of socio-ecological crises,[9] *we cannot go on like this,* an ecological approach to architecture is gaining prominence. Rather than asking: "What can architecture do for climate breakdown?"—a techno-optimist perspective viewing architecture as merely an external factor impacting planetary systems—an ecological approach recognizes that, as the research collective MOULD has boldly stated, "architecture is climate."[10] It considers that "all this stuff came from somewhere"[11]—as IABR contributor Kiel Moe writes—and that the architectural discipline can only assess the nature of its impact if it recognizes how mutually implicated it is with these "somewheres," their ecosystems, and their inhabitants. In an ecological approach, there is no outside; everything is entangled.

Such a radical implicatedness is demanding, and requires skills, tactics, and tools not traditionally part of an architect's repertoire. While the desire for an ecological and regenerative practice is widely shared, it often runs into practical, economic, cultural, and political roadblocks. Transforming the architectural practice therefore means overcoming these roadblocks—and this entails changing the conditions of practice itself. For instance, one practitioner shared that examining the history and potential of timber pile foundations—and subsequently challenging the applicable regulations—had turned them into a political activist.[12] To make room for the collective exploration and creation of conditions for a hopeful and ecological practice, *Nature of Hope* therefore had to be more than a space of display; it needed to turn into a space for assembly.

The "Practice Place" is such a space. Its cake slice-shaped elements made of layers of bio-based and recycled insulation materials, designed by Théo Demans and Clemence Seilles, allow for diverse forms of coming together. Throughout the IABR, the "Practice Place" hosts a series of events, inviting practitioners to collectively imagine, experiment with, and develop the conditions of a regenerative practice. The gatherings are documented in a "Live Archive," an interactive installation designed by meta office. Drawing inspiration from alternative forms of organization, facilitation, care, solidarity and storytelling—found in feminist organizing, resident initiatives, neighborhood theaters, or protest movements—these events aim to engage personal, professional, and political spheres. They facilitate building relations on the basis of experiential knowledge—from architectural workers and civil servants to community arts practitioners, ecologists, educators, and construction workers—forging alliances between those who collectively hold power to enact social and material change.

Rather than a blueprint for the future, hope requires an active practice of engagement, solidarity, and facing what we're up against. By incorporating perspectives that often remain marginalized in the field, this approach broadens our understanding of architectural practice. This is not a radical break but a realignment or repair.[13] From the interstices of the current system, another future is possible—and emerging.

Fig. 9 In Laura Ajola's work *Regained*, anthropogenic materials, such as concrete and steel, are exposed to chemical processes similar to those occurring in buildings over time. The white crystals forming on their surface are called "efflorescence," and can be found on building parts exposed to harsh environmental conditions. The objects, with their similarity to core drills, are a reflection on the uncontrollable nature and porosity of the limits between built environment and "nature," undergirded by an ambiguity about human intentionality in these processes.

Find more information about IABR 2024, held at the Nieuwe Instituut in Rotterdam from June 21 to October 13, 2024, at iabr.nl/en/nature-of-hope or scan the QR code below:

Fig. 10 Installation view

Fig. 11 "Eco-systeem-dienst-plicht" (ecosystem conscription) by the Dutch-based collective -zee -plaats -werk -land (Studio Ester van de Wiel & Studio Joost Adriaanse) investigates the co-production of landscapes by human and non-human actors in the Rhine-Meuse-Scheldt delta, one of the most heavily tamed and domesticated ecosystems on the planet.

1 John Tillman Lyle, *Regenerative Design for Sustainable Development* (New York: John Wiley & Sons, 1996).
2 Cf. Hans-Otto Pörtner et al., *Scientific Outcome of the IPBES-IPCC Co-sponsored Workshop on Biodiversity and Climate Change* (Bonn: IPBES secretariat, 2021), 124–43, 10.5281/zenodo.4659158.
3 See Peter Osborne et al., "A Trait-Based Approach to Both Forestry and Timber Building Can Synchronize Forest Harvest and Resilience," *PNAS Nexus* vol. 2, issue 8 (August 2023), doi.org/10.1093/pnasnexus/pgad254.
4 See Claire LaCanne and Jonathan Lundgren, "Regenerative Agriculture: Merging Farming and Natural Resource Conservation Profitably," *PeerJ*, February 26, 2018, doi.org/10.7717/peerj.4428.
5 See Hakim Bey, *T.A.Z.: The Temporary Autonomous Zone. Ontological Anarchy, Poetic Terrorism* (New York: Autonomedia, 1991), 114.
6 See Irene Feria Prados et al., "Lützerath: Architectures of Everyday Activism," video, 9m 9s, for IABR 2022, *It's About Time*, accessed July 29, 2024, youtu.be/8mDbE7Ga-Ac.
7 See Ivonne Santoyo-Orozco, "Future Commoners," *e-flux Architecture*, June 2023, accessed July 29, 2024, www.e-flux.com/architecture/in-common/529980/future-commoners.
8 See Donna Haraway, *Staying with the Trouble: Making Kin in the Chthulucene* (Durham: Duke University Press, 2016); Audre Lorde, "The Master's Tools Will Never Dismantle the Master's House," in Jane Rendell et al., eds., *Gender Space Architecture: An Interdisciplinary Introduction* (London: Routledge, 2000), 53–55.
9 See Fonna Forman et al., "Democratic Coordination and Eco-Social Crises," *Citizenship Studies* 26, nos. 4–5 (July 2022), 436–46, https://doi.org/10.1080/13621025.2022.2091225.
10 MOULD, "Architecture Is Climate: Chronograms of Architecture," *e-flux Architecture*, February 2023, accessed July 29, 2024, www.e-flux.com/architecture/chronograms/519512/architecture-is-climate.
11 Cit. Niels Groeneveld, "Jonge Maaskantprijs 2021/2022," *Werkstatt*, September 2, 2022, accessed July 29, 2024, www.werkstatt.nu/journal/2022/9/2/jonge-maaskantprijs-teruglezen-de-hele-tekst-nu-online.
12 Cf. "Are Timber Pile Foundations Feasible?," *la-di-da*, accessed July 29, 2024, la-di-da.nl/questions/can-you-use-wood-for-the-foundation-of-a-house.
13 For change as re-alignment from the interstices, see Eva von Redecker, *Praxis and Revolution: A Theory of Social Transformation* (New York: Columbia University Press, 2021); Catherine Koekoek, "Return to the City to Claim It: Temporalities and Locations of Feminist Refusal," *Res Publica* 27, no. 1 (2024), 23–29.

ARGE.CO
The architecture cooperative C/O, ARGE.CO for short, was founded in 2021 and is based in Zurich, Lausanne, Basel, and Bern. The administrative structure's fourteen members work independently as architects but collaborate for competitions, projects, and publications. All members are jointly liable in this model.

Assemble
is a collective working across architecture, design, and art founded in 2010 in the context of a self-building project. Among their multifaceted and award-winning projects are Lot 8 in Arles (2023, with BC Architects and Atelier LUMA), as well as the Goldsmiths Centre for Contemporary Art (2018) and Yard House (2014) in London. Since 2020, Assemble has been teaching at EPFL in Lausanne.

l'atelier, Nomadic Architecture Studio
Spread across two continents and five cities, l'atelier, Nomadic Architecture Studio works on an entirely virtual basis. Founded in 2018 by Pierre Escobar, the office has no physical premises. The staff, who are all freelancers, are paid according to their respective places of residence and work, adjusted for purchasing power. The office's projects include the ongoing redesign of all public spaces in Bon Air, a garden city on the outskirts of Brussels.

Paul Barth
(born 1995) studied architecture in Vienna and Zurich. At ETH Zurich, he was a student assistant at the Institute for Preservation and Construction History and at the station+ Chair. He worked in several architectural offices in Luxembourg and Zurich and was a recipient of the Sto Foundation scholarship at ARCH+ in 2022.

Nick Beech
is an architectural historian who also engages in cultural studies. He is currently a research lead on the Stuart Hall Archive Project at the University of Birmingham. Nick Beech recently contributed to the Translating Ferro / Transforming Knowledge (2021–24) program, which culminated in the Production Studies conference in Newcastle, UK, in 2024.

Oana Bogdan
is an architect and founder of the Brussels-based office &bogdan, which she co-led until the end of 2022 under the name Bogdan & Van Broeck together with Leo Van Broeck. In 2011, 2015, 2019, and 2022 they were nominees, and in 2024 shortlisted, for the Mies van der Rohe Award. Bogdan taught for several years at KU Leuven and was Secretary of State for cultural heritage in the Romanian Government (2016–17). She was appointed chairwoman of the "Good Living" Expert Committee in charge of the reform of the Brussels Region's building code in 2021, and of the Dutch Creative Industries Fund NL in 2023.

Arno Brandlhuber
(born 1964) is founder and partner of the Berlin-based architectural office b+. In his architectural practice, which spans from buildings to research and media, he deals with legislative aspects of architectural and urban production. He has produced several films together with architect Olaf Grawert and artist and filmmaker Christopher Roth, including *Legislating Architecture* (2016), *The Property Drama* (2017), and *Architecting after Politics* (2018). Arno Brandlhuber is professor at the station+ Chair at ETH Zurich and was co-curator of the German Pavilion at the 2021 Architecture Biennale in Venice

Chybik+Kristof
is an architecture and urban design practice founded in 2010 by Ondřej Chybík (born 1985) and Michal Krištof (born 1986). With offices in London, Prague, Brno, and Bratislava, the practice is part of a new generation of designer-makers turned problem solvers bringing Czech architecture to the global stage. Completed projects include the Czech Pavilion at EXPO 2015 in Milan and the Lahofer Winery and Zvonařka Central Bus Terminal in the Czech Republic. The studio has been awarded a number of prizes including the Europe 40 Under 40 Award from the European Centre for Architecture Art Design and Urban Studies in 2019. Their first monograph, *Crafting Character*, was published in 2023.

Leonhard Clemens
(born 1986) is an architect, photographer, and founder of the collaborative architectural office LNCL based in Berlin. He studied at the State Academy of Fine Arts Stuttgart and at the Bartlett School of Architecture and Architectural Association in London. In addition to his architectural practice, Clemens also worked as a researcher at the University of Cyprus and as a research assistant at the Universität Hannover. Since 2022, he has been leading a design studio at DIA Dessau.

Marisa Cortright
is an independent architectural historian based in Zagreb, Croatia. In 2023 she was a Guest Researcher at ArkDes in Stockholm and the Guest Editor of *The Avery Review* at Columbia University's GSAPP in New York. In 2021 she published a book of essays titled *"Can This Be? Surely This Cannot Be?": Architectural Workers Organizing in Europe* with the VI PER Gallery in Prague. She holds degrees in urban and architectural history from Barnard College and the Bartlett School of Architecture.

Peggy Deamer
is Professor Emerita of Yale University's School of Architecture since 2019 and a principal at Deamer, Studio in New York. She is the editor of *Architecture and Capitalism: 1845 to the Present* (2013) and *The Architect as Worker: Immaterial Labor, the Creative Class, and the Politics of Design* (2015), as well as the author of *Architecture and Labor* (2020). As a founding member of the Architecture Lobby, she received the Architectural Record 2018 Women in Architecture Activist Award.

Paola De Martin
(born 1965) is a primary school teacher, textile designer, and historian. In her dissertation *Give Us a Break! Arbeitermilieu und Designszene im Aufbruch* (Zurich: Diaphanes, 2022), she examined the historical correlations between the creative industries and social backgrounds. De Martin now teaches and researches as a postdoc at the Institute for the History and Theory of Architecture (gta) at ETH Zurich. She is co-curator of the antiracist remembrance project Schwarzenbach-Komplex and chairwoman of the association TESORO, which represents migrant working-class families who suffered separation and illegalization between 1931 and 2002 as a result of Swiss legislation. Paola De Martin was awarded the prestigious Swiss Grand Prix Design in 2024.

Elke Doppelbauer
(born 1985) was a project manager at ARCH+ from 2022 to 2024, where she was involved in the organization of the German Pavilion of the 2023 Architecture Biennale in Venice and the 2023–24 exhibition *The Great Repair* at Akademie der Künste Berlin, both of which were co-curated by ARCH+. She has been organizing exhibitions, events, and workshops in the cultural field since her fine arts studies in Linz. Among other things, she was the production manager for the German Pavilion at the 2021 Architecture Biennale in Venice and provided administrative advice to the Berlin-based architectural office b+. She was previously Chief Operating Officer at Muck Petzet Architekten.

Ana Filipović

is an architect and locates her practice between art, architecture, theory, and research. She often works collaboratively, for example as part of the Soft Agency group, which explores feminist perspectives on the built environment, and with Philipp Mecke, with whom she has realized several architectural projects and spatial interventions. In 2020–21, Filipović received the INITIAL-scholarship of the Akademie der Künste in Berlin, where she resides.

Andrea Gebhard

is a landscape architect and urban planner. She previously led the Green Planning Department of the City of Munich, where she also served as managing director of the 2005 Federal German Garden Show (BUGA). She was the president of the German Association of Landscape Architects (bdla) from 2007 to 2014 and chaired the Bavarian regional group of the German Academy for Urban and Regional Planning (DASL) from 2014 to 2021. Currently, she is a partner at the landscape architecture firm mahl gebhard konzepte. She has been serving as the president of the Federal Chamber of German Architects since 2021.

Maria Shéhérazade Giudici

is the founder of the publishing and research plaform Black Square and the editor of *AA Files*. She leads the History and Theory course at the School of Architecture of the Royal College of Art, and heads the PhD Program of the Architectural Association, both in London.

Olaf Grawert

(born 1987) is a partner at the Berlin-based architectural office b+. He studied architecture and urban planning in Innsbruck and Berlin, with a focus on architectural theory and urban studies. He was a guest lecturer at the Joint Master of Architecture Suisse and at the USI Accademia di Architettura Mendrisio and is co-editor of the online platform *What is Architecture?*. Grawert has been a research assistant at the Department of Architecture at ETH Zurich since 2017. In 2021, he was a co-curator of the German Pavilion at the Architecture Biennale in Venice.

Peter Grundmann

is an architect, urban planner, and filmmaker. He studied shipbuilding in Rostock and architecture at the Weißensee Academy of Art Berlin, where he taught architecture and urban planning from 2002 to 2005. With his office Peter Grundmann Architekten, he explores alternative design, construction, and financing methods in architecture to build high-quality structures at low cost. He lives in Berlin.

Gabu Heindl

is a Vienna-based architect, urban planner, and activist. She studied architecture in Vienna, Tokyo, and Princeton, and holds a PhD in philosophy. Her office, GABU Heindl Architecture, focuses on public space, public buildings, common ownership, and non-commercial housing, as well as collaborations in the fields of remembrance politics and critical artistic practice. From 2013 to 2017 she was chair of the Austrian Society for Architecture. Since 2022, she has been a professor at the faculty of architecture at the University of Kassel, where she heads the design and research department ARCHITECTURE CITIES ECONOMIES | Building Economy and Project Development. Her numerous international publications include, as a co-editor, *Building Critique: Architecture and Its Discontents* (2019), and, as an author, *Stadtkonflikte: Radikale Demokratie in Architektur und Stadtplanung* (2020).

Felix Hofmann

studied geography in Erlangen and architecture in Stuttgart. He works as an editor and exhibition production manager for ARCH+. In this capacity, he was involved in the exhibition projects *Cohabitation* (2020–22) and *The Great Repair* (2023–24, at Akademie der Künste in Berlin).

IFUB*

was founded in 2012 by Bernhard Kurz and Johannes Krohne. The common good and fair working conditions are an integral part of the identity of the architecture firm with offices in Munich, Berlin, and Heiligenberg on Lake Constance. 10% of their profits are donated, and full-time employment means a 32-hour workweek. In 2021, the office published a manual with ten guidelines for building for the common good.

International Architecture Biennale Rotterdam (IABR) curators

Janna Bystrykh

is an architect and researcher. She is the head of the Master in Architecture program at the Academy of Architecture Amsterdam, where she is leading the development of a climate curriculum for architecture, and runs her design and research practice BYSTRYKH. Bystrykh has experience with complex urban projects, museum transformations, experimental educational projects, and installations. At OMA*AMO she worked on the *Elements of Architecture* exhibition for the 2014 Venice Biennale and on the research and exhibition project *Countryside: The Future*.

Catherine Koekoek

has a background in architecture and philosophy. She is a PhD candidate in Political Philosophy at Erasmus University Rotterdam. Her dissertation examines how democratic infrastructures—from community centers to the Rotterdams Wijktheater, with which she collaborates—enable democratic coexistence. Together with Veerle Alkemade, Catherine Koekoek produces the feminist architecture podcast *Respons*.

Alina Paias

works as a designer, researcher, teacher, and curator. She uses feminist philosophy, new materialism, and philosophy of technology to explore the work, forms of knowledge, and technologies involved in the production of architecture. She has years of experience as a spatial designer, having worked on projects in Brazil, the United States, and the Netherlands.

Hani Salih

works as a researcher, designer, writer, editor, and curator. He works across a range of disciplines and practices, from architecture to systems and policy. Salih is interested in the broader contexts in which social and cultural phenomena take place, and is currently exploring this in his work as a lecturer in architecture and design, and as a curator of events and debates at De Dépendance in Rotterdam.

Saskia van Stein

is the artistic and managing director of the International Architecture Biennale Rotterdam (IABR). Currently, van Stein is also co-head of the Master's program "The Critical Inquiry Lab" at the Design Academy in Eindhoven. Prior to this, she was the artistic and managing director of the Maastricht-based Bureau Europa platform for architecture and design from 2013 to 2019. Van Stein's curatorial practice started at the Netherlands Architecture Institute (now Nieuwe Instituut) in Rotterdam, where, between 2002 and 2012, she programmed exhibitions at the intersection of architecture culture, political and human sciences, design, and fine arts.

Noortje Weenink

has been working as a junior curator at IABR since 2021 and is active as a spatial designer, writer, guest lecturer, and climate activist. Together with Irene Feria Prados and Wouter Stroet, Weenink ran the design studio "Queer(ing) Space" at the Amsterdam Academy of Architecture. In her professional and everyday life, she explores how disruptive practices can be used for social and climate justice. At Studio Ossidiana she worked on the Prix de Rome-winning project "Amsterdam Allegories."

Sascha Kellermann
(born 1987) studied architecture at the Technical University in Dresden and worked for various architectural offices in Zurich and Berlin. In 2015 he was a founding member of the THFwelcome e.V. association in Berlin. In 2018, together with Omar Barkal and Donata Hasselmann, he produced the documentary *Am Rande Europas* about the effects on the migration deal between the EU and Turkey. He is an editor with the online magazine *kritisch-lesen.de*, and has been an editor with ARCH+ since 2019.

Jan Knikker
(born 1972) is partner and Director of Strategy at the architecture firm MVRDV in Rotterdam, which he joined in 2008 during the financial crisis. He drives business development and public relations efforts, and oversees the office's output. Knikker engages personally in projects such as a resort and estate in Taiwan, the renovation and extension of an estate in France, or the master plan for the reopening of the canals in The Hague, which were paved over in the 1960s. Prior to this, Knikker was Head of Public Relations at OMA / Rem Koolhaas for nearly a decade after a career in journalism.

Jolene Lee
(born 1993) is an architect based in Berlin. She studied in Kuala Lumpur and Dessau and collaborated with Muck Petzet Architekten, FAKT Office for Architecture, and b+. She was a partner at the latter from 2022 to 2024 and a teaching assistant at the station+ Chair at ETH Zurich, and producer of the event and exhibition platform Lab of Intelligence Culture.

Victor Lortie
(born 1996) quit law school to study architecture in Berlin. He has published essays in *trans magazin and Nachglühen / Afterglow* (2024) and co-edited *Überbau: Produktionsverhältnisse der Architektur im Anthropozän* (2021). He was a board member of Roundabout e.V. association at TU Berlin from 2019 to 2023, a founding member of *SITUATION Magazine for Spatial Questions* in 2022, and has worked as an editor with ARCH+ since 2022.

Anh-Linh Ngo
(born 1974) is an architectural theorist, curator, and editor-in-chief of ARCH+. He regularly curates exhibitions and research projects with ARCH+, including *projekt bauhaus* (2015–19), *Cohabitation* (2021), and *The Great Repair* (2023–24). From 2010 to 2016, he was a member of the art advisory council at the Institut für Auslandsbeziehungen (ifa), for which he developed and co-curated the traveling exhibitions *An Atlas of Commoning* (2018) and *Post-Oil City* (2009). He is currently a member of the board of trustees of IBA 2027 StadtRegion Stuttgart, the board of trustees of Akademie Schloss Solitude, and the Goethe Institut's advisory council. He was a co-curator of the German Pavilion at the 18th Venice Architecture Biennale in 2023. Ngo has been a member of the Akademie der Künste in Berlin since 2021, and became its Vice President in 2024.

Will Orr
is an architecture theorist and historian based in London. In 2019, he completed a PhD at the Architectural Association in London, where he now teaches in the undergraduate History and Theory Studies program as well as the History and Critical Thinking graduate program. His research examines shifts in disciplinary and professional ideology from the 1960s to the present.

Ricardo Ruivo
is a Portuguese architect, researcher, and teacher. He is currently Associate Professor at Southeast University in Nanjing, China. Until 2021, he taught in the History and Theory undergraduate program of the Architectural Association, where he also completed his PhD in 2018. His research focuses on architecture in non-capitalist development.

Ruth Schagemann
is an architect. She co-founded VICEVERSA Architektur + Medien in Stuttgart in 2006. She has been a board member of the Architects' Council of Europe (ACE), coordinator of the European Network of Architects' Competent Authorities (ENACA), and member of the European coordination group of the Federal Chamber of German Architects (BAK). She serves as head of the staff unit for national and international professional policy at the Baden-Württemberg Chamber of Architects. In 2022 Schagemann became president of the ACE and, as of 2023, has been managing director of the BAK's EU Liaison Office in Brussels. In 2023, she represented the ACE at the Davos Baukultur Alliance.

Space&Matter
is an Amsterdam-based design studio founded in 2009 by Sascha Glasl, Tjeerd Haccou, and Marthijn Pool. It specializes in architecture, circular neighborhood development, and vision-making by co-creating strategies, buildings, and neighborhoods alongside end users to build strong and fair cities. Neighborhoods are their preferred units of change because they are the place where sustainability meets human experience.

Douglas Spencer
is Director of Graduate Education and Pickard Chilton Professor of Architecture at Iowa State University. He completed his PhD in History and Theory of Architecture at the University of Westminster in 2012 and subsequently taught there, at the Architectural Association, and at the Royal College of Art in London. His publications include *The Architecture of Neoliberalism* (2016), *Critique of Architecture: Essays on Theory, Autonomy, and Political Economy* (2021), and *Architecture and the Ends of Capitalism: Scenes from a Crisis* (forthcoming, 2025).

Jakob Walter
studied architecture in Leipzig, Weimar, and Zurich. For his 2020 master's thesis project *Cohabitation Podcast* at ETH Zurich, he referred to wildlife protection laws to protect residential buildings from demolition by making endangered brown long-eared bats settle in the buildings. He was a co-curator and co-editor with ARCH+ for two years until 2023, when he became a teaching assistant with the Architecture of Territory Chair at ETH Zurich, where he will be teaching a guest studio as part of ZAS* in the fall of 2024.

Susanne Wartzeck
studied interior design and architecture in Nuremberg and Kassel following her training as a carpenter. She co-founded the architecture firm Sturm und Wartzeck in Dipperz, Hesse, with Jörg Sturm in 1995. In 2000, Wartzeck was appointed to the Association of German Architects (BDA), where she has served as president since 2019. Additionally, she volunteers as a jury member in urban planning competitions.

Finn Williams
is the City Architect of Malmö. He previously worked to promote public architecture and planning in the UK through roles at Croydon Council and the Greater London Authority, and as the co-founder and chief executive of Public Practice. Williams is a Visiting Professor of Practice at the Institute of Innovation and Public Purpose at University College London, and was co-curator of the British Pavilion at the 2016 Venice Architecture Biennale.

OCCUPATION / VOCATION

pp. 8–9 © General Motors LLC

Essay Peggy Deamer
Fig. 1 © The State Russian Museum; VG Bild-Kunst, Bonn 2024
Fig. 2 Photo: Felix Oberhage. VG Bild-Kunst, Bonn 2024. Courtesy of Galerie EIGEN + ART
Fig. 3 © Private archive Hollein. Courtesy of Generali Foundation Collection – Permanent loan to the Museum der Moderne Salzburg
Fig. 4 © Wang Qingsong

Essay Douglas Spencer
Fig. 1 CC BY-SA 4.0
Fig. 2 Courtesy of Casa Buonarroti, Florence
Fig. 3 Photo: Marcos Corrêa

Office Profile Chybik+Kristof
Figs. 1–4 © Alex Shoots Buildings
Figs. 5–6 © Chybik+Kristof

Office Profile Ana Filipović
Fig. 1 © Ana Filipović for sub
Fig. 2 © La Mode en Images
Fig. 3 © Balenciaga
Figs. 4–5 © Frank Kleinbach
Fig. 6 © Ana Filipović

Interview Peter Grundmann
Figs. 1–5 © Peter Grundmann

Photo Essay Leonhard Clemens
© Leonhard Clemens

Essay Paola De Martin
Fig. 1 © Paola De Martin
Fig. 2 © RSI
Fig. 3 © Xavier Voirol
Fig. 4 © Zaha Hadid Foundation

VALUE / VALUES

pp. 66–67 © picture alliance / REUTERS / Kristi McCluer

Interview Oana Bogdan
Figs. 1, 4–5, 8 © &bogdan
Figs. 2, 6 © Laurian Ghinițoiu
Fig. 3 © Stijn Bollaert
Fig. 7 © &bogdan, DDS+
Fig. 9 Courtesy of Euclides. Photo from private collection from 1940
Fig. 10 © Luca Beel

Interview Jan Knikker
Fig. 1 © MVRDV; VG Bild-Kunst, Bonn 2024
Fig. 2 Photo: Ossip van Duivenbode. © VG Bild-Kunst, Bonn 2024

Office Profile l'atelier, Nomadic Architecture Studio
Figs. 1–3 Photo: Tim Van de Velde
Figs. 4–5 © l'atelier, Nomadic Architecture Studio

Office Profile Space&Matter
Figs. 1–2 Courtesy of Space&Matter
Fig. 3 © Martijn van Wijk
Fig. 4 © Jean-Pierre Jans
Figs. 5–6 © Space&Matter

Office Profile IFUB*
Figs. 1–4 © Thomas Straub
Figs. 5–7 © IFUB*

Essay Nick Beech
Fig. 1 © Aliaksandr Kazlou | Dreamstime.com
Fig. 2 © Katie Chan under CC BY-SA 3.0
Fig. 3 © National Portrait Gallery, London
Figs. 6–7 © Architectural Press Archive / RIBA Collections
Fig. 8 © Jeremy Selwyn / Evening Standard / eyevine / laif

COMMODITY / COMMUNITY

pp. 116–17 © Dezeen

Essay Maria Shéhérazade Giudici
Figs. 2–6, 8, 10–11 Drawings: Mojan Kavosh

Essay Will Orr and Ricardo Ruivo
Figs. 1–2, 4 © Bernard Tschumi Architects
Fig. 3 Open Parliament Licence v3.0
Fig. 5 © Valerie Bennett / Architectural Association

Interview Finn Williams
Fig. 1 London Metropolitan Archives, City of London, from SC/PHL/02/BOX 136
Fig. 2 Photo: Fiona Finchett

Office Profile Assemble
Figs. 1–8 © Assemble

Office Profile ARGE.CO
Figs. 1–3 © Tobias Fink
Figs. 4–6 © ANA
Figs. 7–8 © Lorenz Bachmann, Andreas Reimann, Rüdiger Kreiselmayer
Figs. 9–11 © Christian Senti
Figs. 12–16 © Tobias Fink

Interview Gabu Heindl
Fig. 1 © Gabu Heindl; © Willi Dorner; VG Bild-Kunst, Bonn 2024
Figs. 2–3 © GABU Heindl Architektur
Fig. 4 © ALLCOLOURS
Fig. 5 © Gabu Heindl

Statements International Architecture Biennale Rotterdam 2024
Figs. 1, 3, 7, 9–11 © IABR / Jacqueline Fuijkschot
Fig. 2 © Open Systems Lab
Fig. 4 © Centro Cooperativista Uruguayo
Fig. 5 Drawing: Yi Zhou; © Remaking Cities Institute (CMU School of Architecture, Pittsburgh)
Fig. 6 © public works and R-Urban Poplar
Fig. 8 © IABR / Sabine van der Vooren

Cover © DS landschaparchitecten

…r Architecture and Urbanism

Publishing Houses
ARCH+/Spector Books

ARCH+ Publishers
Nikolaus Kuhnert, Anh-Linh Ngo

Advisory Board
Arno Brandlhuber, Beatriz Colomina, Philipp Oswalt, Stephan Trüby, Georg Vrachliotis, Mark Wigley, Karin Wilhelm

Editor-in-Chief
Anh-Linh Ngo* (V.i.S.d.P.)

Managing Director
Arno Löbbecke

Editorial Team
Nora Dünser*, Mirko Gatti, Christian Hiller, Felix Hofmann*, Sascha Kellermann* (co-project lead for the German-language publication), Markus Krieger, Daniel Kuhnert, Victor Lortie* (project lead for the English-language publication), Melissa Makele, Alex Nehmer, Jakob Walter* (co-project lead for the German-language publication)

Guest Editors
s+ station+ station.plus
Chair for Architecture and Storytelling
Institute of Design and Architecture (IEA),
Department of Architecture (D-ARCH),
ETH Zurich
www.station.plus

Prof. Arno Brandlhuber*; Giacomo Ardesio, Severin Bärenbold, Brigitte Beck, Ludwig Engel*, Olaf Grawert* (project lead), Pan Hu, Alina Kolar, Meghan Rolvien

station+
D ARCH
ETH zürich

Managing Editor
Nora Dünser*

Editorial Assistant
David Siegrist*

*Editorial team for this publication, which is based on the German-language issue ARCH+ 251: *Unternehmen Architektur* (March 2023)

The English version of this publication has been made possible by the generously support of the International Architecture Biennale Rotterdam 2024: *Nature of Hope*, held from June 29 to October 13, 2024, at the Nieuwe Instituut in Rotterdam.

International Architecture Biennale Rotterdam

Art Direction
Stan Hema, Berlin

Design
Peer Hempel, Finn Rodenberg, André van Rueth

Final Typesetting
Daniel Vandré

Project Management for Stan Hema
Niki Moreira

English Copyediting
Victor Lortie

Translations
Alisa Kotmair (pp. 1–2, 26–29, 58–65)
Victor Lortie (pp. 3, 52–57)
Rob Madole (pp. 4–5, 42–47, 78–83, 144–54)
Jeremy Gaines (pp. 84–87, 100–05, 156–61)

English Proofreading
James Copeland

Head of Research and Exhibition Projects
Christian Hiller

Head of Communications and Marketing
Barbara Schindler

Head of Events
Sascha Kellermann

Publishing Assistant
Tillmann Gebauer

Ambassadors
Martin Luce, Christine Rüb

Prepress
maxcolor, Berlin

Printing
Druckhaus Sportflieger, Berlin

Advertising
anzeigen@archplus.net
archplus.net/de/mediadaten
archplus.net/en/mediakit

ARCH+ Verlag GmbH
Friedrichstraße 23a
10969 Berlin
Tel +49 30 340 467 17
verlag@archplus.net
Managing directors:
Nikolaus Kuhnert, Anh-Linh Ngo

ARCH+ gGmbH (nonprofit limited liability company)
ggmbh@archplus.net
Managing director:
Arno Löbbecke

Donation Account
GLS Bank
IBAN: DE47 4306 0967 1229 2768 01
BIC: GENODEM1GLS
archplus.net/nonprofit

Distribution
Spector Books
Harkortstraße 10
04107 Leipzig
www.spectorbooks.com

Image Credits
ARCH+ has made every effort to notify all copyright holders. Any individual or institution wishing to make a copyright claim is requested to contact the editors.

Acknowledgments
We would like to thank Paul Barth, Manuel Bokanyi, Leonie Wagner, and Sarah Wirth for their in-depth analysis of the statistics on the architecture market. Like their contributions, many of the conclusions and reflections in this publication arose from discussions with students as part of the s+ teaching program (station.plus, IEA, D-ARCH, ETH Zurich).

We would also like to thank Naima Callenberg, Saskia Hebert, Stefan Heidenreich, Gábor Kocsis, Lucia Martínez, Silke Ötsch, Ruth Schagemann, Anna Yeboah, and Nina Zschocke in particular for their productive comments, suggestions, and additions to the content of this issue.

We would especially like to thank all the groups and individuals who have made every effort across various media to raise awareness around the topic of working conditions in architecture to improve them. These include Architects for Future, Failed Architecture, Future Architects Front, Kontextur, The Architecture Lobby, UVW-SAW, and many more.

Germany, Austria: GVA, Gemeinsame Verlagsauslieferung Göttingen GmbH & Co. KG, www.gva-verlage.de
Switzerland: AVA Verlagsauslieferung AG, www.ava.ch
France, Belgium: Interart Paris, www.interart.fr
UK: Central Books Ltd, www.centralbooks.com
USA, Canada, Central and South America, Africa: ARTBOOK/D.A.P., www.artbook.com
South Korea: The Book Society, www.thebooksociety.org
Japan: twelvebooks, www.twelve-books.com
Australia, New Zealand: Perimeter Distribution, www.perimeterdistribution.com

Subscriptions (German issues only)
archplus.net/abo

Direct Orders
of ARCH+ English editions:
archplus.net/en/shop/english-publications

ISSN 0587-3452 (ARCH+)
ISBN 978-3-931435-87-5 (ARCH+)
ISBN 978-3-95905-861-2 (Spector Books)

First edition: 2024
Printed in Germany